CRAZY ABOUT MONEY

How Emotions Confuse Our Money Choices
And What To Do About It

MAGGIE BAKER, PH.D.

ISBN: 0615402909
ISBN-13: 9780615402901
LCCN: 2010915438

DEDICATION

To Bob Grandy, who inspired my confidence to write Crazy About Money, and to my family who lived with me and helped me through the consequences.

TABLE OF CONTENTS

Introduction: Getting Empowered 1

PART I: GETTING READY FOR YOUR MONEY JOURNEY 11

1. The Basics of a Balanced Life: Emotions and Happiness 13
2. Different Strokes for Different Folks: What Does Money Mean? 27
3. Our Biology, Our Hardwiring and Money: The Scientific Bedrock 47
4. How We Act Funny With Money: Predictably Illogical (Behavioral Economics) 61

PART II: WHERE OUR MONEY BELIEFS COME FROM AND HOW THEY DEVELOP 81

5. Building a Financial Self: The Childhood Years 83
6. Transition to Adulthood: The Teen Years 99
7. Getting Set in Our Ways: Money Types 113

PART III: ACTING ON YOUR MONEY BELIEFS 131

8. Starting Money Journeys: Leaving Home (Age 19-21) 133
9. Taking Center Stage: Start-Up Adults On Their Own (Age 21-30) 141
10. Will the Structure Hold? Settling Down (Or Not): (The 30s) 161
11. Time for Reflection: Reckoning (The 40s, 50s and Beyond) 177

PART IV: HOW MONEY AFFECTS YOUR LIFESTYLE 187

12. Flying Solo: Singlehood 189
13. Two's Company: Couples and the Gentle Art of Lying........ 207
14. Suddenly Single: Divorce and Widowhood: 229

PART V: MAKING MONEY WORK FOR OR AGAINST YOU 247

15. Taming the Bulls and the Bears: Investing 249
16. Playing the Odds: Gambling, Debt and Risk........ 271
17. The Third Chapter of Life: Retirement........ 293
18. How Will They Remember You? Leaving a Legacy (or Not)........ 317

PART VI: YOUR MONEY MASTER SELF 331

19. Mission Accomplished! : No More Craziness About Money........ 333

Introduction: *Getting Empowered*

"We must become the change we want to see." Mahatma Gandhi

Crazy About Money is not the kind of money book that will tell you whether to buy gold, how much to put in your 401(k), or whether to rent or buy a house. For many of us, that would be putting the cart before the horse. My goal is to help you become more aware of how you relate to money, so you can change the emotions, beliefs, and attitudes that keep you from making healthier, more sensible choices.

We're often told that our best interests will be served as long as we are rational about money. That sounds simple enough. However, emotions related to money can be so powerful that they prevent us from being fully rational about it. These emotions affect how we manage, spend, save, and invest money, as well as how we interact with significant people in our lives.

You may think about money a lot, especially if you feel you don't have enough. But that's not the same thing as understanding your feelings in order to overcome self-sabotaging beliefs and behavior. To make this a little clearer, think of food. People often fail to improve their bad eating habits because they start trying to change without understanding why they weren't able to succeed before. Similarly, many of us can't change our behavior with money because we don't understand why we make the choices we do. Even financial professionals who make mistakes aren't any more likely to know where they went wrong than the rest of us.

By identifying your emotional reactions to money and reflecting on these experiences, I believe you can learn to deal with money more effectively and enjoyably. You may still make mistakes, but you will be able to recognize them as mistakes and correct them. What usually gets us into trouble, after all, isn't doing the wrong thing; it's failing to understand that it's the wrong thing and fixing it. Repeating the same errors over and over again is what makes people crazy about money.

As a practicing clinical psychologist, I've worked with individuals, couples, their children, and their families for 30 years. I listen to my clients' stories and their concerns as if I were in their shoes, and feel what they are experiencing from their perspective, not mine. I want to know what makes them feel good about themselves, as well as what troubles them. From my empathic understanding of each client, I can help them better understand themselves.

This is important because the more clearly you understand your own feelings, the more successful you will be in reaching your personal goals. If you are unaware of your emotional reactions and thinking patterns, or indulge in extreme expressiveness without regard to its impact on other people (and without understanding why you behave that way), you have less control over your own happiness and your ultimate fate.

Better self-understanding leads to authentic dialogue and the ability to deal with tough issues. As I work with my clients to develop insights that will transform into empowering skills and behavior, I am able to help them feel more visible, understood, and connected.

The insights I've gained have prompted my interest in helping people deal more effectively with the "money devils" behind such issues as spending too much, hoarding too much, or avoiding money matters altogether. Their experiences and the insights from my consulting room can benefit anyone who values money and their relationship with it.

Freeing Yourself from Feeling Bad

Sandy's story illustrates my approach. Her once-brilliant father, 78, had become increasingly confused and disoriented. He resented her attempts to help him, yet at the same time made biting comments about her selfishness and unwillingness to help. Although he prided himself on managing his money well, when Sandy went through his papers she found out he had invested his retirement funds so badly that he had very little to live on. She was terrified that she would feel compelled to have him live with her, but saying no to him made her feel so guilty that she punished herself by withdrawing from her friends.

I believe that Sandy, like the rest of us, is entitled to have a sense of "rightfulness" about herself, to value and focus on her own experience without feeling selfish or "bad." Having a core sense of oneself (i.e., being able to enjoy and feel good about who you are and what you do) is critical to feeling empowered. I call this healthy narcissism.

Presently, Sandy experienced her dad as powerful, stubborn, and self-absorbed. While she was growing up, he was a towering figure she both admired and feared. Although she knew he was now failing, her childhood perceptions of him were so strong that she was unable to say what she truly felt or to act on her present feelings. When she tried to get in touch with her own thoughts, she felt guilty and afraid. Putting herself down and ignoring her own needs were safer than risking a confrontation with Dad.

Through our work together, Sandy came to see that she viewed herself as a helpless, undeserving child. This awareness made her more open to revising her ideas about herself, which helped her get rid of her negative self-image. It also allowed her to challenge her belief about how powerful and deserving her father was. She was then able to confront him with the reality of what he had done to himself, and make it clear that she would help him find a place to live but would not take him in.

As you can see from Sandy's situation, money itself is only part of the issue. It's the complexity of relationships, emotions, and beliefs associated with money that needs understanding and resolution.

Crazy About Money will help you identify the feelings that influence and sometimes control the way you deal with money: how you picture it, how you relate to it, how you use it (or let it use you). You'll learn that there's no need for shame about having issues with money, even though it's a taboo subject both inside and outside therapists' offices. Finally, by better understanding your relationship with money, you will be able to free yourself from its control and make more empowered, healthy financial choices.

~

Crazy About Money? I've Been There

I've earned some of my insights the hard way. More than a decade ago, my husband and I received an unexpected tax bill for $20,000. I was shocked when Howard, who had always taken care of our finances, admitted he had forgotten about the bill and would have to pay it with our credit card. My anxiety and blood pressure spiked, and I launched into a furious interrogation about the state of our finances. Of course he became defensive, and we were soon deadlocked.

This incident awoke me to the fact that money was a huge blind spot in my personal and professional life. I was acting as though somebody else was supposed to be competent enough to look after our money. In fact, not only had I given up the responsibility of daily money management to my husband, but the two of us had handed over our savings to be invested by a broker who was a friend's father. Knowing he would have his daughter's best interests at heart, somehow we took it for granted that he would treat us like family, too.

Realizing this, I was both angry and embarrassed. Why had I assumed that someone who knew more about money than I did would take care of me financially? Worse yet, why did I expect a stranger to look after our money as if it were his own? Yes, he might have more financial knowledge and experience – but it was *our* money!

At the time, it didn't dawn on me that my husband, who is good at almost everything he does, had his own blind spots – his own kind of craziness about money. I also wanted to believe that financial professionals acted logically, at least most of the time. Little did I realize that my trust in their goodwill and capabilities would eventually lead to dire results, teaching me that even *they* can be crazy about money.

These revelations were painful and shameful. As the first step in feeling better about myself, Howard (a psychiatrist) and I agreed that I would take charge of the day-to-day financial operation of our two practices. This took time and organization, but when I saw what money came into and went out of our account, I began to feel more in control and thus calmer.

At the same time I told our broker that I wanted to take a more active role in our retirement investing. To my annoyance, he had little interest in educating me. In fact, this man I had been relying on handed me over to his junior partner, claiming he was too busy himself to entertain my growing interest in the stock market. What he really meant was that *I didn't have enough money for him to make time for me.*

❧

The 800-lb. Gorilla in the Room

It has taken me years to understand my unconscious feelings about money and educate myself to handle it more wisely. In that process, I also learned to listen more closely for my clients' money issues. These issues are the 800-lb. gorilla in many a room, keeping people from being honest with themselves, family members, friends, or a counselor.

People who consult a psychologist typically don't even mention money (unless it's to say they'll have trouble paying for therapy). After all, they're there to talk about their difficulty with relationships, not their bank accounts. So in the past, neither my clients nor I thought of money as a core issue for therapy. For instance, if a client told me about being angry with her husband and going on a buying spree, we would talk about her rage and what it meant for her to seek revenge by running up the balance on his credit card. We didn't discuss her relationship with money or why she chose it as the vehicle for exacting revenge, let alone whether she really wanted what she had bought! That's the classic definition of a blind spot: a gap in the field of vision. If we aren't aware of it and don't correct for it, the result can be a ruinous car crash – or in this case, a financial crash.

After the eye-opening discovery of my own money avoidance, I became more direct in raising the subject with clients. What I discovered was that most people don't see money as an issue in and of itself, because it's so interwoven with other issues.

~

Why a Psychologist Can Help You Understand Money Better

Most of us don't realize that emotions and money have deep and complex relationships with each other. We believe we manage money logically, whether we're running a household or making a long-term financial plan. Rarely do we acknowledge the cauldron of emotions that seethe around dealing with money. For example, say you check your bank account and see the balance is down more than you expected. Do you calmly and coolly assess possible reasons for the discrepancy? No, my guess is that you become alarmed and anxious, wondering if you screwed up, the bank screwed up, or your spouse indulged in a secret spending spree. Even small financial glitches like this can produce strong emotional reactions.

Financial planners are trained to develop strategies that help clients reach their goals. Although they may have a sensitive understanding of these goals, they often lack the psychological training and/or insight to deal with emotionally-based money conflicts.

For example, say a planner asks a client couple how much money they need to meet basic expenses. The husband says $4,000 a month; the wife, $7,000 a month. When the planner asks how much they saved in the past year, the wife says "Not much," and the husband might say, "We did pretty well." What's the truth?

In this kind of situation, the planner might refer the clients to a psychologist who can help them identify the reasons behind their contradictory responses. During a therapy session, the subject typically segues from money to problems with communication, conflicting needs, or underlying psychological issues. Once these are out in the open, a financially savvy psychologist will help clients address money matters, often working in partnership with the financial planner. When the couple returns to the planner, they will have agreed on their truths.

From earliest childhood to the final years, money and emotions are a continuing thread in our lives. *Crazy About Money* will help you recognize this thread and the patterns it creates in your life. As you learn why you act the way you do, you'll find your relationship with money will improve, your financial efforts will be energized and better directed, and you'll be on the path to greater happiness and fulfillment.

How We'll Approach the Empowerment Process

Money plays a huge role as we go through life, and the ways we see and use it change as we age. The first chapters of *Crazy About Money* will discuss what money means to us, where our beliefs come from, and how we develop our money behavior from childhood through young adulthood and into our older years. Later chapters focus on how we use money – be it investing, borrowing, gambling, or leaving a legacy. Throughout the book, you'll hear the stories of people I have worked with. Some of the characters, some of the circumstances, and some of the outcomes may have a familiar ring and help you see yourself more clearly as you witness these struggles, insights, and victories.

By absorbing the stories' lessons, doing the exercises at the end of each chapter, and applying what you have learned to your own money situation, at the conclusion of *Crazy About*

Money you will know how to make better money choices for yourself. Your increased money awareness will help you develop your "financial self": a clear and consistent internal set of positive attitudes, beliefs, and skills that will direct and inform your money management decisions. You'll become proud of what you do with money and happy about what money gives back to you. Instead of feeling "crazy about money," you'll be on your way to becoming a Money Master.

PART I:

GETTING READY FOR YOUR MONEY JOURNEY

We'll begin by looking at how emotions work and what it takes to sustain a vital sense of happiness. To help you think about what money means to you, I will outline the different meanings that money has to various people. Next, we'll walk through a detailed understanding of how your brain processes "information in" and "information out." Included in this discussion are gender differences and aging changes in the brain. Finally, we'll examine the new field of behavioral economics, which addresses the irrational and risky things we do with money in order to protect ourselves from a sense of loss. Once you become familiar with this information, you will be able to apply it forward to understand where your own money beliefs came from and how they have played out throughout your life.

RINO

Chapter 1:
The Basics of a Balanced Life

EMOTIONS AND HAPPINESS

"Just as your car runs more smoothly and requires less energy to go faster and farther when the wheels are in perfect alignment, you perform better when your thoughts, feelings, emotions, goals, and values are in balance." —Brian Tracy

If you walk down a path in the woods and see a crooked stick on the ground in front of you, you'll probably stop in your tracks, heart racing and palms sweaty, before you even have time to ask yourself, "Is that a snake?" Sensing danger, your emotional system prompts you to react without delay. Only later, when you realize you are out of danger, do you actually think about what happened and assess your reactions to it.

As humans, this is how we are wired to respond whenever we perceive threats in the environment. We react the same way to psychological threats. For instance, if you feel you don't have enough money, you may experience a fear reaction when you open a dreaded bill or are reminded that your child's daycare fee is due. If you want more money and can't figure out how to get it, you may feel thwarted or angry, as if you were under assault.

Threats to our psychological self aren't as easy to explain and understand as physical threats. That's because our "sense of self" is a quirky mix of thoughts, behaviors, and values that make us feel good about ourselves. When these values appear to be endangered, we perceive it as an attack on our self. We react emotionally, just as we would to a stick on the path. Someone with a deeply rooted sense of self-worth can easily cope with a threat to their sense of well-being. Someone else, who lacks empowerment, pleasure, and satisfaction in his or her sense of self, may find that emotions prevent him from shrugging off what seems to be a personal insult or hurt.

What Exactly Are Emotions?

Emotions are physical and psychological feeling states that make thoughts and experiences larger than life. Emotions change the world from gray to Technicolor, from deadness to aliveness. Some emotions are negative: for instance, being cheated can make us "seethe with rage." On the positive side, winning the lottery can make us "giddy with excitement."

Emotions have another use. They chunk together facts, ideas, or experiences, allowing us to process information immediately. Faster processing makes emotions more useful and powerful as long as they are based on accurate assumptions. If they're based on flawed data, such as a childhood trauma, emotional reactions can mislead us into making bad decisions.

It takes every newborn *Homo sapiens* a while to learn how to think, but we know how to react emotionally from day one. Babies are born with nine basic emotions, six of which are negative:

- Fear-terror
- Anger-rage
- Anxiety-anguish

- Sadness-grief
- Shame-humiliation
- Dissmell (reaction to things that don't smell good)-disgust

There are only half as many positive emotions:

- Interest-excitement
- Enjoyment-joy
- Surprise-startle

Negative emotions can alert us to danger and thus have high survival value, so it's not surprising that we have more of them. But positive emotions are much more gratifying and, like money, can compound and grow the more we experience them.

Our emotions determine what is amplified in our life, including our relationship with money. They powerfully enhance how we experience specific events, and influence what we think and believe about ourselves. By learning what our emotional states are and understanding how they affect us, we can change our thinking, our beliefs, and ultimately our behavior concerning money.

∾

Emotional About Money

The idea that dealing with money is a precise, rational process is a myth that dies hard. The "experts" on business and investment programs foster this myth by appearing to explain money matters rationally. Even though they too can be misled by emotions, they make their thinking, advice, and predictions appear completely logical. ("The market was up today on good employment news" or "The market was down today because of an increase in mortgage defaults.")

Granted, some people may be able to think about money unemotionally; but for most of us, money's emotional charge colors our thoughts and actions, whether we know it or not. By becoming more conscious of these emotions, we can see how they affect our decisions and learn to create more and better choices for ourselves.

Emotions are embedded in beliefs. You and I, your mother, father, partner, and friends all have beliefs about money that we may or may not be aware of. I like the term "money scripts" (coined by financial planner Rick Kahler and psychologists/financial consultants Drs. Ted and Brad Klontz) as a way of describing the emotional baggage attached to these beliefs.

Unhealthy money scripts develop when our emotions about money are confused or rooted in fear or anger. This can lead to a sense of entitlement, aggressive self-promotion, and ruthless competitiveness. Another way we often deal with a negative emotional charge is to suppress it or try to disconnect it from our thoughts and actions, as if it isn't important or doesn't belong to us. This emotional denial or dissociation is marked by an avoidance of personal accountability, hard work, and financial reality.

Some limiting money scripts are:

- "I'm keeping score. No one is going to ace me out."
- "If others have more, I'm less."
- "Money doesn't count; I'm above it all."
- "Having and spending money is my only pleasure."
- "I'm only safe if I have more than I need."
- "I'll never have enough."

- "Someone will rescue me. God will provide."
- "I should have what I want when I want it. I'm entitled."

We only need to look to the news to see that even smart, well-educated people can let their emotions spur them into poor decisions about money. For example, it appears that many seemingly sophisticated investors joined in Bernie Madoff's irrational Ponzi scheme because it made them feel part of a privileged "in group." Other folks saw people like themselves moving into bigger homes, and became so envious that they too propelled themselves into unaffordable mortgages. Some investment bankers and hedge fund managers took such irrational risks in chasing after the biggest returns, fees, and commissions, determined not to be outdone, that they helped bring on economic catastrophe.

On the positive side, the elements of healthy money scripts are personal accountability, self-assertiveness, emotional stability, and common sense. Some examples:

- "If I work hard and spend only what I have, I'll have enough."
- "Having enough money for my basic needs frees me to focus on what I love."
- "I'm valued for who I am, not what I have."
- "Security is having enough, not amassing more."

Positively charged money scripts are like constantly blooming flowers. They enliven our efforts to take care of ourselves, create optimism, and help us direct our money efforts more constructively. But if you're ensnared by negative scripts, will having more money help free you from them?

Can Money Buy Happiness?

Near the southeast corner of Central Park in New York City is the richest zip code in the U.S. It is also one of the unhappiest zip codes, as Dr. Martin Seligman, director of the University of Pennsylvania Positive Psychology Center, once told me. How can it be that the accumulation of great wealth does not bring the satisfaction and fulfillment it promises? After all, money lets us buy anything we want and do whatever we feel like doing.

In reality, creating extreme wealth is no easy task. You typically have to push other needs and desires to the side, either giving them short shrift or sacrificing them completely. Long hours are the norm.

Perhaps as a result, research shows that people whose primary pursuit is money are more likely to be dissatisfied with their lives. Reaching a financial goal doesn't bring the satisfaction they had hoped, partly because they can always find someone who is wealthier than they are. If getting rich is your main goal in life, you will probably always want more, because you will always compare yourself with those who have more, not those who have less. It's like struggling up a ladder to a destination that is always several rungs above you.

"Money can't buy me love," as the Beatles sang. But all too often, we tend to assume that it can fix everything wrong in our lives. Compared to being poor, having enough money to meet basic needs does increase happiness. But having more money than that usually fails to bring the bliss we imagine.

In fact, having "more money than you know what to do with" can bring big headaches. Rich people often feel vulnerable because of their wealth, knowing that others may envy them and try to take advantage of them. Constantly suspicious and fearful of being befriended for their wealth, not for themselves, they can become aggressively self-protective. A talented family portrait photographer once told me that a multimillionaire customer drove such a hard bargain with him that there was no way for the photographer to make even a meager profit.

I surmise that this wealthy person had not discovered the powerful insights of positive psychology, a newly developed field of study focusing on the strengths and values that enable individuals and communities to find happiness and thrive.

What Makes Us Happy?

Dr. Seligman, who has pioneered the study of positive psychology, believes there are three levels of happiness. The first is immediate and pleasurable. Think of intense moments of joy you have felt, the excitement of taking a physical risk and succeeding, or the rush of sexual pleasure. Although this kind of happiness feels great, it is short-lived.

The next level is the kind of happiness that the Declaration of Independence allows us to pursue. Thomas Jefferson wasn't referring to the immediate sensation of pleasure that characterizes the first level. Rather, he thought human beings were entitled to pursue their own well-being and some degree of personal fulfillment. In positive psychology terms, the "pursuit of happiness" means identifying, exploring, and developing our personality and cognitive strengths, and crafting our life so we use as many of these signature strengths as we can.

Dr. Seligman has identified 24 signature strengths in five categories:

1. **Wisdom:**
    - Curiosity in the world
    - Love of learning
    - Judgment, critical thinking, and open-mindedness
    - Ingenuity, originality, practical intelligence, street smarts
    - Social intelligence, personal intelligence, emotional intelligence
    - Perspective

2. **Courage:**
    - Valor and bravery
    - Perseverance, industry, and diligence
    - Integrity, genuineness, honesty
    - Kindness and generosity

3. **Humanity/Love:**
    - Loving and allowing oneself to be loved
    - Justice
    - Fairness and equality
    - Leadership

4. **Temperance:**
    - Self-control
    - Humility and modesty
    - Prudence, discretion, caution

5. **Transcendence:**
    - Appreciation of beauty and excellence
    - Gratitude
    - Hope, optimism, and future-mindedness
    - Spirituality, sense of purpose, faith, religiousness
    - Forgiveness and mercy
    - Playfulness and humor
    - Zest, passion, and enthusiasm

The last of the three levels of happiness is its highest form: the pursuit of meaning. That may sound like something only a philosopher or a Zen master can experience, but it's accessible to all of us. Happiness of meaning (or purpose) refers to the satisfaction of attaching yourself to something meaningful that's larger than you are: a scientific, artistic, athletic, religious, or business pursuit. The benefits increase still more when you are part of a community of shared goals and values, where you have the potential to influence and be influenced by others as you use your strengths to work collaboratively.

The whole thrust of positive psychology is to encourage us to understand and use our strengths in a supportive, energizing environment. In defining the three levels of happiness, Dr. Seligman wants us to focus on what is good about ourselves and others, not what is wrong or missing in our life.

How does money fit into this three-tiered vision of happiness? Clearly, if we do anything we can to make money, ignoring our unique strengths and values, we're unlikely to feel deeply satisfied. By finding a way to use those values and strengths in a way that provides economic rewards, we're more apt to feel content, and, quite possibly, to be more financially successful.

You may be saying to yourself, "What if I can't find a job that gives me a good paycheck along with the satisfaction of using my strengths? Is it better to be fulfilled, even if this limits my income? Or is a decent wage so important that I should give up the pursuit of happiness for it?"

In my view, if the only available job offers you nothing but a paycheck and some contact with co-workers, that's a starting point, not a dead end. Identify your strengths and find a way to use them in your work.

Consider the story of Rosalee, who worked in the back office of a chain supermarket and hated it. Noticing that she loved to talk with people as much as she disliked doing paperwork in isolation, her supervisor transferred her to the customer service desk. Being able to help customers made a huge difference in Rosalee's happiness. Her productivity increased, and before long she received a promotion and a raise. The moral of the story: Live your strengths and the money will follow!

~

Chapter 1 Exercise: What Are Your Signature Strengths?

Part 1: Take a good look at the strengths listed on page 20 and decide which five of them fit you most closely:

1. ______________________
2. ______________________
3. ______________________
4. ______________________
5. ______________________

Then visit Dr. Seligman's website, www.authentichappiness.com. Take his Authentic Happiness Inventory Test, which will give you a formal assessment of your strengths. How close did you come with your own evaluation?

You'll be able to use the results as a guide to integrate your strengths into daily life. Exercising them whenever you can will create a sense of satisfaction and well-being. You may even find yourself "in the zone," or what psychologist Dr. Mihaly Csikszentmihalyi refers to as "flow." In this highly pleasurable state time stops, self-consciousness evaporates, and you are one with whatever activity you are pursuing.

Part 2: Write down how these strengths play out for you from day to day. Are you surprised by how much or how little you make use of them?

Part 3: With your new awareness of how much you ordinarily implement your strengths, write down some ideas about how to use them more often and more effectively.

By taking time to do this exercise mindfully, you will greatly magnify the value of this chapter's lessons. To help you see how a full and candid answer may help you uncover truths about yourself, I wrote out my answers to the questions. I will answer the questions in the first few chapters. For different ages discussed in later chapters I have included the responses of some of my clients.

Maggie's Response to the Chapter 1 Exercise:

Part 1: As I view myself, my 5 signature strengths are:

1. Love of learning
2. Integrity, genuineness, and honesty
3. Self-control
4. Zest, passion, and enthusiasm
5. Social, personal, and emotional intelligence

Part 2: How do these strengths play out day to day?

In my role as psychologist and writer, I'm constantly learning the details of people's lives and helping them gain insight and think of new ways to improve themselves and their situation. I use my social, personal, and emotional intelligences to navigate with them and help them see themselves better and add to their already existing strengths.

I get constant practice exercising my self-control. A person trying to change has to take little steps toward change, as big leaps usually backfire. Sometimes I'd like to facilitate huge leaps but know the usual consequences so I think them to myself. Sometimes I'd like to scream at the credit card "account executive" but know that will make the transaction more miserable than it already is. And, of course, by the time it is dinner I'm starved and often don't have the self-control to "be good"!

Part 3: **With your new awareness of how much you ordinarily implement your strengths, write down some ideas about how to use them more often and more effectively.**

I use my strengths pretty consistently. I don't often give myself credit for using my strengths because I'm focused on what I'm doing. I can improve my strength awareness by reviewing the day in the evening and focusing on how I have used my strengths. This will help me appreciate what I have and increase my use of them.

~

$
RINO

Chapter 2:
Different Strokes for Different Folks

WHAT DOES MONEY MEAN?

"Don't tell me where your priorities are. Show me where you spend your money and I'll tell you what they are." —James W. Frick

To you, money may mean freedom; to your neighbor, security; to somebody else, love or power. In fact, money has many emotional meanings. To help in understanding where your own feelings about money may have originated, let's look at some of the goals, dreams, and messages I have recognized in my own and my clients' experiences. After recounting each of these stories (I've changed names and details to protect clients' privacy), I will add my own professional views and advice in "Comments from the Couch."

Money Is Security

Fourteen-year-old Christopher bent over the hospital bed, fighting back tears. His father weakly motioned him closer and said in a faint voice, "Take care of your mother, Chris." A minute later his dad — his hero — was gone.

Chris collapsed on a chair next to the bed. Memories of past times passed through his mind. How happy and secure his life had been until the year before, when his dad's once-successful store could no longer compete with large retail chains and went broke. The family had gone from living comfortably to near-poverty.

Ever since then, the specter of his dad's financial failure has haunted Chris. Never, he vowed, would anything like it happen to him. Brought up to excel (and criticized when he fell short), he worked hard for the rest of high school and college. He couldn't relax, fearing that someone else might overtake and defeat him.

Chris's intense competitiveness only increased with his first job in advertising. Long hours of work paid off as he climbed higher and higher on the corporate ladder. His growing bank account should have reassured him that he was creating the security he needed, but it didn't. Each time he reached the goal he had set for himself, he revised it upward because it wasn't enough money.

Chris now works night and day as an advertising consultant. Persistent and determined, he drives himself to amass a fortune because money is the only thing he knows that offers security. He is at his creative best when putting together a complicated campaign for his clients. Whenever he tries to relax, he gets nervous and uncomfortable. He never takes vacations, fearing he might miss an opportunity.

How much money will be enough for Christopher? Now 50, he envisions that by 60 he will have at least $10 million. That new goal, he believes, will make him secure and powerful, not a failure like his father.

~

COMMENTS FROM MY COUCH

The "shock of scarcity" at age 14 has so profoundly affected Chris that, try as he might to achieve security by accumulating wealth, each achievement only pushes him to make more. To experience the comfort and safety his money should afford him, he needs to understand that his youthful feelings of insecurity both drive his success and impede his ability to enjoy it.

I'm reminded that after Philip of Macedon conquered Greece, a philosopher supposedly asked him, "What will you do now?"

The ambitious father of Alexander the Great answered, "Conquer Byzantium."

"And then?" the philosopher queried.

"Then the Persians."

"And then?" probed the philosopher.

"Return home and relax," Philip said.

"Well," said the philosopher, "why not do that now and save yourself all the trouble?"

People like Chris and Philip are driven by unconscious beliefs and emotions to acquire more and more, instead of enjoying the fruits of success. If money represents security to you, it's important to understand the unconscious forces that are keeping you in overdrive and change the belief that you will never have enough. Otherwise, you may find yourself saying on your deathbed, "I wish I'd spent more time enjoying the money I made."

Christopher's bottom-line money belief: If I only have enough money, I'll be safe, secure and "on top."

~

Money Is a Necessary Evil

Another client of mine, Justin, was an interesting contrast to Christopher. Instead of being absorbed by the pursuit of wealth, Justin gave the impression that he couldn't care less about making money. A successful surgeon, he would stay in the operating room for hours on end until the last stitch was perfectly placed. After a restless break, his greatest pleasure was to go back into the OR and perform another procedure with the same dedication and intensity, challenging himself to do it better and faster this time. People came from all over the country to be treated, some in chronic pain, others near death, many of them unable to pay him. He took risky and difficult cases other surgeons would not consider. Weekends were not complete without several operations. Justin dreaded vacations because he could not operate.

His colleagues accused him of being money-driven. Why else would he work so hard? The truth was that operating made Justin feel alive, important, and happy. He loved being a surgeon, surrounded by a cadre of people who acted in concert with him to save lives. He had no idea how much money he was making, and didn't care. He saw himself as working to help people, and believed the profit motive had no place in medicine.

When Justin was forced to retire from surgery because of hand and arm tremors, he was devastated. Although he was nearing retirement age, it depressed him enormously to lose the one activity that sustained his enthusiasm and his self-esteem. Nothing else came close to giving him the sense of purpose he had experienced as a surgeon.

As he worked his way through this loss, he found himself looking for businesses he could become involved in. He had a real entrepreneurial touch, and a number of deals worked out well for him. This gave him no joy, but it was a way to keep himself distracted. Someday, he hoped, he would find something as precious to him as surgery.

COMMENTS FROM MY COUCH

At first I had a hard time understanding Justin. His behavior became clearer when he told me he hadn't claimed his percentage of a deal he had arranged. Although he resented working without pay, when he did have the opportunity to charge a consulting fee, he resisted sending a bill.

In our discussions, we began to understand the complex emotions behind this behavior. It seemed to Justin that once he got his cut, all the wheeling and dealing would be over and he would have to find another project. "Losing" a project felt to him like losing the ability to operate. Sending a bill for his services also made him feel dependent on the person who owed him. He was humiliated to think that someone might assume he needed the money. Deep down he also felt insulted because working for an hourly wage, like a common laborer, didn't reflect his self-image as a skilled and knowledgeable professional.

If Justin had not had enough income to live on, he probably would have thrown himself into a frenzy of money-making activity. However, he still wouldn't care about money for its own sake. He considers money as a necessary evil, and it has no attraction for him. He doesn't want to need it (or anything else) because it makes him feel vulnerable, dependent, and not in control. The term "money monk," coined by Olivia Mellan, is a perfect description of Justin.

Justin's bottom-line money belief: I'm above "dirty lucre"; I just want to be part of the action.

Money Is a Substitute for Love

Money has an amazing power to entwine with a vast number of psychological issues. Mary Lou and Hal are examples of parents who used money as a substitute for love.

This couple worked hard at their small business, but experienced gnawing feelings of guilt that they had missed out on "quality time" with their now-teenage children. To make up for their own unavailability, they bought the kids every conceivable electronic gadget, sent them to expensive summer camps, and on and on.

The two teens reacted by yelling, screaming, and bullying their parents into submission whenever they didn't get what they wanted. The 14-year-old girl, Kirin, stopped handing in her homework, began to bully her schoolmates as well, and secretly started to watch porn. When her younger brother started following in her footsteps, the school intervened and suggested therapy.

Since therapy depended on the parents driving the children to sessions, the kids often missed their appointments. When I suggested they come in together for family meetings, it was impossible to find a convenient or even a possible time for both parents to accompany their children to my office.

~

COMMENTS FROM MY COUCH

Parents so busy they can't find time to bring their children for help? We all know what's wrong with this picture. In fact, many of us know parents just like this. Working too hard to spend much time with their children, they try to make up for their absence by indulging their offspring with all the latest electronic gadgetry, cool clothes, and sports equipment. They rationalize that love has been transmitted, even if they have to go into debt for it. But the kids aren't getting what they need.

In this case, the parents clung to the needs of their business even though the stakes were high with their neglected children. At this late date, they were unsure how to show their love any other way than by indulging the kids with money. Just "hanging out" with their daughter and son made them uncomfortable. For example, when Kirin asked to take a walk to the mall with them, they would say something like "Not now, Kirin; I don't have time. Why don't you call a friend to go with you? Here's twenty dollars. Have a good time." Although turning down these requests made them feel guilty, their guilt didn't push them to develop the capacity for closeness that both parents and children need.

Today, these unfortunate children know their worth only from what their mom and dad buy them. Therapy is still progressing, but I'm concerned that one of the kids will probably get into drugs, become promiscuous, or drop out of school in the not too distant future. The escalated severity of the problem will then take even more time and resources to resolve. Sometimes, however, it takes a catastrophic event to pierce the snug cocoon of "business as usual."

Mary Lou and Hal's bottom-line money belief: Don't bother us; we're busy amassing money.

Money Is Consolation

A full moon shone in the window as Donna sat at her computer, shopping for great buys on the Internet. The night stillness reminded her that her husband, Steve, wouldn't be back from his business trip for several more days. *Click, click, click* —and anything she wanted was hers.

Shopping online was so easy, in fact, that she didn't remember buying the books, the clothes, or the new lamp that showed up on her doorstep a few days later. Shamefaced, she hid the packages. When Steve found them, she told him she had no idea how they got there. Eventually she realized she needed help to overcome this expensive and embarrassing behavior.

COMMENTS FROM MY COUCH

In our discussions, Donna voiced her shame that she couldn't tell her husband how much his frequent traveling bothered her. Thinking she should be independent enough to keep herself occupied and content while he was gone, she blamed herself for giving in to the buying sprees that helped fill the void of his absence.

In the course of our work together, Donna realized that she needed to learn to voice her loneliness to Steve. With his help, she could try to work out ways to feel supported and loved while he was away. Spending money may fill an emotional void in the moment, but it usually doesn't last.

Donna's bottom-line money belief: Buying can fill my emotional need for excitement and connection.

Money Is Self-Esteem

Zelda originally consulted me because of her concern about her daughter's growing coldness toward her, and the girl's expectation that Zelda would immediately buy her whatever she wanted, no matter what the cost. In our ensuing conversations it became clear that Zelda, a beautiful woman, took pleasure in styling herself like a work of art. She enjoyed amazing people with her array of different clothes, and never wore an outfit more than once.

As she explained it, going shopping was like a party for her. Salespeople know her well and they know what she likes. When she visits their stores, they have clothes ready for her to try on while they watch in what she experiences as admiration. Although her husband occasionally gripes that they are running out of closet space for her clothes, which already overflow the bathtub, he is proud to be seen with her.

COMMENTS FROM MY COUCH

Is it any wonder that Zelda's daughter expects her mom to buy her anything and everything? Zelda is enjoying her relationship with money too much to see that her spending is extreme and that her daughter resents her self-absorption. She gets so much emotional "zing" from her forays into the shopping world, and complicit support from her good-naturedly complaining husband, that her behavior is unlikely to change unless they run out of money.

Her husband attended sessions with her and confronted her with his concern about the amount of money she spends. She fought his every word but began to see that her spending was excessive and that there was a real problem. I was able to refer her to a website that offered self-help for spenders. After going through the program, she began to admit that spending as a sole pleasure did indeed have its limitations.

Zelda's bottom-line money belief: Money provides pleasurable buying experiences that lift my self-esteem and make me feel important and safe.

Money Is Self-Importance

While Monty was growing up, he constantly felt overshadowed by his younger brother. Discovering that he could get attention from his teachers and peers by clowning around, he realized that charming other people was an effortless way to get ahead. When his parents realized this might become a problem, he resisted their efforts to make him settle down. Ironically, Monty's acting out only made his brother Robert try harder to be good and please his parents. His mother tried not to show favoritism, but Monty knew she preferred Robert.

Determined not to be second best, Monty decided to show how successful he could be. Bright, handsome, and intense, he charmed others as a stockbroker, using his strengths of zest, enthusiasm, playfulness, and humor. Unfortunately, these qualities were not highly valued by his mother — the one person whose respect and love he craved. As his wealth grew, he attempted to wow her with his new Mercedes, his expensive clothes, and his dolled-up wife; but the more he tried to impress her, the more she drew back. She seemed to prize his brother — now a successful surgeon — all the more.

Monty grew furious with her and with Robert. When she died, his relationship with his brother blew up. Monty tried to obtain as much money as he could from her estate. Since he was skilled at manipulating money and had financial and legal contacts, he was initially successful at grabbing more than his share of the assets. Overwhelmed with grief at his mother's death and unable to match Monty's financial expertise, Robert capitulated in the legal battle that Monty had fomented. Who won this war?

COMMENTS FROM MY COUCH

Monty had some terrific strengths that other people can only dream of. But it wasn't enough for him to enjoy using these strengths; he needed the mirror of his mother's love, which he felt Robert "stole" by developing the kind of qualities she valued and admired. After her death, his ravaging of her estate was a way of getting back at her and at Robert with the weapon of money — the yardstick with which he had hoped to win his mother's recognition of his worth.

Although Monty walked off with more than his share of their mother's estate, is he really the winner? Robert continues to benefit from his past relationship with her. He had felt genuine loss when she died, not the desire for revenge that drove Monty. Until Monty forgives Robert for being himself, and understands that his own value does not depend on his mother's reaction to him, he will have a hard time moving on. Sad to say, he may not recognize the potential gain from working on his relationship with Robert until he experiences the unconflicted loss of a spouse, child, or best friend.

Monty's bottom-line money belief: Money makes me powerful and dominant.

Money Is the Easy Life

Lance grew up expecting to live comfortably. His mom and dad built a successful real estate development firm, planning to someday turn it over to him. However, by age 38 it became hard for Lance to keep up with the physical demands of digging foundation holes and framing houses, even though he still loved it. After working for the business since age 10, he had no idea what else to do. Somehow he needed to earn a six-figure income to support the lifestyle he and his wife Lucy were used to. Physical labor was the only kind of work that gave him a sense of meaning and purpose, but no one else would hire him because he never wrote anything down, hated paperwork, and loathed the tedious process of getting licenses and permits.

Adding to Lance's frustration was the difficulty of collecting his paycheck from his dad, despite all the old man's promises about the great financial rewards the firm would bring him. His father invented all kinds of excuses to avoid paying him, hoping to make Lance tougher and better equipped to run the business. Already feeling resentful and helpless, Lance perceived that his growing physical limitations made him all the more dependent on his dad.

When his father withheld his pay for months, Lance was finally enraged enough to start his own competing business on a very thin shoestring. Lucy was forced to take a demanding full-time job, as well as helping with the fledgling firm. Neither of them is willing to cut back on their lifestyle, because they were promised wealth and comfort and cannot let go of that dream.

COMMENTS FROM MY COUCH

Lance and his wife are locked into expectations they can't break out of. It's going to be hard for him to make as much money as they want because of his limited interests, narrow skill set, and reduced capacity for physical labor. The other obvious choice — to revise their expectations downward — is bound to entail feelings of frustration, loss, and failure. If they insist on maintaining their current lifestyle, it may mean that Lucy will be required to become the primary breadwinner, leaving Lance at home with the children while she develops her career.

Lance and Lucy's inability to confront difficult emotions has led to poor money choices. Unless they are able to disempower the money devils that drive them, they face bitter conflict and painful decisions in the near future.

Lance and Lucy's bottom-line money belief: We are entitled to the money it takes to fund our dreams.

~

Money Is Self-Confidence

Pat and Sal first consulted me about their daughter Lorna, who was not doing well at the performing arts high school she attended. Their fear that she would lose her scholarship brought their financial concerns to the surface. Sal had started a business with the potential to make millions, but his venture was destroyed when it began to threaten a more established company. Dejected, he lost confidence in his entrepreneurial powers. Meanwhile, Pat was working hard to develop a reputation as a painter. Her long hours in the studio meant that Sal took care of ferrying their daughter to and from after-school activities. What with Sal's uncertain income and Lorna's school tuition, there was no money left over for extras.

Many of Lorna's classmates have financially successful parents. Pat and Sal silently fumed when their daughter came home complaining that this friend got a new computer and that friend is going to Paris for the weekend. They had envisioned a future in which Pat would be a famous artist and one of Sal's businesses would soar. The reality that they could barely pay their bills was crushing. To a great extent, they had been victims of circumstance that eroded their hope for a better future. If only Pat's paintings would sell, or Sal's latest hot idea finds traction, they would be able to move on.

COMMENTS FROM MY COUCH

Pat and Sal are industrious, levelheaded people who have had more than their share of bad luck. Although they are both very resilient, too many things were going wrong for them to step ahead with optimism and confidence. Fortunately, they weren't big spenders and wanted Lorna to learn the value of hard work and achievement.

This couple has many strengths — including love of learning, critical thinking and open-mindedness, perseverance, and industry — to serve as sources of confidence and satisfaction. Recognizing that past regrets and comparisons with other people are unproductive, they focused on moving forward. Their strengths and values helped them persist through hard times until Pat's paintings did begin to sell. They learned to focus on what they could control, not what was out of their control. Fortune favors the brave – and the persistent!

Pat and Sal's bottom-line money belief: Great ideas and hard work will bring the money we deserve.

~

Money Is an Obstacle to Altruism

Vonnie and Jose never seemed to have enough money. Jose had earned a law degree but hated his work. Vonnie, a vibrant singer, had difficulty keeping herself organized as a teacher. Unable to mobilize their efforts consistently, they felt unfairly treated by a world that kept them overwhelmed and constantly running to catch up. Whenever they got on top of their finances, some crisis would put them in a hole again. They consulted me because Vonnie's disorganization had gotten to be a real problem. The piles of paper and other accumulated "stuff" crammed into their house was becoming a fire hazard.

Even though they were both well aware of these issues, they couldn't manage to get organized or develop a sustainable budget. Then, out of the blue, Jose found a position he loved with a social justice organization in a nearby city. When he moved to an apartment near his new job, it was a huge shock to Vonnie and their teenage daughter.

Vonnie had not been without Jose for decades. She hated his absence during the week. His new apartment and the extra travel back and forth ate up his salary increase, leaving them no farther ahead. Moreover, Vonnie herself was losing students who found her disorganization hard to deal with, even though they liked her teaching style. She worried that her relationship with Jose would become as bleak as their finances. Upset and worried that their marriage might break up, she started to work hard to change her old habits.

~

COMMENTS FROM MY COUCH

Vonnie and Jose's personal values as artists and social activists made it difficult for them to admit that they wanted more money, or to do what was necessary to earn it. They didn't talk about their discontent easily or often, since they felt it was superficial to be concerned about money.

As a result, a chronic feeling of deprivation colored their life blue — a tint that easily changed to red with envy and anger at the world. The experience of scarcity was so ingrained in their psyches that they constantly felt deprived and demoralized, unable to focus on what they did have instead of what they lacked. They knew what they needed to do, but wouldn't step up to it until they had no choice.

When Jose moved out, the stakes became high enough to force Vonnie to break the frustrating cycle she was in. She started taking medicine that helped her focus, and learned to organize in bite-sized chunks. When she began to see the stacks of clutter shrink, she was encouraged to keep up her new habits. After their house sold, she and Jose found a bigger apartment near his work — but not so big that it would enable her to accumulate more stuff.

Vonnie and Josie's bottom-line money belief: Why try to look after our money, when we've never had enough of and never will have enough?

Money Is Somebody Else's Responsibility

Heather was good at her job as a consultant for multimillion-dollar corporations, but didn't like the aggressive competitiveness of the corporate world. When her advice failed to receive the consideration she thought it merited, she felt discouraged and frustrated. At age 50, she realized that she really loved to create ideas, share them in writing, and teach others. Without worrying too much about how her finances would be affected, she took early retirement from her job and became an adjunct professor of English at a nearby college.

Then her husband, Ivan, left her for his best friend, and Heather's world fell apart. Putting all her energy into her teaching, she tried to forget about what was happening — including the financial fallout of her divorce. Ivan took care of their money, as he always had, until the papers were signed.

Soon afterward, Heather's lack of interest in managing her finances began to cause problems. Faced with big lawyer bills and many others she couldn't pay, she avoided opening her mail for days and weeks at a time. Stacks of bills piled up on her dining room table. When one table got full, she added another. Soon enough that one too, was cluttered with bills.

As her creditors hounded her for payment, Heather consoled herself with computer solitaire. She became more and more resentful and defiant of the collection agencies that pestered her.

COMMENTS FROM MY COUCH

How could this intelligent woman go for months, if not years, ignoring her mounting debt — and seemingly getting away with it? Behind her denial, Heather felt deeply ashamed, partly because of the way her marriage ended but also because she had allowed her finances to get out of control. Her debt was so abhorrent to her, and her shame at the worsening situation was so intense, that she had to deny it at all costs.

Disavowing responsibility for the bills, she convinced herself that the credit card companies and other creditors were being assaultive and unreasonable (much like her perception of the corporate world she had left in disgust).

Heather did not begin to deal with her debts until she learned to trust me enough to talk about what had been happening and feel the support of a neutral, non-judgmental person. It took weeks of baby steps before she opened her bills and thought about how to negotiate payments. During this empowerment process, Heather confessed her plight to her family. They decided to sell property that was no longer of use, generating a cash windfall that saved her from bankruptcy and further shame.

Most situations don't end so happily. Heather's challenge now is to change her relationship with money so she will never again sink into such mortifying debt.

Heather's bottom-line money belief: Someone else will take care of the money; I'm busy doing what I love.

SUMMARY OF COMMENTS FROM MY COUCH

The stories in this chapter illustrate how money can have very different meanings, present a wide range of challenges, and require solutions that vary for each individual. Reading them, you can see more clearly that the way people perceive, think, and feel about money determines how well they will be able to manage it and enjoy it. It's crucial for you to understand what money means to you, and what beliefs, attitudes, and emotions are embedded in that meaning — not just for your own financial well-being, but to avoid souring your relationships with others.

Like a zestful cook, I think of money as the broth of a soup. It permeates the other ingredients and can bring out their flavor marvelously. But if we don't understand how we interact with money, we're likely to find ourselves eating a miserable gruel that offers no pleasure at all.

~

Chapter 2 Exercise: Your Money Story

Write a "money story" or describe a money situation that typifies what money means to you. Then write down what you imagine the Comments From My Couch would be.

1. Do you see any pattern of a good or bad relationship with money?
2. Is there a money devil at work behind the scenes of your life? What has it been telling you? How could you respond to make the money devil feel less powerful?

Again, I include my take on the exercise to inspire you in developing a probing, honest answer of your own.

Maggie's Response to the Chapter 2 Exercise:

1. Do you see any pattern of a good or bad relationship with money?

I marvel at how some people spend so much money on clothes. When I shop and see something at full retail price it shocks me right out of the store. I decided one day to look at some consignment shops for a little price comparison. Just as a car loses a huge percentage of its value when you drive it out of the dealer's lot, the difference in price between a new and "used" dress or blouse is really extreme.

What amazed me was how new many of the clothes looked. There were even some designer names on the racks. It took a little adjusting to feel OK about wearing someone else's abandoned clothes. After a while that worry melted away. I replaced it with the idea that I was ecologically sound by saving a good blouse from going to waste because someone else was sick of wearing it!

I then took the money I had just saved and put it into my money market account for later.

What would I say to myself about this story? First, I would say "good for me" for saving myself some hard-earned money. But I'd add a comment that if I plan to do this all the time, isn't that being too rigid? What is the harm of buying a blouse here and there for full retail price if you really like it and don't do it all the time?

I have a good relationship to money in that I respect its power and necessity and don't waste it. But I am too worried that I might not have "enough." In doing so, I go to an extreme and can sometimes drive myself crazy, not to mention my husband's occasional eye-rolling look of skepticism.

2. Is there a money devil at work behind the scenes of your life? What has it been telling you? How could you respond to make the money devil feel less powerful?

My "money devil" is the fear that I will be blindsided by something and not have the means to cope with whatever disaster I imagine. I need to remember that I have coped with all kinds of losses and am still standing. Taking a moment to step back and absorb my track record is reassuring. If I didn't have such a track record, stepping back would help me gain the perspective to chart a new course and develop the commitment to implement it

Chapter 3:
Biology and Behavior

THE SCIENCE BEHIND OUR DIFFERENCES

"Shaped like a loaf of French country bread, our brain is a crowded chemistry factory lab, bustling with nonstop neural conversations... that dream factory... that fickle pleasuredome, that wrinkled wardrobe of selves stuffed into the skull like too many clothes into a gymbag." —Diane Ackerman

Ever watched a movie with a friend, and discovered when you talked about it later that the two of you had quite different interpretations of what happened? How is this possible when you both saw the same thing?

We assume that we accurately understand what we see and hear. But all information we take in from the world, whether trivial or critical, must be processed and interpreted in order to mean anything. Whatever meaning we find affects the "facts" we use when we choose a new car, an investment, even who we should marry, as well as what and how to teach our children about money. Our brains are the decision engine in this process, using many different emotional and cognitive factors to make simple and complex decisions about money.

But you know what computer programmers say: "Garbage in, garbage out." Sometimes we not only absorb bad information (garbage in), but we also get good information and turn it into garbage. After all, since you and your friend had completely different takes on the movie, it may be that you both took perfectly good information and skewed its meaning. To look at another example, during the real estate boom, most Americans were happily convinced that their homes would increase in value by 10% a year — forever! It didn't seem to matter that there had never been a time in history when that happened. Why did so many of us fool ourselves?

How Our 'Decision Engine' (aka the Brain) Works

All the information we take in with our ears, eyes, nose, mouth, and skin is carried by tiny electrical impulses along nerves to the brain. This new data is held in what neuroscientists call ***working memory*** for a fraction of a second, while we recruit previously learned information stored in long-term memory. By combining short- and long-term memory, our brain creates meaning.

For example, suppose the new data is that the floor is shaking. Hastily checking long-term memory, we recall previously stored memories about earthquakes. We may even remember some advice about what to do. Depending on what this long-term information tells us, we decide to run outside, hide under the bed, or jump into the cast-iron bathtub.

As another example, imagine that over coffee with a good friend, you learn that she has just won $10,000 in the lottery. You hear her good news, and see joy expressed in her eyes, her smile, her excited gestures. Meanwhile, you are feeling reactions of your own, perhaps happiness for her and envy that you didn't win. An instant later her face changes to an expression you don't understand. When you ask about it, she starts to cry. "Rick lost his job three months ago, and almost all the money will have to go to make our missed mortgage payments," she sobs.

That's a lot of data coming into your brain in a few seconds. Amazingly, your working memory can deal with all of it at the same time, allowing you to pull it together into a coherent story.

This happens almost instantaneously, using some of the 100 billion (that's 100,000,000,000) neurons in the brain that interact with each other across 100 trillion (100,000,000,000,000!) connections called synapses. Altogether, the brain contains immense circuits of neurons used to store and synthesize useful information. As we learn (or forget), the circuitry changes. If we change our mind, we *literally* change our brains.

In many ways, our life experiences determine what we have learned and therefore how we have programmed our brains. For instance, there are circuits that represent our attitudes about money. Since we all have a multitude of ideas about money, we are bringing many circuits into play as we try to understand money issues, and some of these circuits represent conflicting ideas. Sometimes we recognize a conflict and decide which side makes sense. When we do that, we may change our brains so the circuits for the "wrong" side become less powerful or even disappear.

What is certain, however, is that we must use our incredibly complicated brain to determine what we do about money, which in turn affects our interactions with other people, who must then use *their* brains to understand what just happened. It's a chain reaction. When you change your mind, you change your brain. What you say and do as a result has an impact on other people, who must use their brains in a similar way to respond. And around it goes.

∾

When the Brain Doesn't Work Right

There are certain times when the brain circuits don't process information properly:

- When you're afraid, angry, stressed out, or tired, you may infer the wrong meaning from something that happens or is said, leading to a hasty decision and a mistake.
- When the brain is impaired by drink, drugs, extreme fatigue, or dementia, you can't "think straight."
- When you have no experience with a particular issue, you have no memories in your brain to bring to bear on it.

Here's an example of this last point. My husband's grandmother, Maude, inherited real estate in Dayton, Ohio, from her father. Living far away in Milwaukee, she had no way to know that the neighborhoods were changing, reducing the value of her property. Her trusted advisor in Dayton, Miss Borgia, kept reassuring Maude that the houses were still excellent investments. (Miss Borgia wanted to keep collecting her inflated management fees.) Maude not only didn't know what was going on, but didn't know that she didn't know it. As important as this property was to her, she didn't pursue the information she needed. Why not? First, she was sure her powerful father would have made wise investments. And when she made her annual visit to Dayton, Miss Borgia was "so lovely," lunching with her at the best hotel dining room in town. Surely Miss Borgia was honest!

Two other pieces need to be added to this story. The first has to do with emotions. Maude was told again and again by her unfaithful husband that she couldn't manage real estate from 300 miles away and that she should sell it. Their relationship was so rocky, though, that Maude refused to go along with his good advice.

To make matters worse, a bout of scarlet fever as a child had left her with heart disease that was starting to affect her brain. She had begun to get confused when presented with balance sheets for her investments. Horrified that she might be getting senile, she denied her increasing intellectual impairment and insisted on hanging onto the properties. Nothing could change her mind. In consequence, her inheritance dwindled as the real estate value sank from what would have been at least $4 million in today's dollars to $300,000 or less.

Obviously money was only a part of this sad story, and it might not have been possible for Maude and her husband to find happiness. Still, if she had been aware of what she didn't know, as well as her silent rage at her husband, she might have acted to preserve part of a hard-earned, modest fortune. In her case, however, there were two complicating factors: emotional barriers that prevented her from admitting that something might be wrong, and faulty mental circuitry due to her illness. Either or both of these factors can make people crazy about money.

Developmental Differences in Our Wiring

We certainly wouldn't expect kindergarteners to be able to make investment decisions. Even if they watched CNBC constantly and had *The Wall Street Journal* read to them at story time, they still wouldn't know what to advise their parents to invest in. Their brains simply wouldn't have developed enough to make complex analytical decisions.

There are many age-based differences like this, but when it comes to financial savvy, only two are really important: the ability to think abstract thoughts and to plan for the future.

Take teenagers, for example. The prefrontal cortex (the front part of the brain), which helps us think clearly about the future consequences of actions, is not completely developed in adolescence. That's why many teens can't imagine the results of what they do. Many times a parent will demand in exasperation, "What on earth were you thinking? Didn't you know that might happen?" The honest answer is, "No, I couldn't think about the future consequences of my actions because my prefrontal cortex wasn't fully online." (What a great excuse!)

That's why adults need to set limits on what adolescents are not allowed to do, and insist that they do things that they don't want to do. For instance:

- "You must be home by 11:00." One reason for this is to prevent kids from getting involved in activities that any adult would know are too risky, but that adolescents can't assess because they actually don't have the emotional/social maturity.
- "No, you can't go out until you finish your book report." Teens often can't look far enough ahead to appreciate the value of being able to plan, a skill that will be essential to them later as workers, household managers, and informed citizens.

~

Gender Differences in Our Wiring

Research is constantly uncovering new differences between the male and female brain. This research must be viewed in perspective, since gender differences are studied by comparing large groups of men and women and comparing the "average man" with the "average woman." However, there's usually a lot of normal variation in these results. For example, researchers may find that the "average woman" is more inclined to avoid risk than the "average man," but that doesn't mean there are no risk-averse men or women who enjoy taking risks.

That said, let's consider some distinctions seen in *most* women and *most* men that can ultimately influence how they relate differently to money.

As you probably know, we humans have two-sided brains. The left and right hemispheres communicate with each other, but there are areas of specialization on each side. Dr. Daniel J. Siegel, a clinical professor of psychiatry at the UCLA School of Medicine, writes in *The Developing Mind: Toward a Neurobiology of Interpersonal Experience* (Guilford, 1999) that women tend to have more ability in left-hemisphere processes. This means they usually outperform men in skills involving the use of language, such as verbal fluency, grammar, and the speed with which they can speak. They're also superior at seeing things quickly, doing exacting tasks with their hands, and performing arithmetic calculations. Meanwhile, men excel at right-hemisphere tasks that are spatial in nature, including putting picture parts together to create a whole, copying a design with blocks, picturing and rotating 3-D objects in their minds, tracking through paper and pencil mazes, and using mechanical skills. Men also outdo women in mathematical reasoning, intercepting moving objects, and finding their way along a route.

Another difference is in aggression. From observations of both humans and nonhumans, we know males are usually more aggressive than females. As retired City College (NY) sociology professor Steven Goldberg points out in *Fads and Fallacies in the Social Sciences* (Humanity Books, 2008), young males engage in more rough-and-tumble play than females, driven toward dominance by high levels of testosterone. Women have less testosterone but more oxytocin, the "tend and befriend" hormone, which is linked to their tendency to be more nurturing and to cooperate with others.

These hormones affect the way our brains work. Although they tend to push men and women to process things differently, life experiences may have enough of an effect to alter these biological tendencies. Some men can be very nurturing, and some women can be very aggressive.

Sex-specific areas of the brain also influence men and women to communicate in different ways. Women seem to have an enhanced awareness of "emotionally relevant details, visual cues, verbal nuances, and hidden meanings," according to Dr. Robert Nadeau, a professor of English at George Mason University, in *S/he Brain: Science, Sexual Politics, and the Myths of Feminism* (Praeger, 1998). Similarly, female infants respond more readily to the human voice, while male infants appear to be more interested in objects than in people.

Since gender-related differences are a consequence of both biological difference and environmental factors, it's possible that the differences between men and women may narrow as contemporary social attitudes erase the rigid expectations of what women and men are supposed to do and not do. Back in the 1940s and 1950s, Maude's husband might well have told her that women should let men handle business matters. If a man made such a comment today, he'd be laughed at.

So how do these research-verified gender differences play out as different money behavior? To begin with, keeping track of money in plans and budgets demands patience and detail work. A woman's natural skill set may allow her to more efficiently perform the arithmetic involved in these tasks. Her greater verbal fluency and ease with language, as well as her tendency to be cooperative and nurturing rather than dominating and/or aggressive, can enable her to work more productively with other people around money issues.

Men's greater facility with math reasoning, with objects in motion, and with dominating others may make them better at seeking out, visualizing, and quickly grasping financial information. On the other hand, their natural aggression, competitiveness, and readiness to take action mean they're more likely to pursue a hot tip in the quest for a big win. Women tend to be more conservative, meaning that they're more concerned with the consequences of a potential loss than the rewards from a big gain.

Dr. Nadeau's research also reports that women often have an enhanced awareness of "emotionally relevant details, visual cues, verbal nuances, and hidden meanings." Money decisions involve complicated emotions as well as facts. If women pick up emotions and subtle shades of meaning, they may be better at detecting who and what to trust compared with men, who are more likely to want "just the facts."

Brain Changes As We Age

Aging is a complex of biological processes, and the human brain is one of the most complicated biological systems we are aware of. A whole host of neuroanatomical changes take place as we get older. For example, while some parts of the brain lose neurons as we age; other parts grow more synaptic connections. It isn't clear how these changes affect us, but we do know that aging affects how we can use our brains. Sometimes the effect is subtle: greater wisdom may compensate for difficulty in remembering or learning. Other brain changes, such as those in later-stage Alzheimer's disease, are not subtle at all.

To get the complete picture, we need to know much more about what is going on at the cellular level. We are aware that cells do what they do because genes order them to make specific proteins. These proteins then carry out instructions from the genes, such as "Repair the damage to the cell wall over there" or "Make a copy of this cell." This process occurs throughout the body and is called "gene expression." Usually, changes in gene expression (that is when the gene is turned on or off) are a part of normal physical changes, including the aging process.

Sometimes abnormal genes are expressed or expression of normal genes are increased or decreased in atypical ways. This causes cells to do unusual things that result in diseases. Alzheimer's researchers have found a particular gene (the so-called APOE-e4 gene) that can be inherited from one or both parents. This gene seems to have a causal effect in Alzheimer's disease. It is likely that this gene is not expressed until later in life (i.e. it has no effect until the person is older when its effect is turned on). Neuroscientists know that APOE-e4 gene is associated with the development of Alzheimer's, but currently they do not know what turns on the gene expression or exactly what "bad" instructions it then gives the cells. It is known that the brain seems to begin forming the plaques and tangles (disorganization within individual cells) that are characteristic of the disease. Plaques and tangles are related to the progressive destruction of neurons that results in the memory loss and other disease symptoms.

A recently published study of gene expression in the aging brain reported some surprising results. Nicole C. Berchtold of the University of California (Irvine) and several co-authors found that the areas showing the most aging-related changes weren't the ones most associated with age-related brain diseases and memory loss. Instead, the most affected areas dealt with self-awareness and the sense of touch. Thus, a person experiencing these changes might be more likely to commit a faux pas or less likely to feel someone touch them comfortingly.

The researchers also discovered that during youth, adulthood, and old age, men undergo three times as many changes in gene expression as women. Most of these changes occur between the ages of 40 and 79. Beyond 80, men's brains seem to stabilize. By contrast, women experience substantially fewer changes in gene expression between the ages of 40 and 79, with a spike sometime between 60 and 99. Dr. Berchtold and her co-authors infer that the rate of gene expression never stabilizes for older women the way it does for older men. Indeed, the risk of dementia for men decreases around age 85 but continues to increase from age 77 to 95 for women.

We're just beginning to learn what these results mean. What's most important for us to understand is that both men and women must make many money decisions even though brain changes may impede this process. As decision-making gets more difficult, aging men and women become worried about themselves and/or anxious for their loved ones, which in turn can make their brain function even less effectively. Since some of these changes occur at a younger age for men, the interaction between a husband and wife may be complicated just when they are faced with financial decisions that will affect their retirement security, such as whether to remain in their home, how much to spend on travel, whether to help a grandchild with college tuition, and so forth.

Thinking About Money: Could Your Wires Be Crossed?

In later chapters, we'll examine in more detail how changes in the brain may affect money decisions. For now, just remember that whenever you think or negotiate, you tend to assume that your brain is working as it should… but it might not be. Your thinking may be skewed by gender-related wiring, normal immaturity that is part of youthful development, or changes due to older age — factors you'll need to take into account when making major money decisions. Other brain differences may affect your relationships, which will also impact your feelings and behavior around money. The more you understand about what to expect at each life stage and how to manage inevitable changes, the better equipped you will be to manage your money well instead of being crazy about it.

Chapter 3 Exercise: How Are You Hardwired?

Write down your answers to the following questions:

1. Have you noticed differences in your memory or your thinking as you grow older? If so, give two or three instances when you've noticed changes in memory, judgment, or ability to express yourself.
2. How have these changes affected your relationship with money?
3. Do you believe your gender influences how you think about money? If so, how?

Maggie's Response to the Chapter 3 Exercise:

1. Have you noticed differences in your memory or your thinking as you grow older? If so, give two or three instances when you've noticed changes in memory, judgment, or ability to express yourself.

In a word, calculator! I bring it with me and use it. Before, I would do more day-to-day math in my head, but now I make little mistakes, get frustrated, and head for the calculator for a double-check. Over the last several years, I've had a harder time quickly recalling names or facts I know are lodged in my brain somewhere. The process of pulling them up "on the spot" often leaves me feeling as if I just walked into a blank hole with no brain circuitry at all. And yet, if I, impatient person that I am, take a deep breath and wait a few seconds with the attitude that my brain will find what I'm looking for, the name or fact rolls off my tongue with ease. I've also taken to organizing my bills so the $20 bills are last, then $10s, $5s and $1s. This slows me down when I get change, so I count it more carefully. When I have to quickly give money out I make fewer mistakes knowing the bills are in order.

2. How have these changes affected your relationship with money?

These changes have made me aware that money takes time and deserves respect. If I organize it instead of having bills flying around my pocketbook every which way, I know what I have and have more of it because I don't lose it out of carelessness. Making these little changes and experiencing how they help has given me new energy and respect both for myself and money. I've also taken to writing down things I have to do. As I've grown older I have assumed greater responsibility and engagement in multiple projects. Writing down what I have to do slows me down and helps me organize exactly how I'm going to do it.

3. Do you believe your gender influences how you think about money? If so, how?

When I grew up the women in my family were really dumb about money. It was exclusively a man's province. I disagreed from as far back as I can remember and wanted to know what I was doing with my money. Learning about it, joining an investment club, and proving to myself that I was just as capable as anyone gave me encouragement to believe in the financial self I have developed.

5
RINO

Chapter 4:

How We Act Funny With Money

PREDICTABLY ILLOGICAL (BEHAVIORAL ECONOMICS)

"Nothing defines humans better than their willingness to do irrational things in the pursuit of phenomenally unlikely payoffs." —Scott Adams

Growing up poor and insecure, Phil vowed to become wealthy one day. That wasn't easy, though, for a teacher with a stay-at-home wife and three children. Hoping to learn the secrets of successful investing, he joined an investment club. However, when the club's portfolio started to do better than his own, he decided to become less conservative. He began to day-trade, often based on tips from his buddies at church.

Why not follow the tried-and-true investment club rules? To begin with, Phil loved the excitement of his pals' enthusiasm for their picks and wanted to be part of this circle of guys trying to hit it big. (Of course, they always implied they had "special information.") When one of these stocks underperformed, he wouldn't sell it. Rationalizing that a lower price meant it was on sale, he would instead buy more, hoping for big-time returns when it turned around. Many times it didn't.

The deeper in the hole he sank, the more paralyzed Phil became. He hated losing, but couldn't seem to stop. By clinging to his dud stocks, he avoided having to admit his poor judgment. The more he lost, the harder he tried, and the more he lost.

Finally Phil's wife demanded to know why he was avoiding her, yelling at the kids, and waking up at night in a sweat. When he confessed what he had been doing with their savings, she insisted he talk with a counselor. He was being *crazy about money.*

The Birth of Behavioral Economics

If Phil had known more about behavioral economics, he might have avoided his financial blunders. This new discipline was established 30 years ago by psychologists Amos Tversky and Daniel Kahneman, who questioned whether people really make financial decisions rationally. Applying the laws of probability, they discovered that we often make choices that aren't in our best interest or aren't based on a full understanding of cause and effect.

For instance, U.S. Air Force decision-makers found that if a fighter pilot was criticized for a poor flight, his next flight was usually better. If he was praised for a flight, the next flight was typically worse. The USAF concluded that criticism worked better than praise to improve pilot performance. What Tversky and Kahneman discovered was that a good flight after a not-so-good one, and a not-so-good flight after a good one, were simply due to chance or probability, not rewards and punishments. When you have a whole series of variable events, they tend to average out — in other words, the highs offset the lows. If you have a high, it's not surprising for the next event to be a low, and vice versa. Statisticians call it *regression to the mean*.

This discovery opened a lot of people's eyes. Since then, behavioral economics has plowed a lot of new ground in helping people see more accurately why certain events occur, so they can apply their understanding to make better decisions about money.

Here are some of the common ways that we (like Phil, the unlucky investor) make illogical decisions that we tell ourselves are completely reasonable.

Loss Aversion

As we saw, Phil refused to acknowledge and cut his losses. Aversion to loss (loss of face as well as loss of money) is a normal human tendency. As social animals, we humans are genetically programmed to form connections with other people. When we lose a friend or a family member, we feel pain. The loss of a pet, a job, or a valued material object has a sting of its own. The result is that whenever we think we're about to lose something that's important to our physical or psychic survival, we anticipate how much it's going to hurt and try hard to avoid that pain.

Loss aversion differs from one person to another, based on their personality and life history. If you grew up with a sense of abundance and security, you might be more tolerant of loss than someone like Phil, who grew up amid scarcity and uncertainty. His desire not to repeat his childhood pushed him (without his awareness) to take dangerous chances. He was so desperate not to be poor, in fact, that he nearly ended up right back where he did not want to be. Fortunately, he was able to make better judgments about money once his counselor helped him gain more insight into his behavior.

Fear of loss shows up in a number of different ways:

- Reacting by making a high-risk decision that feels safer at the moment, but isn't in the long run.
- Preferring conservative investments to more risky ones.
- Selling investments that have gained rather than those that have lost value.
- Wanting to get out of the stock market when prices fall even a little.
- Hanging on to poor investments in the hopes that they will regain their value.

The Sunk Hole Fallacy

The term "throwing good money after bad" describes the "sunk hole" fallacy, which Phil fell into after his hot tips failed to pan out. He kept digging himself in deeper and deeper, while telling himself it was the sensible thing to do.

Here's another example: Suppose you have an old car you love, but it keeps breaking down. After you've sunk a good amount of money into repairing it, you tell yourself that since you've already invested so much in fixing it up, you have to keep fixing it up. Of course, it doesn't really make sense to spend more on repairs than it would have cost to buy another car, but it *seems* logical. After all, do you really want to admit you made a mistake and are wasting money? The upshot is that you ride around in an old car for much longer than may be safe, just because you're too embarrassed to say, "I should have traded this car in, instead of spending so much money on it!"

Status Quo Bias

Another kind of choice is actually a non-choice: a bias toward the status quo. This simply means that we resist change, even if changing would do us good. For instance, suppose you inherit $45,000 in stocks and bonds from your uncle. I bet you'll be tempted to keep the portfolio invested exactly as it is, even if the investments don't make sense for your situation. You may rationalize that you feel too loyal to Uncle Bert to undo his choices, or that you can't afford to pay the capital gains tax that would be due if you sell, but the odds are that you're simply not prepared to make a change.

~

COMMENTS FROM MY COUCH

As I mentioned in Chapter 1, the brain is wired to react instantly to any perceived threat to our well-being. Loss of any kind intensifies negative emotions — grief, fear, anger, regret, or disgust — that alert us to focus and pay attention. Unfortunately, these emotions may not lead to constructive thinking and acting. Instead, we may fall unaware into the trap of loss aversion in any of its forms.

I've experienced many of these behavioral mistakes myself. When the technology stock bubble burst in 2000, not only did I throw good money after bad (the sunk hole fallacy), but I was also so embarrassed about my losses that it paralyzed me. For two years, I did nothing except let money drain away (status quo bias). No matter how often I thought about the carnage in the stock market, I was too ruled by fear, anguish, and humiliation to make any decisions. Worst of all, I couldn't talk to anyone about it. How could I admit these shameful losses?

If my husband wanted an unpleasant argument, all he had to say was, "Dear, I think this bear market will continue. We should get out before we lose more." To me, it seemed he was saying, "Before *you*, you idiot, lose any more of *my* money!" My defensive anger discouraged his efforts to get us to sell, especially when our broker chimed in, "Hang on, the market's bound to go up soon." (Brokers also let emotions interfere with their advice. After all, he didn't want to feel ashamed of having advised us to buy the stocks we owned.)

I could not act until I was figuratively on my knees with the exhaustion of losing so much money. What helped me recover was hearing little snippets of stories from other people who had suffered similar losses, and realizing I was not the only one who had been blindsided by the bubble. It taught me about the importance of talking openly about problems. Otherwise, you begin to think you are the only one so afflicted, which can make you feel even more depressed and discouraged.

Another tactic that can help in this situation is to put the loss in perspective. When you open your 401(k) statement and see you lost $2,000 last month, you feel immediate "in the moment" pain. But step back a moment and think about how this loss affects your overall financial position. Say, for example, you originally had $100,000 in your account. If you lost $2,000, that was 2% of your portfolio. Assuming that you feel you're properly invested, remind yourself that such losses are normal stock market behavior and are likely to be offset by gains (regression to the mean).

Mental Accounting

This concept was developed in the early 1980s by Richard Thaler, a financial psychologist at the University of Chicago. He was intrigued by the fact that people value some dollars less than others, depending on where the money came from.

For instance, let's say Doug goes to a casino with $100. He has some big wins early in the evening, boosting his funds to $1,800, but later his luck sours. He ends up leaving the casino with only $500. Did he lose money or gain money? It depends on how he frames it. He could have walked away with $1,800, so he really lost $1,300. However, Doug reacts strongly to loss, like most people, so he prefers to think that he won $400. Do you think he will deposit the $400 in his checking account to pay household bills? Richard Thaler's research indicates that on the contrary, Doug will put this "found" money in a separate mental account to buy something fun for himself.

Here's another example. Imagine you bought a $150 ticket for a concert featuring your favorite group. At the arena, you realize you left the ticket at home. After hopping up and down, bemoaning your luck, and possibly yelling at your best friend for not reminding you to bring the ticket, would you spend another $150 to see the performance?

Now imagine the same scenario, except that you plan to buy the ticket at the box office. But when you get there and pull out your wallet, you realize you've lost $150 somewhere in the parking lot. You still have more than enough cash to buy the ticket. Would you?

Most people say they would buy another ticket if they lost $150 in the parking lot, but not if they left the ticket at home. Why? It's mental accounting. If you had to buy a replacement ticket, which means you'd end up spending $300 on entertainment (your original $150 plus $150 for the second ticket). However, money lost in the parking lot doesn't come out of your mental "entertainment" account, so you'd buy a ticket even though the bottom line is that you're still $300 out of pocket.

As you can see, mental accounting is often a sneaky way to protect yourself from the pain of loss. Spending $300 on entertainment feels like a more painful loss than losing $150 to bad luck in the parking lot and then buying a $150 ticket.

~

The Anchoring Effect

Anchoring is a concept related to mental accounting. Specific numbers stick in our head as "anchor points" that we use as a reference for future decisions.

For example, suppose you buy a stock for $48 a share. Based on analysts' projections and your own research, you believe the price will go up to $65 in a year. However, it hangs up at $59, and your financial advisor tells you she believes it probably won't go higher than that. You want to hold on to it until it reaches $65, because that's the number stuck in your head. When your advisor finally prevails on you to sell, you feel no satisfaction with your $11 per-share profit, only disappointment that you didn't make $17 a share. Does this sound greedy? It isn't really. The way events get framed in our perception can determine our behavior and emotional reactions without our awareness.

Rena's story is a good example. When her adored father died, he left her stock in the bank he had worked for all his life. Rena didn't sell any of this stock, even though its value had already dropped from $800,000 the previous year to $750,000 when she inherited it. She kept it in a separate mental account, determined to hold onto it until it returned to its previous peak of $800,000. Even then she really didn't want to sell it. She was a savvy investor with her own money, but this was different; it represented her father's hard work over a lifetime. If she treated it like her own investments and lost any of it, she would never be able to forgive herself.

So she watched the bank stock drift downward, unable to think of it as the same kind of money she was successfully investing elsewhere. Denying that "Father knows best" would have meant being disloyal and going against her beloved father's wishes.

~

COMMENTS FROM MY COUCH

Rationally speaking, mental accounting is bogus. If you had 100 one-dollar bills stuffed in your pockets and lost ten of them, I doubt if you'd say to yourself, "Thank goodness I lost the ten from my shirt pocket and not the ten from my left front pants pocket!"

However, most of us do keep separate mental accounts, so we're not as rational as all that. For example, if you have savings in the bank and also carry a balance on your credit cards, you're prone to mental accounting and anchoring. After all, you probably earn less than 5% on your savings, while paying anywhere from 10% to 20% in credit card interest. It would be more logical to pay off the credit card debt out of your savings, wouldn't it?

Here are a few other signs of mental accounting and anchoring:

- You wouldn't dream of withdrawing savings for a vacation, but happily splurge with your tax refund.
- You tend to spend more with a credit card than when you use cash.
- Most of your retirement savings are invested conservatively, but you put your year-end bonus in a risky junk bond fund.
- You aren't willing to sell your house for less than what it was worth three years ago.

Think about the way you manage your own money. Do you consider "saving" to exclude paying off debt? Do you limit your use of certain financial tools for illogical reasons – for example, refusing to put any monthly expenses on a credit card, even if you get into a serious cash crunch? You may be practicing mental accounting.

The Endowment Effect

Richard Thaler was also interested in what he termed the "endowment effect."

He was astonished to find a huge disparity between people's expectations of buying and selling prices. His beginning research asked participants two questions:

- How much would you be willing to pay in order to eliminate a 1-in-1000 chance of dying immediately? (Average answer: $200.)
- How much would you have to be paid to accept a 1-in-1000 chance of dying immediately? (Average answer: $50,000.)

Thaler further demonstrated the "endowment effect" by randomly giving mugs with the college logo to half his economics class. He then conducted an auction to see how much money mug owners would require to part with their mugs and how much the students who didn't have mugs would pay to own one.

The mug buyers were unwilling to pay more than a median price of $2.75. However, the mug owners would not sell the mugs below a median price of $5.25. In other words, the owners felt their possession was worth almost twice as much as potential buyers did. After listing other examples of large differences between the prices at which a person would be willing to buy and sell the same item, Thaler concluded that people tend to overvalue what belongs to them and undervalue the same thing if it belongs to someone else.

The endowment effect is another manifestation of loss aversion: we focus more on cost (what we'd have to sacrifice in order to act) than on opportunity (what we could miss if we fail to act). The possibility of an enjoyable gain in the long term has a hard time competing with the sting of parting with money right now.

The endowment effect is very much with us in everyday life. Let's say you're selling your house. Of course you want to get every penny it's worth, and then some. (Don't you deserve to make a profit?) Your real estate agent's pleas to lower the price don't make you budge, because you *know* how valuable your home is. But wait a minute here. Understanding that the endowment effect makes people overvalue what they already own, you should rethink holding out for a higher price. Plus, the owner of the house you plan to trade up to will also overvalue his house. So if you want to get a good deal from him, you're going to have to get around *his* endowment effect. Is it any wonder negotiations so often reach an impasse?

∾

The Herd Instinct

There's a bluff on Chesapeake Bay known as Turkey Point, so called from folklore that Indians used to stampede flocks of turkeys off the cliff to become turkey dinners. True or not, the birds' behavior is a good illustration of the herd instinct, which prompts individuals in a group to act together without planned direction. By extension, herd instinct also applies to the tendency for investors to pile en masse into a rising stock market, flee together when the market slumps, and crowd into the bond market instead.

By taking on the protective coloration of the herd, individuals hope to reduce the risk to themselves. But when danger actually threatens, they usually take flight with everybody else in the group. Unless they are careful, they may end up on the table with creamed onions and cranberry sauce.

~

Confirmation Bias

Confirmation bias is our tendency to search for, welcome, and absorb information that confirms our initial impressions or preferences. Once we develop preferences (big or small), we're alert for any information that fits our preconceived opinions and feelings. At the same time, we filter out data that doesn't support these preferences. Literally, we only hear what we want to hear! Since we're usually not aware of confirmation bias and anchoring, we don't seek out discrediting information to counter its effects.

Let's say you have just purchased stock in an exciting new company. You eagerly peruse reports of its high growth potential, while discounting warnings of a possible strike. Loss aversion — manifested as anxiety to be reassured of your investment acumen — drives you to concentrate on good news, while bad news goes in one ear and out the other.

~

MORE COMMENTS FROM MY COUCH

The ideas born of behavioral economics research have practical value for everyone who has a relationship to money. That means all of us, of course. Now comes the advice part.

As I offer the following suggestions, try to stay aware of your personal reactions. Do you tell yourself, "Well, that sounds good; but with my track record, there's no chance I'll really follow through with it"? Or do you say, "Oh, I can't wait to try that!" but then forget a few hours later what you were going to do?

We all have voices in our head like those. Let them sing their merry tune, while you ask yourself what the outcome could be if you actually followed the advice. Imagine the benefits in as much detail you can, and let that mental image lead your charge toward exploration of the new and the possible.

1. Recognize that every dollar, no matter where it comes from, has the same buying power. Suppose your budget limit is $800, but you want to buy something that costs $850. It's human nature to say, "What's $50 more if I'm already spending $800?" Now say you expected to pay $100 for an item, but the lowest price you can find is $150. Do you still say, "What's $50 more?" Probably not! Yet $50 represents a certain fixed amount of hours worked or interest earned – an amount equally hard to replace in either case.

2. Accept losses and move on. Being extremely loss-averse, we hate losing much more than we enjoy winning. For example, we rant and rave if we lose $10 to a cashier who gave out the wrong change, but if we win $10 on a lottery ticket, our tepid response is often "Well, it's about time."

If you have a perfectionist, self-critical streak, you may start to blame yourself for a loss, whether or not you had control over it. "I knew I should have counted that money again" or "Why did I listen to what Joe said about that stock?" inevitably leads to "How could I do such a stupid thing?" Of course, you could always blame someone else – the cashier, Ben Bernanke,

Bernie Madoff, or your advisor – but that makes it harder to learn from past mistakes.

Interestingly, heightened loss sensitivity is true in relationships as well. Dr. John Gottman, a leading marriage and parenting researcher, suggests that one critical comment aimed at a partner may take up to five positive comments to repair. Why? Because negative comments from someone we trust can make us lose our sense of well-being and security, and usually our self-esteem.

3. Be open to change. We human beings love to feel connected and attached to others. We also get attached to our house, our car, our clothes, our money, and our investments. When the attachment turns into glue and we are stuck to a particular item, we find ourselves making excuses for its flaws. Reluctance to sell it or look for other alternatives limits our scope so much that we may repeat mistakes.

Awareness is the first step toward change. To pry yourself away from a "golden cow," consciously direct your attention to other possibilities. Keeping a notebook and writing thoughts down can help you shift your awareness.

4. Remember, it's not worth more just because it's yours. When something is ours, we tend to overvalue it. That can lead to rocky negotiations or lost sales. Again, awareness is key. Do you have an emotional attachment that colors your perceptions? Have you taken into account that most things depreciate in value after they're bought? And if the item in question is your house, are you so fixated on its resale value that you've forgotten how long it provided a roof over your head? Armed with knowledge of the endowment effect, you have a better chance of countering the tendency to inflate the value of what you own.

The most important lesson of behavioral economics is that we all tend to frame events in particular ways mainly to avoid loss. The more we know about these tendencies, the easier it can be to look at our experiences and choices about money with a clear head.

Neuroeconomics: The Next Frontier

A hybrid field interweaving neuroscience, psychology, and economics, neuroeconomics uses new imaging technology to actually see what our brains do when we interact with money. For instance, when we're excited about the possibility of making lots of money, our nucleus accumbens lights up with activity. When we anticipate or experience a loss, our amygdala (which performs a primary role in the processing and memory of emotional reactions, particularly negative emotions) brightens with activity and we experience fear. Seeing the brain working to process emotions helps us understand that emotional reactions are a big part of human behavior and need to be taken seriously.

One of the most recent discoveries is that the hormone oxytocin increases our sense of trust in others. When we interact in a friendly manner with others by shaking hands, hugging, smiling, or kissing, our brain releases oxytocin and we feel trusting and relaxed. Oxytocin is also released when we eat deep-fried foods and carbohydrates, which helps explain why frustration or unhappiness often drives us to "comfort foods" like ice cream and French fries in hopes of feeling better.

Dr. Paul Zak, the economics professor at Claremont Graduate University who researched oxytocin, has also investigated the neuroeconomics of distrust. Since low levels of trust can keep us from managing money effectively, his results are valuable. Dr. Zak found that when trusting someone else in a money transaction is questionable, men and women respond differently. Men react to untrustworthy behavior with increased levels of dihydrotestosterone (DHT), a "high-octane" testosterone. Although everyone produces DHT, men have 5 to 50 times more than women. The implication is that men, unlike women, in general react more aggressively to signals that someone can't be trusted.

The trust-distrust dynamic is a vital part of the ways we relate to others around money, as well as the ways we relate to money itself. Being able to see and measure components of the trust response helps us understand how to make these relationships more effective.

~

Where Do We Go from Here?

With all the new and interesting findings of behavioral economics and neuroeconomics, it's easy to feel swamped with information. After all, our prefrontal cortex (where logical thinking and strategizing happen) can effectively handle only five to seven bits of data at a time, as Jonas Lehrer reports in *How We Decide* (Mariner Books, 2010).

As research uncovers how normal people frame or cognitively perceive particular events, we will be better armed to understand ourselves and our reactions to dealing with money. Although behavioral economics deals with thinking processes, what is fascinating to discover is that, at base, people are trying to protect themselves from the emotion of loss with deceptive thinking strategies. Loss of any kind is an emotionally charged event that we as normal human beings go to great lengths to avoid, not only in our thinking and in our feelings, but in our actions. Clearly, no one likes to lose money (or anything else, for that matter).

But as you come to understand your personal relationship to money, knowing the basic findings of behavioral economics will help you gain insight and awareness about your behavior. In the next chapter, we'll discuss how childhood experiences with money influence the development of attitudes, beliefs, and emotions through the teenage years and into young adulthood. By then, these beliefs and emotions have become part of our basic character, and largely determine how we will use money for the rest of our lives.

∾

Chapter 4 Exercise: Your Money Behavior Quirks

Let's put some of the behavioral economics ideas you've read about in this chapter to work for you. Since money is imbued with different emotions (such as excitement, fear, or anguish, to name dominant ones), the first step in making money management a more consistently positive experience is to become aware of how you feel about it.

Negative emotions need to be understood before you can turn your attention away from them to more positive feelings. Once you have identified the negative emotions, then focus on how you would like to feel and imagine that good feeling state.

1. Remember the "sunk hole" fallacy? Think about one or two instances in your own life that this fallacy has influenced your behavior. Write them down. After reflecting on your answer, write down how you could avoid throwing good money after bad next time around.
2. Do the same for one or two more of these ideas:
   - Status quo bias
   - Mental accounting
   - Anchoring effect
   - Endowment effect
   - Confirmation bias
   - The herd instinct
3. What did you learn about yourself from this exercise?

4. Now put your learning into practice. Commit to changing something each week and write down the results. Visualize yourself following through on this exercise and imagine the good results you are going to get. The practice of visualizing and experiencing yourself in a state of good emotions, just like imagining yourself executing a perfect golf swing or skillfully and gracefully winning a ballroom dance contest with your partner, will help you achieve your goal. When you consciously practice in your mind and in your actions what you want to achieve, you'll be halfway there.

Here's an example that may help you identify your emotions. Imagine you have just lost $100. If you were asked the following questions, what is the first thing you would think of?

1. How did you lose it?
2. What emotion are you experiencing (sad, mad, frustrated, dejected, overwhelmed)?
3. What are the consequences for you of losing $100?

What could you have done differently to prevent the loss of the money? How would you feel knowing you had avoided the loss? What positive benefits would your different behavior afford you?

Maggie's Response to the Chapter 4 Exercise:

1. Remember the "sunk hole" fallacy? Think about one or two instances in your own life that this fallacy has influenced your behavior. Write them down. After reflecting on your answer, write down how you could avoid throwing good money after bad next time around.

I love my 1995 Toyota. It is full of memories of family trips and car pooling. It bears the endearing scars of my son's introduction to driving. When the muffler blew at 100,000 miles there was no question about fixing it. When the shock absorbers failed I wondered what was coming next and thought about getting another car. But that is a huge expense and Toyotas are made to last up to 200,000 miles. So I got new brakes. And on and on. When the car started leaking oil I again questioned what I was doing but kept getting it repaired even though I knew rationally that I was throwing good money after bad. It wasn't until my son said, "Mom, I know you love the old jalopy, but how safe could it be with outdated airbags and iffy innards?"

That comment woke me out of my illusion. Thinking that I was unsafe driving it and might endanger other people provided me with a good enough reason to say goodbye to the Toyota while keeping all the memories it held in my heart.

How could I have avoided throwing good money after bad? Maybe by not getting lost in all the memories the car held for me and sitting down and adding up the total amount I put into the car. A repair here and a repair there doesn't allow you to see the grand total. If I encounter any more "sunk holes" I will whip out my calculator and start adding and imagine myself feeling great walking away from a "sunk hole" seduction.

2. Do the same for one or two more of these ideas:

Anchoring is closely tied to expectations and cues we pick up from other people. For instance, if I hear about a sale from a friend who says, "Relax the Back is having a great sale on chairs. Really nice ones are marked down 35% and are going out the door for $250. You gotta check it out," I run over expecting to spend $250 on a fabulous chair. When I get there all the $250 chairs are gone and the least expensive chair on sale is $325. But the $250 price sticks in my head. I get a good chair at 35% off, but I'm weirdly upset that I'm spending $75 more than my friend. Trying to talk myself out of my "irrational" reaction doesn't work. I realize that my expectations were ANCHORED to $250. That price is lodged in my mind as the comparison deal I should have gotten. Once I am aware of this, I can more easily let go of the anchored number and enjoy the chair.

3. What did you learn about yourself from this exercise?

Sometimes I think I belong in the "stupidly stubborn" category. I can hold on to things and ideas long after they are worn out. At the same time, knowing that all that I think, feel and do are human tendencies I can learn to outgrow and change if I channel my energy to change rather than hold on.

4. How I put my learning into practice:

I will focus on what I really want. For instance, if I want my office to look and feel really good I'm going to imagine a great chair. If it costs anywhere form $250 to $500 and it enhances my office for years, then it is worth getting, anchoring effects aside. As I practice imagining how my office looks and the comfort the chair will bring, the price shifts to the background and the good feelings of doing something positive for myself and my clients soar.

PART II:

WHERE YOUR MONEY BELIEFS COME FROM AND HOW THEY DEVELOP

In the next chapters, you'll examine how we form our money beliefs, emotions and attitudes as children, then as teenagers. Early in life we tend to learn about money in indirect and subtle ways, witnessing our parents' behavior as well as picking up information (accurate or not) "on the street." As teenagers, our allegiance—and our financial attitudes—shift from our parent to our peers. By the time we are ready for college or a first job, our emotions and behavior have begun to crystallize. Before long we emerge as a full-blown money type: a Spender, Worrier, Risk Taker or a subtle mix of types, with all its strengths and weaknesses.

RINO

Chapter 5:
Building a Financial Self

THE CHILDHOOD YEARS

"Children have never been very good at listening to their elders, but they have never failed to imitate them." —James A. Baldwin

So far we've looked at general ways attitudes toward money are expressed. But each of us is an individual with a unique identity. How does our personal relationship with money evolve? How do we shape a financial self?

This process begins when we're young. We absorb messages about money from observing our parents, whose reactions, attitudes, and beliefs concerning money are often communicated indirectly to us. For instance, when children are asked what they think their parents need, they frequently answer "More money." That's because they hear their parents fight about money, so they figure that having more of it will make Dad and Mom happier. What these children really want are parents who have a harmonious relationship with each other and can give their families more stress-free time.

It's easy to see how a child may think more money will ease family tensions. Just as important, or even more so, would be the whole family having good times together. Even very wealthy families can be unhappy.

Early Environmental Influences

Babies are very social creatures. From birth on, they're in almost constant contact with others. They instinctually want to connect and interact. Infant researcher Beatrice Beebe, clinical professor of medical psychology at Columbia University's College of Physicians and Surgeons, and New York psychologist Frank Lachmann, Ph.D., have discovered that interactions between a baby and its caregivers during the first several months of life can (and usually do) become lifelong patterns, some of which will influence how that person later builds and lives out a unique relationship with money.

Say, for example, that a mother is very sensitive to her baby's first strivings to make contact. She imitates her baby's vocal rhythms, she smiles, she gently tickles and thoroughly enjoys her baby's reactions. The baby learns to expect smiles, fun, and contentment from interacting with Mom. From this secure base, its development unfolds naturally and fully.

But suppose the mother is depressed from having just lost one of her own parents. As much as she loves her new baby, her face, posture, and way of handling the child convey sadness and indifference to its communication cues. At first the baby will react with anxiety, trying to rouse a response. If that fails, the baby begins to learn it can't count on other people for love, security, or communication. Unless the mother changes her behavior to make the baby feel loved and cared for, it won't receive the psychological nourishment it needs. A false kind of independence may develop, but the child will have a core sense of sadness, disconnection, and insecurity. Growing up, it may distrust and avoid intimacy with others.

Of course, very early experiences don't necessarily set in stone the course of a baby's development. Young children are still unformed and resilient enough to be affected by other influences; and as a boy or girl grows, there are opportunities to interact with all kinds of people who may respond differently from the early caretakers. The child's own talents and abilities can also make a big difference in what happens.

Still, our very early childhood patterns tend to form the basic model for what we can expect throughout life. Sometimes we do succeed in changing our expectations and behavior, but usually they linger despite the pain they may cause. When they crop up later in financial discussions or transactions, they will influence how we think about and behave around money.

~

Understanding Limits

An understanding of limits and boundaries – a developmental task that starts at birth – is essential for dealing with money. If children are given everything, or are deprived of having anything, they don't know what to expect from others.

In order to develop a healthy financial self, it's critical for children to understand what they must do for themselves and what they can rely on from others. Parents can use money to help set reasonable expectations of behavior. For instance, offering an allowance for chores and praising children for tasks well done can teach them to value themselves and the work they accomplish, laying the foundation for success as adults.

The factor that seems to correlate most with success, according to George Vaillant, M.D., a professor of psychiatry at Harvard Medical School, is whether a person was industrious as a child. If children experience themselves as "able to do" by having a paper route, babysitting, or pursuing a special interest like reading, music, or sports, they tend to carry that attitude into adulthood and become successful. Even family dysfunction – alcoholism, depression, divorce – doesn't matter as much as the child's ability to be industrious and feel good about her- or himself as a result of that work.

At first blush, this may seem a little far-out. What does youthful industriousness have to do with money? But when children find ways to earn money, they develop a sense of effectiveness and strength. For example, young Mike started helping his dad with small construction and painting jobs at the age of 5. He developed a reputation in the neighborhood for being very handy. By the time he was 10, he was earning money from small jobs of his own. Money spoke loudly to him: when he worked, he could buy himself video games and a new bicycle! This early connection between work and rewards stuck. Mike started his own business at 21, and today is the highly successful head of a public relations firm that has flourished for 30 years.

How Money Scripts Evolve

Another major influence in the evolution of a financial self is the set of attitudes, beliefs, and emotions that we learn to associate with money. If the examples we absorb as children are primarily healthy, we're likely to make wise financial decisions later in life. Unhealthy attitudes and beliefs, on the other hand, tend to lead to poor and self-defeating choices.

Using myself as an example, let's look more closely at how early experiences with money can affect growing children, potentially forming the bedrock of money roles that shape our behavior as adults.

What I Learned

When I was almost 4, my father and I played a game I loved. As I jumped up and down around him, he'd pull out some shiny coins from his pocket and toss one my way. If I missed the catch, I'd scurry after the coin and bring it back to him. If I snared it, I got to keep it and would proudly drop it into my piggy bank. Over time, I got pretty good at capturing the coins, and my piggy bank filled up. I felt happy, powerful, and proud that my dad saw I was good at the money game.

But my early joy and excitement about money soon faded. By age 6, I felt tense and anxious whenever money was mentioned. What happened?

Despite my father's apparent largesse during our game, our family was always on the brink of going broke. When Mom asked Dad for grocery money, he'd blow up, and when she spent more than he thought she should, he'd complain. Piles of unopened mail sat on a shelf above his bed. If I messed up one of the piles, he'd yell, "Leave those damn bills alone!"

When my father, Jack, and my mother, Essie, weren't arguing over money, they'd talk about how much more money there was when they were young. Growing up in a sleepy town of 3,500 on the banks of the Connecticut River, I heard many stories about the lives they had led as privileged teenagers in Manhattan. They'd both come from wealthy families. Jack's father, a distinguished Navy captain, made tens of millions of dollars in marine salvage. Spending extravagantly, he lived the high life in Paris and New York. Then a salvage job went sour and he lost millions. His fortune all but disappeared before he was 50. Essie's dad, a mining engineer, had less money but kept a firmer grip on it — so firm that he was able to retire at 45. He and my grandmother moved just a mile away from us to a large house with a big garden filled with flowers. I spent many happy hours with him as he lovingly tended and tagged his plants with their proper Latin names.

My dad, handsome, bright, and argumentative, didn't take to working hard like his father, but he did carry on his father's tradition of extravagance and carelessness. As a young man he dreamed big, looking forward to the day he'd inherit what was left of the family fortune. He was still waiting for his ship to come in when he married Essie, a pretty, sheltered young lady who liked poetry and Albert Schweitzer. He kept waiting while my brother and I arrived. Even when his father's death showed there was little inheritance to speak of, he never pursued a serious career or even held a steady job. Although he dabbled in real estate and investments to put food on the table, he couldn't quite make ends meet.

Dad and Mom relied on the weekly check her parents gave her. Every Thursday Mom would drive over to her parents' house with our dirty laundry, ostensibly to use their washer and dryer. While she was there, her mother would hand over the check, her eyes cast down to hide a look of distaste. Mom's face would turn red with embarrassment as she quietly slipped the check into her pocket.

Sometimes money tensions centered on me. I'd hear my dad shout, "Why did we spend so much on *that*?" Mom would reply weakly, "Because she needed it." He'd retort, "We spend too much on things we think she needs. If this doesn't stop, we'll all go to hell in a hand basket!" My needing and wanting clothes and toys evidently made our problems worse. I blamed myself, as children do. If I didn't need or want anything, there would be more money and my father wouldn't be so angry and my mother so sad. Not having money gave me a panicky, unsettled feeling.

When I was 4, I'd ride my bike every day to my grandparents' home. My very proper grandma, her white hair in a neat little bun, served Granddad and me tea and cakes precisely at 4 p.m. I loved being with them. They were wonderful to me: cozy and warm and always smiling. One day, while looking through my grandma's purse, I discovered a fat roll of bills.

I quickly peeled off a few of them and stuffed them into my pocket to give Mom and Dad. But I never did — I just kept the money. Somehow, having those bills in my pocket made my feel more secure.

When I was 7, my parents decided to give me a $5 a week allowance for helping with the chores. I did the chores, but they forgot my allowance. When I asked for it, my mom got angry but finally gave it to me.

So far, I had learned from Dad that money was fun and he had a lot of it. But when he talked with Mom about money, he always had an edge of irritability and anger in his voice. He treated her as if she were a spendthrift, dumb and overindulgent with me. I learned that men controlled money, women were stupid with money, and that my needing anything that cost money caused tension. From these early experiences I developed the attitude that money was scarce, and that I, like Mom, would never have money of my own or be able to use it well.

It was a different story for my brother Johnny. 18 months older than I was, he soon became a brilliant entrepreneur. At age 8, he set up a walkie-talkie system for his friends, and got them to pay for it. At 9, he built a slot machine and sold that to his friends. Johnny got the same bottom-line messages I did: that money was scarce and our parents could not be relied upon to fulfill our needs. However, experience showed him that his exceptional intellect and skills would bring both monetary reward and freedom from the pain of scarcity. Realizing that he could earn good money on his own, he was able to counteract our parents' message.

Luckily, I too learned that hard work could be a salvation, but the lesson didn't come from either of my parents. It was my granddad who took me under his wing and taught me the value of industry, persistence, and saving. His teachings and actions ran counter to Mom's and Dad's, but to me had the ring of authenticity and calm.

~

Financial Confidence: Shawn's Story

Contact with my friends' families also tempered the feelings and attitudes I absorbed from my parents. My best friend Shawn got $4 a week for her allowance. Every Friday afternoon her parents gave her four crisp new dollar bills along with huge smiles. When we played after school at her house, her parents smiled and laughed about the things they bought her. They bought me things, too. This taught me that unlike my parents, other people not only had "enough" money but (amazingly) liked to share it.

Shawn's dad believed that he would always have enough money, partly because he received regular checks from a trust established by his mother, but also because he loved his job of designing and manufacturing furniture. Shawn's frugal mom, by contrast, grew up poor and never entirely lost the fear of not having enough. Even though she didn't need to work after her marriage, she sold her own handmade clothes to earn money for herself and contribute to the family.

Shawn's parents implied that she deserved nice things and that they were happy to give them to her. She grew up with the expectation that she could ask for and get what she wanted, because there would always be enough money. But she also learned that she could work to earn her own money, which could be used to improve her life and that of those close to her.

~

Money Is Power: Julia's Story

Our friend Julia, a cute redhead, was always so well-dressed that she couldn't roughhouse with us. She got $10 every week, for which she didn't have to do a thing. She felt sorry for Shawn and me because we had to do chores to get our allowances.

Julia's parents came from impoverished backgrounds that they had both vowed to escape. Julia's dad started a McDonald's franchise and did very well. He was so proud of the money he made that he wanted everyone to know it. Giving Julia whatever she wanted helped him look and feel good.

At age 8, Julia loved to show off to us that she could buy anything she desired. We were all jealous at the attention she got from teachers and classmates. She learned that money has power to buy and influence friends, and that that she could always get more without having to work for it.

൴

Money Anxiety: Sally's Story

When Sally's best friend got a hamster, Sally begged for one too. Her mom frowned: "Hamsters are cute, and I'd like to get one for you. But they're expensive, especially if your sister and brother also want one. Let's add up what it will cost for the hamster, the cage, and the food." Sally helped her mom write down all the expenses, which added up to almost $40. Her mom said, "Good grief, that's just the initial cost! We'll have to keep buying food, too. And forty dollars times three takes it over the top."

Sally's mother didn't want to veto something Sally really wanted, just to teach her to be thoughtful and wise about spending money. Deep down, she was concerned about who would take care of the hamsters. However, Sally perceived her mother's concern as an indication that she had asked for too much.

If this dynamic became established, it could result in a long-lasting money belief like "Everything costs more than I have" or "Thinking about money makes me nervous." If Sally's experience continues to reinforce her mistaken impression that money is scarce, she may end up living out an unhealthy money script, such as "I'll always have to worry about money" or "I'll avoid thinking about money altogether."

~

Feeling Inferior: Carsheena's Story

Carsheena, a pretty, active 8-year-old, was excited to have been invited to her classmate DeeAnn's birthday party, but couldn't figure out what to get as a gift. Her mom suggested an iTunes gift card. When Carsheena gave DeeAnn the gift card at the party, DeeAnn's face lit up. Then another young guest, peeking over DeeAnn's shoulder to see the card, blurted out, "Only ten dollars? Your mom is cheap!" Carsheena was crushed. She hadn't realized that people make judgmental comparisons.

Such an experience could create the unhealthy belief that giving, caring, and affection are measured in dollars, and that spending more means you care more. Carsheena might conclude that her mother was stingy or that her family was poor. This in turn could lead to a negative belief like "My parents embarrass me" or "I want to spend lots of money on buying things for people, so no one will ever call me stingy."

Carsheena's experience could also make her feel "less than" or "inferior to" her peers. The worst part is that she was too embarrassed to tell her mom or dad how she felt, so this belief got planted quietly. When beliefs "go underground" (i.e., become unconscious), they develop even greater power to influence our behavior for a long time.

Another outcome of the birthday incident, especially if it's reinforced by other experiences, may be that Carsheena vows never to feel "less than" again. This can serve as a powerful motivator to succeed. On the other hand, it may discourage her if she can't figure out how to get past this perception. Childhood experiences and beliefs are like a kaleidoscope: seemingly unrelated events, interactions, thoughts, and feelings can come together in unique and surprising ways.

When we're starting out in school, what we see and hear at the moment is our reality. Our eyes and ears tell us who is taller or shorter, more talkative, or getting more attention. Our tendency to compare ourselves to others, usually our peers, accelerates as we progress through school: we are constantly assessing who gets the most attention, who is the prettiest, who is the smartest, who has the most friends, who gets more money for snacks or for an allowance, and so on. By the age of 11 or so, we can imagine and reason more independently.

The Need for Control: Paul's Story

Twelve-year-old Paul's odd jobs after school had taught him that hard work yielded money to spend and save. Worrying that the $392 he had saved might get misplaced, his father explained the concept of putting money in the bank to earn interest.

A little mystified by this new idea, Paul and his dad went to the bank. When Paul saw the huge vault door, he understood why his money would be safer there. However, the savings passbook they gave him when he deposited his money seemed like a poor substitute for his hard-earned cash, especially when the teller explained that the current 2.3% interest rate meant he would earn $2.30 for every $100 saved.

Paul left the bank thinking that $2.30 wasn't much. He wanted to have his money near him, in a box on his dresser, so he could see it, count it, and watch it grow when he added to it. A money belief that might evolve from his attitude and experience is "I need to control my money and guard it myself to feel successful."

~

The Uncoolness of Earning One's Way: Tony's Story

Tony got a cell phone for his 13th birthday — inexpensive insurance in case of trouble, his parents thought. Tony felt cool calling and texting his friends, but was unhappy that his mom and dad made him pay part of the monthly bill out of his allowance. His friend Myrna, who was also given a phone for her birthday, bragged that she didn't have to pay anything because her parents were rich.

That made Tony mad. When he complained to his parents, they said he was luckier than Myrna because paying for the things he needed and wanted would prepare him better for the way the world works. Tony wasn't so sure about that reasoning. He was more inclined to believe "I am worth less," "I'm not as cool because I have to pay," or "I feel cheated because some people get things easily while I have to work for them."

~

The Childhood Roots of Money Roles

Understanding the childhood origins of our money behavior helps us make sounder decisions and avoid financial pitfalls. It can also alert us to the unhealthy attitudes of others to whom we might consider entrusting our money.

Remember, everyone has certain beliefs, attitudes, and emotions that characterize their relationship with money. We need to uncover and assess these feelings, and when necessary reconfigure them, to make money decisions that will be healthy, effective, and satisfying.

Children acquire healthy money beliefs when their parents and other significant adults model good money behavior and are comfortable in their relationship with money. Openness and willingness to discuss money can also help us evolve to healthier beliefs. Sadly, in our culture it's easier to talk about almost anything (including sex) than money.

By age 13, our experiences with our parents and extended family have instilled in us specific beliefs and feelings about money, creating the role that it will play for us. In the next chapter we'll see how in the teenage years our peers become the dominant influence, superseding even our parents, in shaping our relationship with money.

Chapter 5 Exercise: Getting to Know Your Money Self

Take some time to think about the following questions, and write down your answers:

1. When did you first become aware of money? Relax your mind and your memory to recall images, situations, or conversations about money?

- Were you 3 or 4, or possibly younger?
- What emotions did you feel: sad, mad, glad, bad?
- What impact did this experience have on you at the time? Did you make any promises to yourself? Did they last?

2. What money beliefs did other influences have? How did they communicate these beliefs to you?
   - Your parents?
   - Aunts, uncles, grandparents?
   - Friends?

3. What are some of the money beliefs you had as a child? Do you find them still valid, or would you like to change them?
4. Do any of the stories in this chapter about children's emerging money beliefs ring especially true to you? How is your money story similar? How is it different?
5. How would you teach your children about money? Did this chapter give you any ideas?

Maggie's Response to the Chapter 5 Exercise:

1. When did you first become aware of money? Relax your mind and your memory to recall images, situations, or conversations about money?

My first remembered money encounter was finding change in my father's favorite lounge chair when I was about 4. I'd gleefully show him my exciting discovery. He thought it was cute, so we made a game out of it (as I described) where he would toss me a coin and I'd try to catch it. If I did I could keep it. If I missed he got it back. I loved the game and so did he. The positive emotions have lasted and helped develop my amassing bent. I made no promises or vows at such a young age, but I still cherish the feeling of excitement of the game and the connection it created with my dad.

2. What money beliefs did other influences have? How did they communicate these beliefs to you?

I learned as I grew up that my mother was not interested in money. It made her nervous. It was Dad's territory and she was just as glad. That made me feel special to my dad, as we shared the interest without Mom's participation. I have no idea how my aunts and uncles felt about money, except that they had it and spent it.

I figured my grandfather had plenty of it because he was so generous with me. He paid for my clothes, bought me whatever I wanted at the drugstore and even let me charge things to his account, as I grew older. Finding so many big bills in my grandmother's wallet (and one time stealing a few with no consequence) confirmed that they had lots of money, though they never talked about it.

3. What are some of the money beliefs you had as a child? Do you find them still valid, or would you like to change them?

Through elementary school I became aware that some of my friends had more money, some had less. It didn't seem to matter much at the time, as long as we had enough to play and have fun. By our sixth grade prom, though, things changed. We compared how much money each of us had to get a graduation dress. I remember feeling mad that some of my friends got a lot more than I. The older I got, the more I wanted that cost big bucks and the more I realized that some of my friends were luckier than I.

As a kid I was aware of money sources and tensions around it, especially from my mom and dad. I had to figure out how to get it from my family and didn't really have a sense of empowerment about earning much on my own. The unhealthy belief I developed was that someone else would have money I wanted and I would have to figure out how to get it from them. As I review it now, the common money belief that "someone should take care of me" was playing loudly to me.

Because there was such a strong emotional sense from my parents that money was scarce and uncertain but something that was constantly and nervously debated, as I grew older it was clear to me how important it was to have a job to make sure you could earn your own money. Many people I grew up with lived off income and didn't really work much. I made a vow as a teenager never to be like that, though I still carried the underlying, conflicting belief that "someone would take care of me."

4. Do any of the stories in this chapter about children's emerging money beliefs ring especially true to you? How is your money story similar? How is it different?

The children's stories in the chapter rang true to me. Clearly, it is not what people say but how they say it that influences growing children. When a subject like money has so many unexamined emotions and beliefs embedded in it, it isn't surprising that information is conveyed very indirectly and in ways that people do not consciously intend.

5. How would you teach your children about money? Did this chapter give you any ideas?

The way to teach children is to be aware of your own money beliefs and emotions and how you convey them to your children and your partner. A crucial way to show both money and children your caring and respect is to give age-appropriate allowances for tasks accomplished and to discuss with children their ideas about money and what they think is fair.

Chapter 6:
Transition To Adulthood

THE TEEN YEARS

"I get by with a little help from my friends." —John Lennon

Everyone is familiar with the physical changes that mark the beginning of adolescence. Girls become shapelier, boys grow like weeds; girls can't stop talking, boys start to grunt. These physical changes spur desires to be more independent and form relationships with peers. Preferring to hang out with a group of friends who are close to their own age, teenagers shove aside their parents, often rather thoughtlessly. This thoughtlessness isn't necessarily premeditated, though. Dr. Lawrence Steinberg, a professor of psychology at Temple University, has shown that adolescents are far more emotionally sensitive and reactive to their peers than to older people. This is hardwired into humans, just as mothers and babies are hardwired to bond. The young person's former dependence on his or her parents transfers to teenage friends, so what those friends are doing, thinking, and believing becomes a very powerful influence.

Cognitive changes amplify the physical changes of puberty. By 11 or 12 years of age, adolescents generally have a strong capacity for abstract thought and can imagine, strategize, and plan better than they could as children. Thus equipped for independence, they blossom with excitement about what they can achieve without so much parental supervision. There's just one little wrinkle: with the rush of newfound hormones and the beginning surge of biologically driven social-emotional growth, they are largely incapable of putting brakes on their eagerness to explore life. While cognitive reasoning is well-developed and stable by the age of 16, it's not until the mid-20s that young people are fully able to exercise good judgment and restraint when faced with the lure of stimulating activities.

What's going on here? Social neuroscience tells us that increased risk-taking in adolescence is a result of changes in the brain's social-emotional system. These changes encourage reward-seeking, especially in the presence and under the influence of peers.

Why Risk-Taking Increases in Adolescence

Starting in early adolescence, the brain's dopaminergic system undergoes massive changes. (Dopamine is a neurotransmitter that allows us to feel excitement and pleasure.) The growth of new receptors disturbs the old way dopamine flows through the brain. To make up for the resulting dopamine deficit, we crave stimulation — in this case, the excitement of risk-taking. Consequently, adolescents in their late teens are more likely to binge-drink, smoke, have casual sex, engage in violent or other criminal behavior, or cause serious automobile accidents.

The remodeling of this system results in greater dopaminergic activity in the prefrontal cortex, the area of the brain that strategizes, organizes, and plans. This activity spikes in early adolescence. Some researchers speculate that the resulting "reward deficiency syndrome" in young teenagers is similar to the behavior of people with certain types of functional dopamine deficits. Dopamine-deficient people seek out addicting drugs and thrilling experiences to make up for the dopamine they lack.

An example I know of is Betty, a woman who became dopamine-deficient in her 40s. Formerly a quiet, reserved individual, she suddenly began gambling for high stakes. It calmed her down for a short time. Then she'd start to get irritable and crave the calming fix that gambling created for her. Her thrill-seeking behavior became so driven that she actually mortgaged her house to play the slots. This pattern eventually got so out of control that she ended up hospitalized and broke.

Why Teens Care So Much About Peer Opinions

The adolescent brain also produces increased amounts of oxytocin, a hormone that undergirds social bonding and trust and regulates the ability to recognize social stimuli. As I mentioned earlier, oxytocin is also released after eating foods high in fat, one reason why these "comfort foods" taste so good and calm us down when we're stressed. The abundance of this hormone makes young teenagers abnormally aware of others' opinions of them. In fact, they may imagine that their behavior is the focus of everyone else's concern and attention. After the age of 15 or so, this hypersensitive self-consciousness declines.

The Power of Peers

Adolescents are not irrational or deficient when they process information. Nor do they feel omnipotent or invulnerable, or assess risk differently from adults, according to Dr. Steinberg. The reasoning power and basic information-processing ability of a 16-year-old are similar to those of an adult. (Executive functions such as future orientation and planning continue to improve through the early 20s.) The reason teenagers take more and bigger risks is because their social-emotional capacities are still immature. They do think, but their thinking is swept aside by the intensity of their emotions and impulses.

The biological changes taking place also play a part in how sensitive teens are to their peer group and its norms. Their behavior in groups will be more risky because they can ignite each other's enthusiasms and passions. For example, 16-year-old Joey knows his parents don't want him to drink. When his friends urge him to crash a party where booze is available, he's pulled into it because his investment in the group is of paramount importance. Of course he knows the consequences of being caught, but they're only a shadowy possibility far in the background while the lure of the party is compelling and immediate. If his peer group should get into computer hacking or shoplifting, he will have an equally hard time saying no. Despite knowing it's wrong, he would be unable to regulate himself well enough not to join in.

Risk-seeking tends to decline after the late teens. It is thought that maturation of the prefrontal cortex helps strengthen the biological brakes, allowing adolescents to control their behavior more effectively.

Biology sets teens up for a rocky ride towards extremes. How they deal with money provides another venue where their ability to exert independence and control will be tested.

Teens and Money: A Recipe for Risk

Teenagers don't forget the money attitudes and beliefs they acquired in childhood, but may push them into the background because the influence of peers is so strong and forceful. They hang out with their friends 90% of the time and are constantly assessing who has the cutest clothes, fanciest cell phone and computer, coolest music and video system, and sweetest car. In this ongoing process, their friends' attitudes and behaviors almost always trump parental opinions. Since teenagers' "brakes" are still weak, they may goad each other into risky financial behavior, fully aware of what they are doing.

~

Paul, Julia and Carsheena As Teens

In the last chapter we learned about Paul, the industrious youngster whose parents instilled in him the idea of hard work and saving. Now in his first year of high school, tall, athletic Paul already belongs to one of the popular groups. Its leader, Andrew, is a daredevil type who pushes his followers to join him in borrowing his older brother's car when his brother is at work, or in cruising the mall to check out girls and electronics.

Paul likes being part of the gang in these adventures, although he sometimes has second thoughts when he is by himself. At the mall, his friends spend money on upgrades for their computers or cell phones, buy lunch and snacks, and go to the movies. At first Paul was reluctant to spend so freely, since he had always been careful with money. But when Andrew got some cool shoes and chided Paul for being reluctant to buy a pair for himself, the other group members chimed in, making Paul feel dumb for not going along. In the heat of the moment he relented, though realizing he wouldn't be able to put money in the bank that week. The bad feeling passed as all his friends gathered round and told him how cool he looked in his new Nikes.

As the months go by, Paul continues to work hard but doesn't save very much. However, now he doesn't care. He is a core part of the "in crowd," and the fun he is having sure beats going to the bank every week. After all, he tells himself, he has his whole life to make money, but he'll only be a teenager once.

What about Paul's classmate, redheaded Julia, whose once-poor parents vowed she would never feel deprived? Julia still loves to display her expensive new clothes, pedigreed Jack Russell puppy, and iPad to her friends. Although they admire everything, they get sick of her constant showing off, and it aggravates them that she doesn't have to lift a finger to get all this cool stuff. Julia enjoys the feeling of power that her possessions give her. She begins to gravitate to a different set of friends who have also lots of stuff and won't be jealous when she shows off what she has.

Carsheena learned from her childhood birthday-party experience that it was important to avoid being thought cheap. She now uses her mother's credit card to treat her other teenage friends to meals and movies. When she hears that some of these "friends" have made snide comments behind her back, she becomes even more lavish instead of easing up on her generosity. Determined never again to feel "less than" her peers, she believes that spending lots of money is a way to win power and popularity – even if it makes her friends envious of her.

Chapter 6 Exercise: The Influence of Others

If you're in your teens complete the first part of this exercise. If you're older, Do the second part.

FOR TEENAGERS:

1. How would you describe your relationship with money? How are your ideas different from your parents', brothers', and/or sisters'?
2. Do you have money memories from childhood? If so, write them down. How have these memories influenced the way you relate to money?
3. Have your friends influenced how you think about and use money? How so?
4. How much do you think about money? Does it play a part when you are dreaming about your future?

FOR OTHERS:

1. When you remember your teenage years, how did you think about money? How were your attitudes and ideas different from your parents' and/or your siblings'?
2. Did your friends influence how you thought about and used money? How so?
3. What still endures from your teenage years in your relationship with money?
4. Are you doing as well financially as you dreamed you would when you were a teenager?

A 12 Year Old Boy's Response to the Chapter 6 Exercise:

1. How would you describe your relationship with money? How are your ideas different from your parents', brothers', and/or sisters'?

As a teenager with no job and no time to get a job because of after school activities, money is a problem especially during the weekends when every one of your friends wants to go eat. Parents think I should get a job, but if I do I would not be able to play soccer and keep the grades up.

2. Do you have money memories from childhood? If so, write them down. How have these memories influenced the way you relate to money?

I remember asking my parents for a dollar or two for a bag of chips or a candy bar but now it turned out to be $10 or $20 dollars because as I got older there were other more expensive things to buy such as a video game, music or just a movie. Every time I get money, I try to save it or spend it on the weekend.

3. Have your friends influenced how you think about and use money? How?

I guess they have influenced me because I usually just spend money during the weekend and that is when I'm with them.

4. Are you doing as well financially as you dreamed you would when you were a teenager?

When I think about the future and money I think always having money for whatever I want to buy or get, but the truth is that I don't think about money a lot. I might think about it when I'm working hard on something and it will benefit me and make me more successful in the future.

A 14 Year Old Girl's Response to the Chapter 6 Exercise:

1. When you remember your teenage years, how did you think about money? How were your attitudes and ideas different from your parents' and/or your siblings'?

My relationship with money is fairly simple. My parents pay for most of my things such as food, housing, school, vacations, etc. I don't have a regular job; I babysit and sometimes work for my parents or the neighbors, so I don't have much of an income. The main thing I spend money on is clothing. When I think about my life nothing really money related comes to mind. I think that my siblings and I relate to money in the same way and have never had any problems with it. However my parents and us don't always agree about money. Nothing big, just little things, like for instance how much money clothing should cost, or the types of places we stay on vacation, and eat out at. They think things are pricier than my brothers and I, Which I think is due to the fact we live in an affluent area.

2. Do you have money memories from childhood? If so, write them down. How have these memories influenced the way you relate to money?

I don't really have money memories from childhood. However I think I relate to money the way my parents have raised me. We've always had plenty of money but they have tried to teach us not to waste it, and how we should be saving it. It taught me not to spend all my money and be more careful about what I do with it.

3. Have your friends influenced how you think about and use money? How so?

My friends have influence the way I have used money in many different ways. They have shown me how to spend less money and get more by shopping in different stores. But they've also taken me to shopping at places like Nordstrom's which is very expensive. Sometimes I've been jealous of the things they have, like nicer cars, clothes and better vacations. Some of my other friends don't have as much money as we do so that makes me grateful for what I have. So my friends have influenced the way I think about money, but since I have friends with both more or less than I do , they haven't influenced me very much.

4. **Are you doing as well financially as you dreamed you would when you were a teenager?**

I don't think about money that much because I've never had any problems with it. Sure I want more expensive things than I can afford, but I know I don't need them. When I think of my future money is a big factor. When I think of my future I think that both my husband and I will work and we'll make as much or more than my father does. I think about my future and I want to be able to afford the great trips I go on now with my family, the great house we have and the nice things we have.

A 17 Year Old Boy's (Older Brother of the 14 Year Old Girl) Response to the Chapter 6 Exercise:

1. **When you remember your teenage years, how did you think about money? How were your attitudes and ideas different from your parents' and/or your siblings'?**

I don't have a job, so I only get money from my parents or the occasional odd job. It has never been a very close relationship, I guess. If I need it, I get it. It has never been a big problem.

2. **Do you have money memories from childhood? If so, write them down. How have these memories influenced the way you relate to money?**

Yes, but not many. Money never played a huge role in what I did. I remember my taking my money sometimes or I may have just lost it. And saving up for toys and things.

3. Have your friends influenced how you think about and use money?

How so? Money means different things to my friends. One of them always has lots of money, never works and spends liberally. Another has a bunch always but works for it. Others rarely have any and are very stingy. I don't really like to bring money together with my friends, because I usually have enough for myself and I rarely ever borrow money. I would rather go without. And generally among friends, if you lend money you won't get paid back, but who you lend it to is important. Money and friends is a bad combination, because the smallest amount of money can provoke an argument. As I've gotten older, I have become more liberal in terms of sharing and lending because it feels good to share and hard feelings over it are never worth it.

4. Are you doing as well financially as you dreamed you would when you were a teenager?

I don't think about it much at all. Fairly recently my parents gave me a credit card to buy things that basically they would buy for me if they were around. Essentials. And I pretty much only use it for food, which now at least is the only thing I buy. So I rarely think about money because it is never a problem for me. When I get cash, I might save some for non-essentials like rowing [he's a competitive rower], but most of it I put into an account and save. I'm not sorry for anything in particular and have never withdrawn from the account. I don't think about it much when I think about my friends. This may be because I don't think about it much now, or because most of the things I see myself doing in the future are not at all high paying. Money is just not a huge motivator for me.

Maggie's Response to the Chapter 6 Exercise:

1. When you remember your teenage years, how did you think about money? How were your attitudes and ideas different from your parents' and/or your siblings'?

I remember my older brother constantly talking about all the money he was going to make from his inventions and his general brilliance. I, on the other hand, was much more focused on figuring out what would make me happy to do or be. I countered what I thought was his greed and narrow focus on money with thinking about a job I could do passionately. My father's income was up and down and caused him grief. He expected more than he was willing to work for. I wanted to be different and love what I did so much that my earning would be constant and secure, but not the primary focus of my life.

2. Did your friends influence how you thought about and used money? How so?

Some of my friends had more money, others had less. I envied the ease with which some of the richer kids spent money and how they showed themselves off using it. Always seeking to be different, I wanted to show what I could do, not what I had.

3. What still endures from your teenage years in your relationship with money?

The belief that money is used to fuel my passions.

4. **Are you doing as well financially as you dreamed you would when you were a teenager?**

Valuing who I am and not what I have is a lasting lesson from my teenage years. I am making more money than I would have dreamed as a teenager. What I didn't realize back then is how much it costs to live!

RINO

Chapter 7:
Getting Set In Our Ways

MONEY TYPES

"Money itself is also neutral — neither good nor bad. You can raise a cathedral with money; you can build a death camp with money. What you do with it is up to you. You can become obsessed with acquiring money; you can become equally obsessed with avoiding it." —Jerrold Mundis

Brain wiring, behavioral quirks, and our early life experiences around money combine to shape each of us into a particular "money type" or combination of types.

The better you understand not only how you use money, but how you think and feel about it, and how you organize it (or it organizes you!), the easier it is to figure out what is holding you back from having a more balanced attitude toward money. This balance is what Olivia Mellan, a Washington, D.C.-based psychotherapist who has worked in the field of money psychology for over 20 years, has aptly named this concept "money harmony."

Mellan has identified several different "money types," each with a unique relationship to money. Keep in mind that none are essentially good or bad. In many cases, your money type simply characterizes the basically healthy attitude you have toward money. If your attitude or behavior is obsessive — too intense, too extreme, too rigid, or even destructive — it is time to examine your money type in depth.

The Spender

The first money type, the Spender, enjoys using money for immediate pleasure. Spenders typically have a hard time saving and prioritizing for the future, since they love the "now" of instant experience and gratification. In fact, they often enjoy the activity of shopping and spending more than the subsequent pleasure of wearing the shoes or watching the new TV they've bought. Anything that constricts spending, like following a budget, is anathema to them.

Remember Zelda, who loved to go to small boutiques and other stores? A Spender with an artistic flair, she liked to think of herself and the way she dressed as a work of art. The salespeople were glad to help her find exquisite clothes that showed off her stunning figure and long, wavy blond hair. Time flew while she reveled in their attention and praise. Although this excitement waned after she left the shop, Zelda was left feeling good about herself and eager for another shopping experience that would give her that same intoxicating high.

For Spenders, buying things affirms that "I'm important" and "I deserve this special gift." To deny a spending impulse feels like saying, "I'm not worth it," and leads to feelings of deprivation. The problem is that the glow of spending lasts only minutes, hours, or perhaps a day or two after the purchase. By the time the credit card bill arrives, the thrill is long gone and depression can set in over the size of the balance due. This may trigger another round of shopping to feel good again. If this cycle of spending is out of control, it becomes an addiction.

Extreme Spender behavior shouldn't be confused with enjoying a new car, a better computer or a beautiful new sweater. Remember that emotions amplify an experience. If a moderate Spender buys something truly needed or wanted, the experience rewards her (or him) with a good, hefty dose of fun, as well as a way to feel special or important. That intensity of good feeling can be healthy, energizing, and memorable.

~

The Hoarder

Hoarders are the polar opposites of Spenders. Hoarders like to save money, and may have trouble spending it on themselves or their loved ones. They carefully prioritize financial goals and don't mind following a budget in order to achieve them. Staying within boundaries is the name of the game, just like a kid who enjoys coloring within the lines of a picture. They tend to be very practical and hate to waste anything, especially if it costs money.

Angie was a Hoarder who loved the security of knowing exactly how much money she had in the bank. She liked nothing more than tracking her daily spending, so she could analyze it at the end of the week. In fact, she focused on this so much that her friends wondered if she was in dire financial straits. When she went out to dinner with them, she never offered to treat and always left the minimum tip. They felt offended, and she began to have a reputation for being cheap.

Hoarders' sense of self-esteem comes from being frugal and careful. Because they derive satisfaction from denying their impulses to spend, they may feel superior to Spenders. They feel contentment and pride in their self-discipline, rather than the spontaneous pleasure that Spenders experience.

~

The Binger

Bingers tend to save obsessively, then spend all their savings in a flash without really knowing why. You might think of a volcano or an earthquake as an analogy. Tension builds inside the Binger as he or she restrains the impulse to spend, over and over again. The pressure can only be contained for so long before it erupts into a buying explosion.

Arthur, a Binger, had worked in his dad's auto repair shop for as long as he could remember. As an adult, he stayed late at his own shop to tinker with his classic Thunderbird. When he came home at night, full of excitement about his car, all his wife could muster were comments like "Don't you care about me or our kids? Men are so selfish — and you take the cake!" Shamed and quietly seething, Arthur would mutter promises to limit the time and money he spent on his passion. He could usually keep this vow for about a month, congratulating himself on being thrifty and virtuous and pleasing his wife. Then he would feel compelled to go online to a store that always featured some "must-have" accessory for his T-Bird. Before he knew it Arthur would be keying in his credit card account number, feeling elated about the new enhancement he just acquired for his classic car. Sometimes, without realizing it, he bought duplicates of items he already had.

As you can see, Bingers have two sources of emotional amplification and satisfaction: the pride and contentment of saving, along with the spontaneous relief of splurging. That makes a Binger a hybrid of a Hoarder and a Spender. If this save/spend behavior causes financial problems, they usually originate in the intense, overboard spending phase.

∾

The Money Monk

Linda, a senior university librarian, is a Money Monk. To her, the ultimate pleasure is spending a whole day lost in an intriguing book. The exterior of her life is very simple and almost Spartan. What she lacks materially she makes up for with a rich and active imagination. And she likes it this way, with no material desires to clutter up her fantasies. When her sister calls and talks about a fabulous trip, Linda conveys disapproval that her sister would spend so much money on pure pleasure that was bought, not created. Sometimes she has trouble with friends who want to go out for a fancy dinner. Although she has the money, she considers that using it for expensive food is just plain wrong. Linda maintains her superior attitude, but once in a while admits that she is on the rigid side.

Essentially, Money Monks believe that there is something immoral about liking money, that the love of money is the root of all evil and that it will be a corrupting influence. A Money Monk's self-esteem comes from the satisfaction of feeling superior to money and those who seek it. Their sense of self is centered in the essential values in life. They don't want to be dirtied by glossy, earthly pleasures or corrupted away from a sense of value.

The Money Avoider

Money Avoiders feel overwhelmed and anxious at the thought of dealing with anything money-related. They don't balance their checkbooks, review their account statements, or investigate their financial choices. The idea of taking charge of their money creates so much anxiety and confusion that it seems easier just to avoid it.

Alisha, a Money Avoider, lived on her own. Since she earned $80,000 a year, she was able to indulge her money avoidance. As long as she paid her bills and the checks didn't bounce, she was happy. But when her car broke down, her avoidance really complicated her life. She had no idea what kind of new car she could afford or how to find the best auto loan. Instead of devoting the time and effort to figure it out, she decided to keep fixing her old car. The repairs cost only $300 here and $500 there, and she knew she had these smaller amounts of money. In the long run, she ended up spending nearly as much to keep her old car running as it would have cost her to buy a new, safer car.

Extreme Money Avoiders may experience a feeling of being paralyzed by the need to make a financial decision, much like someone with math anxiety. More often, they just do not think about money. You can imagine the trouble that can lead to.

The Amasser

Amassers are happiest when they have large amounts of money at their fingertips. Who wouldn't, right? But for Amassers, it's a primary life focus. They tend to see their self-worth as an extension of how much money they have accumulated.

Peter started saving in his 20s. Coming from a poor family, he knew what it was like to not have enough money. Every time he was able to save even a little money, he envisioned himself as one day amassing a good-sized fortune. Knowing the power of compounding, he meticulously examined his initially small investment portfolio to watch dividend reinvestments making his money grow. (Each time he was paid a dividend, he reinvested it to buy more shares.) He fantasized that in 10 years he would have doubled his money. It intoxicated him to feel the power and safety of his growing fortune.

For Amassers like Peter, accumulating money provides a sense of power and security, a kind of invulnerability to the vicissitudes of life. Their sense of self is so tied up with gathering more and more wealth that they may feel terrible if they have to withdraw any of it. When they don't think they have enough, they may feel they are failing and become depressed.

~

The Risk Taker

Most entrepreneurs take some risks with money, but success usually results from a careful balancing of risks and rewards. Risk Takers enjoy risk for its own sake. Loving the thrill and adventure of the ride, they tend to throw their money around in the hope of winning big. If they do win, they are on top of the world and feel invincible.

Avram, a classic Risk Taker, loved to gamble and let everyone know it. Whether he was going to the casino or investing in a new business idea, he would brim over with excitement at the thought of a big win. Although he made good money, it didn't stay with him long because people were always plying him with ideas for a "can't miss" new business. He usually dove headfirst into these opportunities, fixed on how much money he was going to make. If the returns were disappointing or problems cropped up, Avram slumped into depression and rage because events were not unfolding the way he had expected.

Risk Takers' sense of self is generated by the excitement they feel about their risky adventures. They're adrenaline junkies who come down in a big way when they experience a financial loss. With their sense of self deflated, they can quickly become depressed — at least until the next risk comes along.

~

The Conserver

Conservers — an addition of mine to Olivia Mellan's existing money types — are determined to find the best value for their money, no matter what it takes. They'll spend hours on the Internet finding the best value, drive hours to save a dollar, or deprive themselves of something they want or even need in the short run in order to get a bargain that takes weeks to obtain.

What's the payoff? They are not wasting resources, they are not being taken advantage of, so they are safe from the perils of being exploited. What they tend not to see is how much it costs in terms of time and energy to get the best deal. But their behavior makes them feel safe, and for that reason it is hard for them to act any other way.

For example, Greg loved computer research. A diehard Conserver, he'd spend hours online (particularly when he wanted to buy something for himself) finding the best deal on a pair of socks, a new stereo, or an efficient woodstove. He had plenty of disposable income, but told himself he wanted to keep it that way. If his wife reminded him that he was ignoring friends or wasn't playing catch with his son, he'd mutter acknowledgment and continue to search the Web. He once pointed out to her that his frugal ways had helped put them in good financial shape, but she retorted, "When you're on your deathbed, do you want to remember the two dollars you saved on a pair of socks, or the smile on your son's face as he caught one of your tough pitches?"

Deep down Greg knew his wife was right. However, he was so rigidly locked into his Conserver money type that he could not bend for fear of missing out on a bargain.

~

The Dealer

Dealers, another money type I've identified, come in two varieties. The aggressive Dealer loves nothing better than to show his/her power and ability to get a better deal on whatever he/she buys, whether it is a new house or a piece of furniture or a bag of nuts! They like the kick it gives them to overpower another person and dominate the deal.

Marvin, an aggressive Dealer, was a real estate mogul who loved to take his wife shopping for expensive jewelry. He'd wait patiently while she picked out what she wanted. After being told the price, he would look at the salesperson indifferently and ask how much of a discount the store was willing to offer. After many rounds of bargaining he would succeed in lowering the price at least 30%, if not more. To his wife's embarrassment, he behaved this way whether he was buying diamonds or doughnuts. Even in stores that wouldn't be expected to discount anything, he found a way around sticker prices. Marvin derived such a sense of power and gratification from his bargaining experiences that he never realized what a jerk his wife thought he was.

Passive Dealers are more subtle. They like exercising power, but they go about it by surrounding themselves with like-minded and "like-moneyed" people. When it is time for a deal, they are wolves in sheep's clothing, intent on getting what they want.

For instance, Karen was the head of a foundation that supported her family's interests. A highly social person, she could be a delightfully pleasant hostess when she entertained. Whenever she negotiated business deals, though, she didn't hesitate to display an iron fist inside the velvet glove of her charm. Anyone who knew her socially would be surprised in any business negotiation, because she always got what she wanted.

~

The Risk Avoider: An In-Depth View

Risk Avoiders choose safety and security in all things financial. They hate financial surprises and setbacks. Taking a risk feels to them like bungee-jumping off the Golden Gate Bridge.

Joel, a master musician and teacher, began to think about the possibility of expanding his website to include teaching, publishing, and product selling. However, he would need financial backing to add all that capability. He filled out an application for a substantial business loan; but as much as his adventurous idea excited him, he was afraid that taking such a big financial risk would be foolhardy, even dangerous. He never sent in the application.

To Joel's parents, who grew up during the Depression, the idea of seeking a bank loan or investor capital was not only foreign but a bad way to do business. They paid cash for everything and prided themselves on being independent and self-sufficient. Whenever Joel expressed one of his expansive ideas to his parents, they would make comments like "Son, you're going out on a limb; better watch yourself."

As much as Joel tried to suppress these old childhood money scripts, they still played loudly, making him feel ashamed and afraid to reach for something more. At the same time, he really wanted to move ahead with his business plans. He tried to convince himself that his parents were living out the values of a different generation. Sick of listening to those old scripts and feeling bad, he decided to forge ahead with the loan. But after filling out another application, he found himself waking up in the middle of the night with bad dreams.

Joel tried to feel strong about his decision, but his guts had turned to jelly. Torn between excitement and terror, how could he tell whether getting a loan was a good idea?

COMMENTS FROM MY COUCH

When I counseled Joel, the first thing I asked him was to identify and name the emotions he was feeling. When he heard his parents' cautionary voices in his head, what feelings did their comments arouse in him? For example, if he heard his parents say that doing business on anything but a cash basis was fraudulent, risky, and bound to lead to failure, that might elicit emotions of fear, resentment, and disappointment that they weren't more supportive and encouraging. At the same time Joel felt excitement about moving forward, which conflicted with the negative messages from his parents.

Next, I asked Joel to rank his negative feelings on a scale of 1 (least upsetting) to 10 (most upsetting). Quantifying our emotions, especially negative ones, helps us gain control over how overwhelming they feel. (For somewhat the same reason, doctors and nurses ask patients to rate their physical pain.) Simply denying negative feelings may make them seem to disappear, but they are still around and will eventually return.

Joel rated his negative emotions as a 9. His challenge then was to let them exist in the moment, while imagining how he wished to feel. His self-talk went something like this: "Well, I've been running my business for decades, and I've done pretty well. I'm really resentful that my parents can't acknowledge that. I'd like to ask them directly for that recognition."

By identifying his need to be recognized, focusing on what it would feel like, and asking himself if this was what he really wanted, Joel took a huge step in reducing the fear and shame that interfered with his experience of himself as competent and powerful. From then on, he was able to feel a positive level of excitement with less interference from those negative old scripts. This emotional change helped him decide more clearly what his new venture would entail and whether he had or could develop the skills he needed.

Heightened negative emotions are "sticky." That is, they tend to cling as if they were made of Velcro. And because emotions are there to get us to pay attention to what is happening, they can take over until the perceived danger has resolved. Initially, Joel's fear "stuck" and did not allow him to act on his excitement. If he succeeds in working through his fear and connects strongly to his enthusiasm, he will be much better positioned to rationally evaluate the risks and rewards of his potential business venture.

If you, too, are hearing negative old money messages that keep you locked in unproductive behavior, I would suggest following the steps that Joel did:

1. Examine your negative emotions as you feel them in the present moment.
2. Quantify them. How intense are they on a 1-10 scale?
3. Reassess how accurate the feelings are.
4. Reflect on your experience with fresh insight, thus diminishing the negative emotions and leaving room to experience more positive feelings.

∾

The Money Worrier: An In-Depth View

Money Worriers worry about their money all the time. Sometimes Worriers are also Money Avoiders, which means they worry unproductively. Often, though, Money Worriers want to control their finances.

Alice was a good example. A math major in college, she had all the tools she needed to worry about her money well. And that she did. She made Excel spreadsheets of her earnings and expenses; she called her financial advisor every day, and she researched investments at night to check on the recommendations the advisor made. She had nightmares of going to the bank and finding her account overdrawn and her savings gone. When friends tried to console her, she would listen politely and keep worrying inside. Even looking at her growing net worth had little effect on her anxiety. She would acknowledge that it was increasing, but would worry about unforeseen expenses that could whittle it down.

Behavior like Alice's isn't an appropriately cautious form of financial management, but an extreme form of worry. Money becomes a preoccupation that these Money Worriers fret about all the time. They obsess over spreadsheets and personal finance programs, constantly checking their investments for fear that something catastrophic will happen. Worriers often think that if they had more money, they would stop worrying. Actually, more money just gives them more to control (or to lose), so they worry at least as much — if not more.

Sylvia was another Money Worrier. When she came for a therapy session, she somewhat jokingly asked if I did exorcisms. She felt possessed by a demon she couldn't throw off: money. As the executive head of a successful venture, she was responsible for her organization's budget. They were having a so-so year, and she needed to borrow funds for operating capital on her credit card. However, the card was in her name, which meant she would be personally responsible for the loan.

Sylvia comes across to her staff as very rational and matter-of-fact when money is concerned, but realizing that she would be liable for the debt left her feeling furious, scared, and immobilized. What would happen if the business couldn't pay back the loan? She might end up on the street helpless, poor, and alone.

~

COMMENTS FROM MY COUCH

Sylvia grew up in a family that was somber and religious. Her dad, who had a good management job in a large corporation, always competed aggressively with her, whether they were playing a word game or a set of tennis. Meanwhile, her anxious mother demanded that Sylvia, the oldest daughter, measure up 100% to her expectations. Being a sensitive child, Sylvia tried to be perfect in order to avoid disappointing her parents. It was a no-win situation. If she excelled, her father viewed it as "winning" against him; if she fell short, it upset her mother. Their agendas were more important to them than how Sylvia felt.

Consequently, Sylvia learned to hide her emotional needs. She grew up with grave doubts about herself and her own worth. As an adult, she feels self-pride and joy only when she pleases other people. These days, those people are her business colleagues. If they mirror to her that she is an effective leader, she feels affirmed; but she can't generate feelings of pride and satisfaction about herself on her own. Moreover, if one of her colleagues seems competitive, she wonders if she herself is too aggressive. No matter how hard she tries, she can never fully win.

Given all this old emotional baggage, it's understandable that Sylvia felt worried and self-critical when confronted with her company's money shortfall. Her childhood ability to absorb high levels of self-blame had transformed in her adult years into a belief that when things go wrong, it was her fault. Therefore, she must be to blame for her businesses' not-so-hot year. Not only did she have to fix it, but she would be punished if she didn't.

Silvia's intellectual realization that this was irrational didn't diminish the panic she felt. When I asked her to reflect on her emotional state, she reported feeling frightened, anguished, and ashamed. On an intensity scale of 1 to 10 where 1 is low and 10 is extremely high, she told me her fear was at 8, her anguish at 6, and her shame at 5.

I would like Sylvia to feel so solid about herself and her competence that she could see her businesses' so-so year as being about the business, not about her self-worth. I would want her to know that she has valuable skills and that she is valuable. When she is emotionally flooded, she cannot perceive that she is not her business, or that there is more to her business than just her effort and skill.

Once she replaces the negative scripts from her childhood, she will be able to think more clearly about the answers to questions like these:

- "Is last year's so-so performance part of a normal business cycle?"
- "Is our business being affected by the overall economy?"
- "Are we facing real problems from a change in customer behavior or in the competitive environment?"

~

The Importance of Acknowledging Emotions

The way we deal with money — as a Hoarder, a Spender, a Money Monk, or some other money type — often derives from old childhood patterns as you have learned. While young, we now know that we unconsciously absorb how our parents handle money (or, more accurately, how we perceive they handle money), as well as how their attitudes affect us. The resulting emotions can interfere with our rational adult decision-making. In particular, anxiety about money choices is heightened when people have insecure beliefs about themselves and their personal power, as Joel, Alice, and Sylvia did.

All the self-talk in the world will not ease this kind of deeply-experienced anxiety unless we make an effort to reflect on the emotions that get churned up in dealing with money. If our emotions are not acknowledged and experienced, they can distort our perceptions about ourselves and our relationships, leading us into flawed decisions.

Many people are skilled at disconnecting their emotional reactions from events, from other people, and even from themselves. For example, you may be very effective at phoning a client who owes you money, even though you are secretly afraid the client will yell that your services aren't worth anything. Obviously, if you are too afraid of this possible negative result, your mind won't be clear to present your case logically to the client. You may have to remind yourself that if you take time to process the emotion you are feeling (e.g., fear that the client will refuse to pay the bill), you will have far more control over the outcome of the interaction.

The impact of unacknowledged emotion on behavior and self-esteem is powerful and leaves people with little control over what is happening to them. By learning to experience emotions and reflect on them, you will become more creative, solve problems more effectively, and feel better about yourself.

~

Chapter 7 Exercise: Your Money Type

1. What is your money type? Are you one type or are you more a mixture of types?
2. What impact has identifying what type(s) you are had on how you perceive yourself and how you behave?

Maggie's Response to the Chapter 7 Exercise

1. What is your money type? Are you one type or are you more a mixture of types?

I'm a money amasser. I love to see my money grow. I'm always looking to the future and anticipating how happy I will be to see MORE than I had before. I feel excited and powerful that I have more now than I did and am building AND NOT WASTING!

2. What impact has identifying what type(s) you are had on how you perceive yourself and how you behave?

What I don't like is that sometimes I want something NOW, maybe something I don't really need but just like because it is fun. The consequences are that I have the pleasure of shooting for more sometime in the future, but sometimes I worry that if I drop dead I won't ever see that growth and I will have missed out. I'd like to change not having to amass ALL the time and be more balanced — save some and play with some NOW!

OK, so if I want to play with more money now and not save everything, what is my first step? First, I need to figure out how much money I'll allot for play. I'll start with maybe $40. Now what do I want: a book I won't have time to read, a CD I can already listen to on YouTube, a good lunch out with a friend, exactly what? Realization: I've put off any "unnecessary" spending for so long that I don't know what I want that I don't need. NOTHING comes to mind that doesn't cost a lot more, like a GPS for my car (that I don't really need either).

Wait a minute — how about putting the $40 toward something more expensive? I can think of a number of pricey things. But isn't this what I always do? SAVE? Ah, there is a difference. What I'm saving for isn't going to amass and I don't really need it. So this is a small, bite-sized step. Writing down my thoughts has shown me how hard it is to break out of my money type and try and do something against the grain of my established habit pattern. At the same time it has given me access to my thoughts and feelings and has put me one step closer to being more flexible and balanced.

PART III:

ACTING ON YOUR MONEY BELIEFS

Having seen how money types develop, we'll take the next step of looking at how we behave with money, based on the beliefs and patterns that are now part of our financial self. For better or worse, this relationship with money will play out over the rest of our lives. If the results are disastrous, it's a signal to become more aware of underlying beliefs, emotions and attitudes that we need to change.

Chapter 8:
Starting Money Journeys

LEAVING HOME (AGE 19-21)

"The most difficult phase of life is not when no one understands you; it is when you don't understand yourself." —Anonymous

From birth to age 12, we are most influenced by our parents and relatives. Peers play the strongest role when we are between the ages of 13 and 18. By the end of our teenage years, our beliefs and attitudes about money are set. We have established the foundation of our particular money type and are behaving in accordance with it, albeit unconsciously.

By age 19, although we may still be financially tethered to our parents in big ways (such as for college tuition), we are usually free to make most day-to-day money decisions on our own. Whether we go off to college or full-time work, many of us are living away from home. Dad and Mom may be watching our back, but at least they're no longer looking over our shoulders. Between the ages of 19 and 21, we take the first big steps toward total responsibility for ourselves. Personally, professionally, and financially, we have a chance to soar – or stumble.

A Future Money Master?

Alec began his first year of college with a lump sum from his parents, who emphasized that if he spent it all before the year was out, he would have to make up the shortfall. He didn't pay much attention to his spending, though. Daily living cost more than he expected because his parents had paid so much of the basics when he lived at home. And instead of eating inexpensively at the student union, he enjoyed treating his friends to beer and pizza (which also helped him gain the "freshman 20" pounds). By spring he was running low and beginning to complain.

Alec's parents refused to help; reiterating their view that careful planning and spending was the only way to stay out of money trouble. Realizing that he had to get a part-time job to make it through the semester, Alec vowed that the next year he would plan better. And he did. He created a spreadsheet of all his expenses and categorized them so he could see exactly where his money was going. Not wanting to live like a tightwad, he kept the part-time job so he could have some jingle in his pocket.

Alec has a very balanced approach to money. He spends to indulge his interests and appetites, but doesn't go overboard. Although he takes the time to get a good deal, he doesn't waste hours looking for the ultimate bargain as a Conserver would. He is realistic about what he can afford, and feels confident that he can earn money if the need arises. Although he hasn't put much money aside so far, he plans to start a savings program after graduation, once he is working full-time. All in all, I would say that Alec is on his way to becoming a Money Master.

The Education of a Spender

Hank, also starting his first year, was told by his parents that he would have to manage his own money. They weren't clear about how much they would help him, although they had often come to his rescue throughout high school.

In his first weeks at university, Hank was inundated with offers for credit cards. He signed up for one, intending to use it only as a short-term backstop if he ran out of money. Not expecting to carry a balance, he didn't pay much attention to the interest rate: a whopping 18%. But his expenses — for books, food, beer, concerts, movies, and so on — always seemed to exceed the money at hand, and he never succeeded in paying off what he owed on the card. In fact, the balance kept mounting. When the monthly statement came, Hank would assuage the momentary prickle of alarm and anxiety by buying himself a $250 pair of sunglasses or a $170 pair of cross-trainer running shoes — a self-defeating habit that only added to the problem. Still, he figured his parents would come to his rescue. Even if they didn't, he would be able to pay off the bill with a great-paying job after graduation.

When Hank graduated, he owed nearly $5,000. There was no great-paying job in sight, but his parents bailed him out again. Although they wanted him to do some work for them in return, he knew they wouldn't follow through. Instead of helping him to learn how the real world works, their support deprived him of the opportunity to be responsible for himself and the satisfaction it brings.

Clearly, Hank is a Spender money type. An impulse buyer, he gets immediate satisfaction from buying expensive items he can show off to his friends, no matter what the cost. Knowing his parents will not hold him accountable for his spending, he feels no guilt about it. In fact, he lives so much in the moment that he rarely thinks about its consequences.

Hank may hope that his parents never change or run out of money. We might hope for the opposite: that one day he will have to be responsible for his own financial behavior.

~

Taxiing Down the Runway

Up to now, we've absorbed how our parents, grandparents, aunts and uncles, older siblings, and adult family friends relate to money. We've heard them talk, we've seen them act, and we've soaked up the feelings that swirl around money: pleasure, satisfaction, pain, anger, fear. More recently, we've felt the prodding of our peers to buy this or that, to go here or there, to do one thing or not do another.

Now, as fledgling adults, we're in a transition period. We begin playing out our embedded money scripts or roles, pointing to the way we will handle money-related challenges once we are fully on our own. Soon we will be able to do what we want, when we want, and how we want. No one will tell us what to do. We'll live our life just the way we want to!

In the next chapters, you'll see how the money beliefs and emotions we've acquired play out in the major developmental phases of our lives as adults. Each phase presents its own array of financial challenges. Our ability to meet these challenges head-on will determine whether the result is money harmony or chaos.

~

Chapter 8 Exercise: Analyzing A Money Issue

If you are a young adult in the transition years, consider the following questions and write down your responses. If you're no longer in this age group, you may find that completing the exercise reveals some attitudes you weren't aware of.

1. Think of a money issue you have and write it down in terms of how it affects your behavior. For example, "I should spend less money on impulse buying, but when I see something I want, I have to have it." Or "I keep lending money to my friends expecting they will pay me back, but most of the time they don't."
2. Draw a picture representing your issue. If it's impulse buying, for example, you might draw a magnet to symbolize the intensity with which you're impelled to buy things.
3. Does behavior caused by this issue make you feel negative about yourself? If so, in what way? (A negative feeling might be something like "I'm such a jerk; I have no self-control," or "Why do I let people take advantage of me when I know better?")
4. If you could stop your problem behavior, would it change how you think of yourself?
5. As you focus on your money issue right now, what emotions do you feel? Regret, guilt, fear? Where in your body do you feel them? In your chest, your stomach, somewhere else?
6. Sitting in a quiet place, focus on your money issue and how you have responded to these questions so far. Let your mind wander. Jot down your thoughts and feelings, even if they do not seem to be related to your issue.

7. Reflect on what you've written. Is there a theme? For example, you may have written about feeling deprived when you can't buy something you want, or about pleasant memories of going shopping with someone you love.
8. Now think about what you could do differently the next time you get an urge to act under the influence of your money issue. Write these options down and choose one. Write it on a card and tape it on your refrigerator or your car's dashboard.

It takes 90 repetitions of a behavior to make it a habit. Writing your goal(s) down and seeing it in a familiar place, such as on a car dashboard or bathroom mirror, will help you focus on the goal and achieve it.

A Young Adult's Response to the Chapter 8 Exercise:

1. Think of a money issue you have and write it down in terms of how it affects your behavior. For example, "I should spend less money on impulse buying,

My money issue: I don't plan a monthly budget so I'm not sure where my money is going. I could probably save more and spend more responsibly if I planned.

2. Draw a picture representing your issue. If it's impulse buying, for example, you might draw a magnet to symbolize the intensity with which you're impelled to buy things.

I drew a picture of a dollar sign with question marks floating around it:

?$$$?

3. Does behavior caused by this issue make you feel negative about yourself? If so, in what way? (A negative feeling might be something like "I'm such a jerk; I have no self-control," or "Why do I let people take advantage of me when I know better?")

My behavior makes me feel sad and frustrated.

4. If you could stop your problem behavior, would it change how you think of yourself?

If I could stop this behavior, I would feel proud and in control. I'd probably have a lot less anxiety.

5. As you focus on your money issue right now, what emotions do you feel? Regret, guilt, fear? Where in your body do you feel them? In your chest, your stomach, somewhere else?

Things feel chaotic when I focus on this issue.

6. Sitting in a quiet place, focus on your money issue and how you have responded to these questions so far. Let your mind wander. Jot down your thoughts and feelings, even if they do not seem to be related to your issue.

My "to-do" list is growing but I get little done. I keep thinking that if I were more organized, I would be happy. Not sure where to find the happy medium between "perfection" (unrealistic) and unreliable/unorganized/ IMMATURE.

7. Reflect on what you've written. Is there a theme? For example, you may have written about feeling deprived when you can't buy something you want, or about pleasant memories of going shopping with someone you love.

The theme seems to be immaturity and disorganization.

8. Now think about what you could do differently the next time you get an urge to act under the influence of your money issue. Write these options down and choose one. Write it on a card and tape it on your refrigerator or your car's dashboard.

Is it realistic to write down every time I spend $$$? Or maybe take the first step and set up a monthly budget?

Chapter 9:
Taking Center Stage

START-UP ADULTS ON THEIR OWN (AGE 21-30)

"Money isn't the most important thing in life, but it's reasonably close to oxygen on the 'gotta have it' scale." —Zig Ziglar

Our 20s mark the emergence of money as a major concern in our lives. We face a new reality: all the freedom we want, but all the financial responsibility that comes with it. We have to work to pay for rent, utilities, food, clothing, transportation, health care, and entertainment. The bill for our cell phone, cable TV, and high-speed Internet may easily top $100 a month. Many of us are also saddled with student loans and credit card debt that carve further chunks out of our salaries.

As a result, we may be forced to downsize our lifestyle from the way we lived when our parents were footing the bills. If we can't bear this constraint, we continue to spend extravagantly, figuring we'll worry about the bills later. We live almost exclusively in the present and don't think very far ahead. Although the best time to launch an aggressive savings plan is during our 20s and early 30s, our attention is usually focused elsewhere: on building a career, keeping up with day-to-day expenses, establishing intimate relationships and friendships, and perhaps settling down. Financial security 30 or 40 years from now is hardly on our radar screen.

Vic, a 24-year-old actor, was a good example of this mindset. When he won a speaking role in an upcoming movie, he upgraded to a more expensive apartment. Two weeks after signing the new lease, he was notified that the shooting schedule had been postponed for eight months. With his dreams on hold, he went back to bartending and scurried around for a roommate to help pay the rent.

In therapy with me, Vic learned that he had been operating under the unrealistic money assumption that "The universe will provide." Once he accepted that this magical thinking wasn't rational, he worked to develop planning and strategizing skills based on the healthier mantra of "Spend only what you have — not what you think you *might* have one day."

Generation X and Millennials

The dependence on technology that characterizes today's young adults differentiates them from all the generations that preceded them. Generation X, born in the 1960s and 1970s, was the first to transition into the brave new world of mass-market credit cards, personal computers, and mobile phones. Millennials, born between 1980 and 2000, are the first generation to have had access to computers before first grade. They can hardly imagine life without e-mail, instant messaging, texting, iTunes, iPods, iPads, Kindles, Facebook, and You Tube.

GenXers and Millennials are skeptical of authority and the information it puts out. They're more likely to be influenced by their peers in the online world via Facebook and the like. Their heroes tend to be real-life successes like Bill Gates, Steve Jobs, and Oprah. When they have questions, they turn to media stars, media information, and Internet sources, not the great books of Western civilization. Instant contact in a networked world has created knowledge-sharing possibilities that didn't exist 40 years ago.

When they finish college and get their first job, young Millennials expect to find work that rewards them with personal satisfaction and fulfillment. They've been told they can be whatever they want to be, from the next rock star to a Buddhist monk to a genius software developer. Not having much of a long-term focus, they tend to have little idea of what is required for great success.

They also expect to earn terrific salaries. As the offspring of a relatively affluent generation, they're likely to be shocked that they can't live as well as they did under Mom and Dad's roof. They are often unaware of how much their parents worked and scrimped to get ahead.

As these young adults struggle to make their own way, a critical factor is how realistically their father and mother have set limits and expectations for them. Can doting parents tolerate seeing their child unhappy in a low-paying entry-level job? Can the young folks overcome their frustration at having to cut back the free-spending habits they've enjoyed for years?

Experimenting with Life: Jake's Story

A typical GenXer, Jake was bright and verbally articulate. He skated through high school and talked his way into a good liberal arts college without ever learning good study skills. It was much more interesting to experiment with drugs, sex, alcohol, and different identities from Gothic to New Wave to world traveler. After two years of college, he decided he would rather go to art school. After two years of art school, he realized that he enjoyed performance art more than graphic arts, so he became a theater major. After a number of years, he eventually graduated with a total of 235 college credits.

With a degree in theater under his belt, Jake discovered how difficult it was to earn a living. His acting skill and natural gregariousness led him to become an MC for parties. These jobs allowed him to keep up with payments on his low-interest student loans.

Contemporary critics might say Jake is typical of the experimental mentality of young adults today. Try what you like; and if that doesn't feel right, move to something else. Experience is the teacher, and pleasure is the guide. Commitment to what you "should" do has no value, since there is no overarching authority to respect or follow.

Jake loves being on his own and living in the moment. He doesn't waste time worrying about what will happen in the future. To him, money is a tool for desire and fun, and success is letting life take him wherever it will.

COMMENTS FROM MY COUCH

Many psychological and cultural influences combine to influence young adults through their 20s. Questions like "Who am I?", "What do I want?", and "Where am I going and with whom?" are uppermost in their minds.

Their parents' role in setting limits around money and being emotionally supportive is crucial for GenXers' and Millennials' development. Because so many present-day young adults have grown up in comfortable circumstances, they expect the same when they strike out on their own. Parents who want their children to grow will stay emotionally supportive, while resisting the temptation to over-help with financial handouts. It's a good idea to clarify expectations by sitting down with the kids and drawing up a plan (or even a contract) that outlines what support they can expect and for how long. This will help young people to learn to distinguish actual needs from wishes that simply feel like needs.

Fear of Failure: Rachael's Story

Rachael, at 28 a GenXer by age but not by character, consulted me because she couldn't decide what kind of work she wanted to do. She had always struggled in school because of learning difficulties and didn't feel she was especially good at anything. Although she was lucky enough to have well-off parents who were willing to support her, she lived with an undercurrent of shame because she had to rely on them.

Her career coach came up with several ideas, but when Rachael tried to follow up on them, she easily became discouraged and would backslide into anxiety and self-pity if anything went wrong. She spent days criticizing herself and feeling defeated. This reaction would frustrate her parents, making them feel helpless and trapped into supporting her.

It never occurred to Rachael that everyone, especially beginners, makes mistakes, or that mistakes can become learning experiences. As the Dalai Lama has said, "When you lose, don't lose the lesson." Young adults like Rachael tend to think, "When you lose, you're a loser."

This cycle continued for months. It wasn't until Rachael found something she felt good at that her confidence began to grow. She took a design class, found she wasn't the worst student, and realized how much she liked it. Although she will need support during the training program she has embarked on, her enthusiasm has encouraged her parents to hope she is on her way to a job that pays well.

Rachael has been very lucky to have parents who can afford to support her through her 20s. What might have happened had she been forced to fend for herself with no confidence and no money?

~

Seeking the Just-Right Job: June's Story

June, a young GenXer who graduated from a good college and had a wonderful job upon graduation, was a case of suspended development. After a year, she was laid off when the project she worked on was canceled. Unable to find another job, she began to drift. Her parents, who were retired, began to worry about June when she asked for money to pay her everyday bills. What was going on that made their talented only child unemployable?

For June, who had been brought up in the expectation of finding a highly respectable profession or a husband (or both), the painful loss of her wonderful job had been compounded by a feeling that she was overqualified for other jobs she might be able to get. Although very capable, she worked in spurts and resented having to work hard. Her parents patiently encouraged her over the next year and a half while she continued to search for a job. By the time June turned 27, a hole had developed in her resume that she could not explain.

When she consulted me, she mentioned that her parents thought she would be more marketable with a master's degree or a Ph.D. They were willing to underwrite her education in any field she chose. After we explored several options, June chose fashion design although she had no previous training in art. She attended art school for a semester, then decided it was wrong for her. She considered another bevy of options, from getting a doctorate in English literature to buying and running a bar.

However, nothing worked. June became more resentful and her parents more worried, with no resolution in sight. When I suggested to June's parents that they talk with her about gradually reducing the amount of financial support they gave her, she flew into a rage and threatened them with suicide. They in turn became paralyzed at the thought of losing her.

By chance, June ran into a marketing executive who was looking for help. She was hired as his Girl Friday, with opportunities for advancement. Though the job didn't pay much, it had enough status not to be an insult to her. Everyone breathed a sigh of relief.

I counseled her parents to develop a plan for gradually reducing her allowance over the course of a year. Earlier in therapy, June had started to become angry with me because she felt I was expecting her to find work. Now convinced that I was plotting against her with her parents, she abruptly refused to talk with me any more. Her parents still planned to discontinue financial support over time, although they were terrified about what might happen.

COMMENTS FROM MY COUCH

This standoff might have been prevented if June's parents had had an open dialogue with her from the start. June was determined that life should conform to her desires, with good things only a mouse-click away. Her conviction that she was entitled to a highly paid job and nothing less is a variant of the money belief, "Someone else should provide for me in the style to which I am accustomed."

This sense of entitlement masked June's emotional vulnerabilities. Underneath all her bravado, she felt like a helpless youngster. She was bright enough not to have had to work very hard to get good grades; but when things did not go her way, she had never learned how to follow through with persistence and hard work. Instead, her embarrassment and shame were so painful that all she could do was to run away from what caused them and strike out at her parents. This pattern will continue until they stop enabling her. Of course, cutting off their support may mean a more prolonged battle of wills before June learns to become accountable for herself. Until she makes time to reexamine her priorities, it will be hard for her to get to the next developmental stage: settling down into a rewarding relationship with her work and/or a family of her own.

Start-up adults seldom realize they are playing out money scripts programmed into them as they grew up. Let's look more closely at how one young adult, Sharon, succeeded in rewriting a faulty money script with the help of a financial therapist.

~

Sharon's Story: An In-Depth View

Sharon, a 23-year-old with curly blond hair, enters my office dressed in a bright skirt and blouse, a flashy necklace, and dangly earrings. However, the cheery attire can't hide her slumped shoulders or sad face. She's here because she feels socially isolated after leaving college and moving to Philadelphia.

"In the two months I've been in this ridiculous city, I've spent too much time alone," she says, tearing up. "I love to have fun; I'm a people person."

"Moving is tough," I offer. "Feeling isolated at the start is normal; it takes a while to make new friends. How often do you go out?

I expect her to answer once or twice a month, but she surprises me. "Oh, at least five nights a week," she says. "I've found some cool bars. But I hate the two nights I spend alone. I miss my old friends. I don't get much sleep because I text and Skype and create wall posts on Facebook all night. That screws up the next day, but I don't care — I'm connecting with my friends."

"Not getting enough sleep sounds like it could be a problem."

"Not compared to being alone."

"Is your job OK? Does it pay enough to cover your expenses?" I ask. "You must be spending a lot on bar bills."

"Well, yes, maybe a hundred dollars a week. Maybe a little more. It's OK, though," she adds quickly. She shifts in her chair, curling one foot under the other thigh. "Except that my pitiful salary does leave me short here and there."

"If you run short at the end of the month, how do you handle it?" I ask. "Do your parents help out?"

Sharon replies with striking indifference: "I pay the minimum on my credit card; that's all I care about. I figure I'll have lots of time to make money later. And I haven't asked my parents for anything since I left college. They don't like how I spend my time. They've forgotten what it's like to be young and have fun."

"You don't mind carrying a credit card balance every month?"

"Why should I?"

"It's up to you, but if your goal is to take the best possible care of yourself, you might think of changing how you view yourself, and understanding your relationship to money. Are you up for that?"

"Not really," she says, then adds after a long pause, "I mean.... What choice do I have? I hate the way I feel now, and I don't want to make it worse."

I'm thinking to myself that Sharon has both a loneliness problem and a money problem. Which is the primary issue: the loneliness or the money? I suspect that each feeds the other. To help Sharon understand her view of money better, I suggest an exercise (Olivia Mellan, personal communication) that can be very revealing. "Pretend you're having a conversation with Money," I tell her. "Imagine what it looks like and what it might say to you if it got a chance. Write down your dialogue — back and forth, with questions and comments. It's not an easy exercise, but try it."

Sharon breezes into my office the next week and sits down with a smile. She tells me she imagined Money to be a fun-loving companion, just like her, and dressed in Gothic-style black to attract attention. This is how her conversation with Money went:

Sharon: I wish you'd hang around more often. It seems like every chance we have to get together, you leave me.
Money: Well, ditto. I enjoy your company as well. But truthfully, I'm not sure you want to hear what I have to say.
Sharon: Go on, I can handle it. I want to know how you feel. I mean, c'mon, look at all the things we've done together.
Money: See, that's just what I mean. I don't think you take our relationship seriously. You look to me for fun and entertainment, like that is all I can provide. It makes me feel cheap, used. I have so many more qualities that you don't seem to have noticed. I guess you make me feel worthless.

Sharon: Really? I thought you enjoyed the things we've done. Fun times make you feel worthless? Fun times are made possible because of you. I'm shocked, Money. I didn't sense that you were struggling with anything.
Money: That's just the point. You didn't sense it.
Sharon: What do you mean?
Money: You are so involved with your good time that you neglect the larger picture. You're so focused on the present, you don't see that maybe I have more to offer than just being a social support system. I do enjoy that, don't get me wrong, but even chocolate loses its appeal if that's all you eat.
Sharon: I see. I had no idea you felt this cheap.
Money: I don't think I'm the one you should be apologizing to.
Sharon: What? You just told me my actions make you feel cheap.
Money: I'm not worried about my well-being. I am, however, concerned about the well-being of our relationship. I don't get what sort of life you're living.
Sharon: Yeah, but I don't know what I can do about it.
Money: You can change. I'm sure you have more that interests you than those hoppin' bars.
Sharon: I guess so, but I panic without other people.
Money: Why don't you challenge yourself?
Sharon: Money, you are tough. But you're right. Too much chocolate.... OK, I get it.

"I felt silly starting the money dialogue," Sharon tells me. "But once Money and I started speaking, it got easier. What I learned about myself hurt and embarrassed me. I've been so abusive with money and I've damaged myself. When I'm out having a good time, that's all I feel, that great feeling of being connected and belonging. But I guess my 'hot state' of connection disregards Money, and in the end that hurts me."

"Do you think you can make some changes?" I ask.

"I don't know," Sharon says honestly. "I love my social life, but I'm starting to think I can't afford to continue it. Mom and

Dad gave me money in college when I needed it, but I kind of sensed I was hurting them by asking. That made me feel selfish and angry. I sure don't want to ask them for help now and get back into that."

"Did you ever talk directly about money with your parents?"

"Not really. Whenever I asked them they got vague and evasive, so I stopped because I didn't like making them so uncomfortable." She pauses. "Deep down, maybe I felt I didn't deserve to get money. My parents don't go out much and they never seem to have much fun. They should do a money dialogue and learn what I'm learning!"

I say, "It sounds like the way your parents dealt with your money requests left you feeling bad about yourself. Your friends encouraged you to go out to parties and concerts with them. When you were out having a good time, you didn't feel those guilty feelings about asking for money."

"You're right, Dr. Baker. What a mess!" Sharon pauses again, then adds, "I wish thinking about money didn't make me so confused and angry."

"That's another reason why lots of people avoid talking about money, but it's not really a good one. You and I can think about money and the emotions we feel about it, and sort our feelings out as we go along together."

"Yeah, I guess so. I really have to stop this whirlwind."

"Why not plan how much you can afford to spend if you only go out twice this week? Then stick to it. Take note of how it makes you feel, but don't judge yourself. Write down your observations and bring them with you next week. OK?"

Sharon nods resolutely. On the way out of my office she says, "I'm scared to do this, but it will be disastrous if I don't."

A week later, she reports on the experiment: "I stuck to my fifty-dollar limit, but I hated it. I tried to find someone to buy me drinks and that made me feel creepy. I couldn't believe what I was doing and how desperate I must have come across.

I wanted to curl up and die. So I left, raced home, and cried myself to sleep. In the morning, the only thing that made me feel better was that I didn't go over my limit. On the nights I stayed in, I had no idea what to do. I thought about my parents never going out to have fun. Being home alone made me feel like them."

I counter, "But, Sharon, look what you accomplished! You stuck to your fifty-dollar limit, observed your behavior, and felt some pretty painful feelings without denying them. I'd like you to appreciate your progress. Keep it up."

Sharon arrives for the next session looking proud. "My credit card bill came, and I can actually pay more than the minimum," she announces gleefully. "And when I went for a walk with a new friend of mine at the condo, we thought of a couple of things to do that don't cost anything." She adds with a laugh, "Money is really proud of me!"

COMMENTS FROM MY COUCH

Sharon's original complaint was loneliness and lack of friends. She needed to stay connected to others in order to get affirmation that she was loved. The best place for her to get this was at parties and bars where everyone was more generous with compliments.

As we talked, Sharon became aware that money issues also played into her self-esteem problem. She so desperately needed the approval of others that she never considered the cost of going out or the cost of paying for everyone's drinks on many occasions. Thus, money became intimately connected with her need to be included and esteemed. Since her parents' discomfort with money matters had caused her to develop

Money Avoider attitudes, she was in danger of getting in over her head financially.

In therapy, Sharon evolved from feeling desperate and empty to being confident and satisfied. Now this young adult is free to act in her own best interests with her money, her activities, and her time. Did she have a money problem or a loneliness problem? She had a self-esteem problem and self-control problem that are now well on their way to being resolved.

~

The Importance of Parental Boundaries

From the beginning of a child's life, limits and boundaries are a critical part of developing a confident, cohesive sense of self. Parents are meant to be givers of love and structure to help the emerging individual flourish. As you've seen in this chapter, young adults struggling to stand on their own feet are rarely helped when parents can't set limits with money. Worse, over-giving can inadvertently create devastating long-term problems. In order to feel powerful and effective, we have to learn that good things result from our own efforts. When we are indulged, this process cannot flourish. It's like feeding a baby before she is hungry, so she never learns that communicating by crying is the way to secure nourishment for herself.

Many parents today try to be their child's friend first, rather than focusing on supporting, directing, guiding, and challenging. Saying "no," when it's necessary to set limits and provide structure, can be supportive and growth-enhancing.

There's a story that Mrs. Vanderbilt (or maybe Mrs. Astor or Mrs. Rockefeller) was taking her son to the Plaza Hotel in Manhattan for lunch. After the chauffeur helped her out of the car, he took a wheelchair from the trunk. Then he opened the curbside door and helped her 30-year-old son into the wheelchair. Bystanders asked, with great sympathy, what was wrong with the poor fellow that he couldn't walk. Amazed at the question, the *grande dame* replied, "Why, of course my son can walk. Thank goodness he doesn't have to!"

Even if you have millions to burn, I doubt you'd want any child of yours to be so incapable of an independent life. By the start-up years, young adults should be ready to stand on their own two feet.

~

Chapter 9 Exercise: Challenges Of The 20s

If you're in your 20s, the questions below will help you explore how embedded money beliefs influence your response to challenges during this phase of life. If you know someone in this age group, encourage them to think about these questions and write down their answers.

1. Whose story in this chapter do you most closely relate to? Why? Does it suggest a possible way to improve your own situation?
2. Describe yourself as if you were writing to a pen pal. Are you who you want to be? If not, what would you need to change? What steps would you need to take?
3. What role could money play in helping you become your ideal self?
4. What do you believe money is and can do for you? How do these beliefs affect your behavior?
5. What role does money play for the people you feel closest to, and in the activities you enjoy together? Are

you satisfied with what you spend on them? Would you change anything?

6. How did you choose your current job? Was money an important factor in the decision?
7. Do you plan for the future? If so, how far ahead – two years, five years, 10 years? Is money a significant part of your planning?
8. You learned about money scripts that you develop through childhood and your teens. Can you identify one or two that influence your present behavior?

As young adults, the better we understand our embedded money scripts and current money issues, the more clearly we will see what changes are necessary to build a stronger financial self. This is a task we need to embrace as we search for our grownup identity, independence, and personal fulfillment.

A Twentysomething Adult's Response to the Chapter 9 Exercise:

1. Whose story in this chapter do you most closely relate to? Why? Does it suggest a possible way to improve your own situation?

I relate more to Hank because I knew I had my parents to back me up. The difference was that I didn't run up a lot of debt...but I didn't also have a fear of running out of money.

2. Describe yourself as if you were writing to a pen pal. Are you who you want to be? If not, what would you need to change? What steps would you need to take?

Writing to a pen pal (or online dating) I'd describe myself as responsible but a bit scatterbrained and easily overwhelmed.

I am not who I want to be just yet. I need to take more responsibility for myself—I need to plan for the future and STICK to the plan

3. What role could money play in helping you become your ideal self?

Money would help me in terms of my appearance—I'd like to budget to buy new clothes and jewelry and update my look. I'd get an occasional pedicure or manicure. It could also help me pursue my interests in attending art events and traveling.

4. What do you believe money is and can do for you? How do these beliefs affect your behavior?

Money is a means by which to live. It can't buy you happiness—that has to come from within. But my interaction with money can affect how I live my life and how I feel about myself. Having money and spending (or saving) it wisely would probably make me very happy, or at least make me feel secure. I live very hand to mouth but have the luxury to know that my parents won't let me starve "on the street." Still, not having enough money to live AND do what I want causes me a lot of anxiety

5. What role does money play for the people you feel closest to, and in the activities you enjoy together? Are you satisfied with what you spend on them? Would you change anything?

Not answered.

6. **How did you choose your current job? Was money an important factor in the decision?**

I chose my current job because of status (better title) and more responsibility. Money was definitely a factor but not the greatest one. I asked for a significant raise but only got about 60% of it. That was frustrating because I like the job and feel like I'm learning a lot, plus I get paid in other ways like attending events and conferences. I'm really OK with my salary for now.

7. **Do you plan for the future? If so, how far ahead – two years, five years, 10 years? Is money a significant part of your planning?**

I tentatively plan for the future. I do it in my head and don't write it down. I usually only plan a year or two in advance. Money plays a small part—it becomes more important when I'm considering big purchases (renting vs. owning) or going on a big vacation.

8. **You learned about money scripts that you develop through childhood and your teens. Can you identify one or two that influence your present behavior?**

One is that "someone will always come to my rescue and take care of me." Another is: "If I focus on money I'll feel really restricted and have to give up too many things I like." Just writing them down helps me see they are real barriers to moving in a healthy direction with money and for myself.

LOAN

Chapter 10:
Will the Structure Hold? Settling Down (Or Not)

THE 30S

"There are two ways of being happy: We must either diminish our wants or augment our means." —Benjamin Franklin

Now life gets more serious. Thirtysomethings are typically forming relationships with significant others, getting mortgages, and having children. This puts them in the driver's seat — hopefully with a full tank of gas and good brakes.

In the late teens and early 20s, as we've seen, a young person's attention is on issues of personal identity: who they are, who their friends are, what kind of work they want to do, and what their dreams are. By age 30, most young adults are well on their way to settling into a life they have constructed. Perhaps for the first time, they are using their own emotional and financial resources to make major decisions for themselves.

During this phase, many of us are curious to know how we're doing compared to our peers. For instance, suppose you went to an Ivy League college and all your classmates are now in high-powered corporate jobs or have launched successful businesses. You, however, have been experimenting in several different fields since college and are still not sure what you want to do. If you find yourself not measuring up to your pals' achievements, self-doubt is likely to creep in. You wonder, "What's wrong with me? Why can't I decide what I want to be when I grow up?"

On the other hand, you could be doing better than some less happy peers because you took the time to find work you are passionate about. You may have fallen behind in some ways, but if you've discovered what you truly want to do, you have the makings of a platform that can launch you into further success.

The Growing Importance of Money

Money gains significance during the settling-down phase because most of us are paying our own bills by now. Having been in the workforce long enough without substantial help from our parents, we understand just how far our money can go. If we're not earning as much as we need or want, we have the choice of improving our value in our current field, changing fields, or lowering our standard of living. Now is the time to make changes. Once we start raising children, family responsibilities will narrow our career options.

Pressured by growing financial obligations, many of us become preoccupied with immediate concerns. Planning for retirement or a child's college education is still far enough away to be put off indefinitely. Yet if we haven't started planning by now, we'll go through life continually reacting to financial crises in a haphazard and stressful way.

∾

The Rule of 72

Settling down requires the maturity to plan ahead. That means setting goals for the short term and longer term. Make time in your schedule every month to consider where you are going and whether you are on track to achieve what you want. People with a plan save twice as much money as those without a plan, according to a survey by the Consumer Federation of America.

Also, the sooner you start saving, the more you can benefit from compound growth (earning interest on the interest you've already received). One way to understand how time and interest work together is to learn the Rule of 72. This simple rule lets you find out how long it will take to double an investment by dividing the interest rate into 72. At 3 percent interest, for example, an investment will double in 24 years (72 divided by 3 = 24).

The higher your interest rate, the sooner your money will double. As this chart shows, increasing the interest rate to 6% cuts in half the time required to double your investment. Remember, this growth occurs without having to save another penny!

The Rule of 72

At This Interest Rate...	$1,000 Will Double to...	In This Many Years
3%	$2,000	24
6%	$2,000	12
12%	$2,000	6

The point is that you're not "losing" the money you save. Instead, you gain – often in a big way, depending on the interest rate you receive!

~

Knowing Your Relationship with Money

Effective planning requires you to think about the roles money plays for you. This is especially important before getting into a long-term relationship, where you will find yourself reacting to how your partner or spouse feels about money. Your money type will probably remain the same, but the dynamics of a relationship can cause interesting things to happen.

Let's say two Spenders marry or live together as partners. They both like to spend money, but one is bound to be a bit more of a Spender than the other. This means the lesser Spender will be better able to put on the brakes and may indeed become a relative Hoarder, creating balance in the relationship. The couple may still overspend, but probably not as seriously as if each partner were on his or her own.

If you know what you are all about money-wise — or, better yet, if both of you know and understand your money types — it will be easier to work out your money relationship as a couple. Recognizing the pitfalls of your money type can also help you grow beyond the limits of that type. For instance, let's say you are a Money Monk — a money type that (as we saw in Chapter 7) doesn't believe money is important. When you hear about a fantastic conference, you make plans to attend it, then realize you'd have to give up a week's pay that you can't afford to lose. Had you thought this through in time to ask your employer, he or she might have been willing to give you the time off with pay, or even fund your trip. But since you're a Money Monk who believes that being concerned about money is beneath you, you let time go by until it's too late to ask.

No matter what money type you are, try to think ahead of time about what you might do to get what you need. You'll have to ask yourself a couple of tough questions:

- "Would the action I'd have to take be in conflict with the characteristics of my money type?" If so, you'll have to do something that's not habitual for you.
- "What would I have to change in myself to be free to act in my own best interest?" Is it an emotion like fear, or a belief about yourself like "I'm not worth it"?

Once you've outlined what you need to change, you have the basis of a plan. Take the plunge and do what you're not used to. If you have trouble reducing a fear, discarding a belief, or executing an action, ask a friend for support. Keep trying even if the results aren't perfect, and be sure to congratulate yourself on the baby steps you take. Being your own cheerleader can make the arduous task of change more fun and effective.

~

In a Financial Fog: Joan's Story

Just a few days after their honeymoon, Joan's new husband, Stuart, went out and bought an SUV. Though Joan wasn't happy about this, she didn't tell him what she really thought. Stuart could be very persuasive, while Joan didn't have the arguing skills or persistence to get what she wanted.

A day after he drove home in the SUV, Stuart took Joan to the bank and pressured her to sign loan papers so that both of them would now be liable for his $200,000 of premarital debt. Joan, who knew very little about managing money, had no confidence in her ability to understand what was happening. She did know that she was being bullied and was overwhelmed with fear and disappointment, but couldn't stand up for herself. She only knew she felt trapped and wanted to get away. Desperately unhappy, she began to lose weight. When Stuart's family noticed how thin she was getting, they chided her for not being a better cook. What if poor Stuart should lose any of his 275 pounds?

After six months of Stuart's bullying, Joan took a job at a summer camp 800 miles away. Much to her anguish, Stuart insisted on getting a job at the same place. He did such a poor job as a camp counselor, though, that he was soon asked to leave.

Free of her husband for the rest of the summer, Joan became more confident and was hoping to stand her ground when she went home. However, the pressure from Stuart and his family became so intolerable that she decided to leave him. Her parents did not offer her financial help, but they gave her a place to stay and found her a good lawyer. When the judge understood how Stuart had coerced Joan into co-signing for the premarital debt, he ruled that responsibility for paying the debt would revert solely to Stuart.

This made Joan realize it was up to her to take charge of her life. As she gained strength to express her feelings, she decided to divorce Stuart and go back to school. By good fortune, an insurance company settlement of $50,000 came in from an automobile accident she'd been involved in before her marriage. This gave her the funds to start a new life.

COMMENTS FROM MY COUCH

Joan and Stuart's story illustrates the importance of understanding one's emotions about money in order to make rational decisions when they count the most. Clearly, their relationship was troubled from the start. The first manifestations of this trouble were his impulse purchase of the SUV and his insistence that she share his colossal debt.

Joan had always been a passive person who let life happen to her. She was attracted to Stuart because he seemed so definite about what he wanted. He treated her like a queen until they got married, at which point his focus shifted from her to his own needs and wants. He was a Spender, while she was a Money Avoider.

After their relationship failed, Joan sought psychotherapy to help her manage her sadness and confusion. As for Stuart, he could not see that anything he was doing was a problem. He blamed Joan for not acting "right" (i.e., not doing what he wanted). His parents backed him up, pressuring Joan to comply with his wishes. Nothing much will change for Stuart until he is able to look more clearly at his own behavior.

∾

The Money Manager: John's Story

John's aunt, uncle, and cousin were all doctors who loved their work. Somehow, though, he didn't acquire the doctor gene. Majoring in economics instead, he landed a job after graduation as an account manager at a big bank. Through this window into other people's finances, he discovered how shockingly much debt young adults in their 20s and early 30s were accumulating. John considers himself pretty good at thinking up ways to spend money too, but his memories of working hard as a teenager to save for college remind him how important it is to be a smart money manager.

Luckily, he's both a planner and a realist. Knowing that one day he'll want to retire and enjoy himself, he figures that starting to fund his 401(k) now should give him substantially more money than if he delays making contributions.

Still, like many young people, John struggles with impulse spending. He would love to buy a new stereo system with all the bells and whistles. Occasionally he'll check the specs, look up user reviews, and comparison-shop for the best price, but then catch himself as he's loading up his online shopping cart. Mildly annoyed, he won't finish the transaction and will send the money to his 401(k) instead.

Settling Down Right: Donna and Clark's Story

What does good financial balance look like for a couple in their 30s? Consider Donna and her husband, Clark. Donna, who works in financial services, has been supporting Clark while he finishes law school. They have some debt because of education loans, but her salary has steadily increased and Clark is confident he will do well as a lawyer. They are close to Donna's family but get no financial support from them.

Donna and Clark spend countless hours talking about their values, what they want from each other, and how they feel about money. Although they don't agree on everything, they have learned to be tolerant of their differences and tease each other affectionately about their silly quirks. They both agree that Donna will work for another year, and then Clark will take over as the primary breadwinner so they can start a family.

COMMENTS FROM MY COUCH

It's easy to say that this couple will do fine because they will have plenty of money. However, many affluent people still end up in money trouble. More important for Donna and Clark is that they've learned to talk with each other, negotiate differences, anticipate, and plan. They have a strong social support system, they enjoy each other, and they have established clear and reasonable boundaries with each other and their parents. I would expect them to navigate their way through the settling-down period in a way that holds a good deal of promise for their future financial security.

Making Time to Plan

With the responsibilities of a house and children, the ability to organize and plan becomes essential. Day-to-day stresses can be so consuming that even if a couple has good planning skills, they may be too exhausted at the end of the day to think beyond the next weekend.

For example, the only time I thought about money in my 30s was when I tried to pay down my credit cards as much as possible every month, hoping to have enough left over for a vacation at the end of the year. If you'd asked about my financial plan for the future, I probably would have laughed. I barely knew what an IRA was, and what little I had heard didn't interest me at all.

Although I was married, my husband and I didn't talk about money with each other or with our family or friends. It was just a necessary evil. We felt fortunate to be able to afford what we needed. When our children were learning to recognize what a penny, nickel, and dime were, we never thought of using that learning experience to teach them about spending and saving. Even though my husband's employer provided a generous retirement plan, we discussed it so rarely that I was hardly aware of it. Of course, I didn't realize at the time how much it could benefit me to know more.

Now that my sons are in their 20s, I'm much more aware of how important it is for them to have sound money beliefs and skills. Just as they have to figure out who they are in their work and love lives, they need to know who they are in relationship to money.

Don't Throw Away Money By Failing to Save

As a young adult I would laugh at the Lennon and McCartney song, "When I'm 64," as if 64 were so far away that it didn't matter. Now the humor has waned (though it's still a great song). I wish I had understood in my 20s and 30s that saving some money every month, even $25 (the cost of a biweekly Starbucks latte), lets time work its magic in transforming a few dollars into a supersized balance.

Unless you're a Hoarder or an Amasser, how can you start saving if there's so little incentive to act? Here are some ideas:

- **Minimize the pain with automatic debits.** You can authorize your bank to move money automatically into a savings account once a month or with every paycheck. If you pay off a loan or get a raise, use the extra cash to boost your savings contribution.

- **Get a buddy to back you up.** Find a friend who also wants to save money. Discuss what you could do together to get started and help each other stay on track.
- **Challenge yourself.** Promise yourself a reward: "If I save $1,000 in the next six months, I'll treat myself to 'the works' at a day spa." Or if you have a family, get them all involved: "If we can save $2,500 by next summer, we'll all go on a camping and canoeing trip to the state park." You'll also be challenging yourself to overcome procrastination and short-term thinking.
- **Think of it as getting in shape for the future.** When you start a new fitness program, it feels like you'll never be able to work out enough to get really buff; yet systematic effort over time can produce great results. The same is true of saving.
- **Scare yourself.** If all else fails, fear can be a good motivator for a systematic savings effort. Do you want to be a financial burden on your children and grandchildren? Of course not! Do you want to live in a refrigerator carton and shuffle around on the street with a shopping cart? Start saving!

Whatever works for you, start now. Don't put it off until later, as I did. If you wait too long, you'll have to deal with the anxious realization that there may be too little time left to create a nest egg that will support you into your 90s or beyond.

"For all sad words of tongue or pen,
The saddest are these: 'It might have been.'"
John Greenleaf Whittier

~

Chapter 10 Exercise: Meshing Money Types

During the settling-down stage, your job is most likely stable. For those who are in a relationship, two money matters usually crop up: how to blend your money type with your partner's; and how to plan for a future that may include buying a house, starting a family, and negotiating your chosen lifestyle and work patterns with your partner.

A Settling Down Person's Answer

1. What money type(s) are you? What do you think your partner is? See if your partner agrees with this assessment.
2. Discuss how your individual types work together and/or conflict with each other. Listen empathically to each other's opinions until you agree on how you can work comfortably together around money. Write down your consensus.
3. Write down what you most value in your life. How much money do you need to implement those values on a month-to-month basis?
4. If you don't have enough money to live out your values, which would you think of first: getting a better paying job or re-organizing your values?
5. Are there any money scripts you can identify that are currently influencing your behavior?

A Settling Down Person's Response to the Chapter 10 Exercise:

1. What money type(s) are you? What do you think your partner is? See if your partner agrees with this assessment.

Philosophically, I am drawn to the Money Monk's "above material gain" attitudes; I would love to excuse myself from financial issues. I have grudgingly accepted how untenable that position is for someone constantly struggling to make ends meet. From a more realistic perspective, I would prefer to Avoid Risk, Conserve, and occasionally make good Deals. However, my disconnectedness regarding money results in sometimes thoughtlessly spending money (i.e., Spender type). More commonly, when I am unable to quickly resolve financial challenges, I fall into the behavior of the Money Avoider type. I suspect that I sometimes intellectualize my Avoidance in terms of Money Monk behavior, thereby making it seem nobler, or at least more palatable. In any case, my money avoidance clearly prevents me from overcoming or even managing my difficult financial situation.

I think that my wife would ideally prefer to combine the better aspects of the Conserver and Risk Avoider types. She aspires to handle money frugally, as her mother does, even though her mother is a stereotypical Hoarder. In practice, she spends most of her time as a Money Worrier. Like me, however, when her worries become too extreme she lapses into the Money Avoider's behavior. Of course, avoidance usually worsens the financial condition, leading to more worrying, thus creating a vicious circle.

2. Discuss how your individual types work together and/or conflict with each other. Listen empathically to each other's opinions until you agree on how you can work comfortably together around money. Write down your consensus.

Comparing what I perceive to be my behavior with what I perceive to be my spouse's behavior, I am struck that we both are afflicted with avoidance problems. While our behaviors would be problematic enough if we each functioned separately, by operating as a financial joint venture, we are prone to dysfunctional money behavior that becomes much more severe. For example, if one of us "overdoes it" somehow, by overspending, or by missing a good opportunity in an effort to avoid risk, and that person lapses into avoidance (either monk-like or fear-paralyzed), then the other one of us might assume that things are OK... nothing to worry about... we're safely conserving. "So that's good, I guess I can do some Spending, or some Dealing, or just be a Money Monk." In reality, however, any one of those behaviors would significantly exacerbate the problem, leading to much more worry, to the point where Avoidance becomes the shelter of last resort. And on and on.

3. Write down what you most value in your life. How much money do you need to implement those values on a month-to-month basis?

I value my own contributions to the world as a teacher and scientist, and I value being able to provide for the well-being of my family, especially my two children, so that they can grow up to be healthy, reasonably well-adjusted and well-educated. This will allow them in turn to make valuable contributions to the world. In terms of money needed to implement these values, a central issue is being able to keep a stable dwelling for my kids to call their home. I also need to plan to have sufficient money for them to go to college when that time comes.

However, instead of being able to save money for college or anything else, I have been "jogging in place" (and sometimes going backwards) financially. I occasionally have to dip into our home equity credit line to cover some expenses. So although I'm not sure how much it would take to implement my values, I know it must be more than my gross income of $6,500 per month.

4. If you don't have enough money to live out your values, which would you think of first: getting a better paying job or re-organizing your values?

This is a very difficult question because many of my values are tightly intertwined with my current job. I have some financial stability (although I would prefer a greater monthly income), and enough work-time flexibility to spend time with my children. While it is difficult to make headway on paying off my debts, my relatively low-paying job easily suffices to make our monthly mortgage payment, thereby providing a stable home for my kids. It will also provide a guaranteed partial tuition benefit for their college years.

My values, at least those stated above, are relatively non-negotiable, which logically means that I need to find a better-paying job. However, these same values (especially wanting to contribute by teaching and doing science) put severe limitations on my options for getting a better job. It seems imperative, therefore, that I find ways to make more money on a yearly or monthly basis while retaining my current job.

If I had known how financially constrained things were going to be at this point, I probably would have made some different choices earlier in my career and/or marriage rather than struggling to support a house, wife, and kids.

5. Are there any money scripts you can identify that are currently influencing your behavior? What about your spouse's money scripts?

Yes. One is, "it's unseemly to talk about money constraints or let money constraints be a big consideration in my thinking." Another is, "Intellectual and emotional happiness trump financial happiness," and "I have a social obligation to share my wealth with less fortunate people even if I don't have much."

My wife grew up financially strapped. She remembers her parents saying: "Avoid ever being in debt," and "always look after your employees before looking after yourself."

Chapter 11:
Time for Reflection

RECKONING THE 40S, 50S AND BEYOND

"Time is like money; the less we have of it to spare, the further we make it go." —Josh Billings

As I approached 50, I became acutely aware that we had not planned carefully enough for our sons' college educations. Somehow, I'd figured we would come up with the money. Costs had increased fourfold since Howard and I went to college, but the stock market's great returns had made us hope it would offset our lack of planning.

Our sons' grandfather had put $10,000 away for each of them in the early '80s. In the intervening ten years, these accounts had grown tremendously. When our first son went off to college, he drew $60,000 from his account to cover his costs. Unfortunately, the market dropped like a rock as our younger son approached college age. He was left with only $30,000, and had to get student loans to pay for the rest.

I was rudely awakened to the need to focus on and learn about money. Family and work had been my consuming passions over the years; I had assumed I wouldn't have to worry about money as long as I could keep earning more. Of course, that wasn't enough.

Evaluating Our Lives

Through the 40s, we begin to perceive that things won't go on forever. Children graduate from high school; gray hair sneakily appears in the mirror. Many of us start to realize, perhaps for the first time, that we may not be able to fly higher or faster. At 50, we probably have fewer years left than we have already lived.

This is often when people start to reevaluate their lives. Am I doing what I really want to do? Do I want to ever stop working? How much money would I need? Yikes, can it be time for our 30th high school reunion already?

Pedal to the Metal: Christopher's Story (continued)

Remember Christopher from Chapter 2, haunted by the memory of his late father's business failure? Chris's ambition pushed him through college and into his first job in finance. Expecting his bosses to relate to him the same way his father had, he sought out older, more experienced businessmen who could help him develop his career. Finding them was the easy part. But when they took him under their wing, he was always disappointed that, unlike his dad, they didn't put his interests above or even on a par with their own. It never occurred to Chris that he simply expected too much.

Feeling betrayed and embittered, he became grew suspicious and distrustful of others. Sometimes he tried to even the score in ways that might be called either shrewd or selfish. He was determined not to come out on the short end of a deal.

Approaching 50, Chris found the courage to strike out on his own. Once he started his own business, the intensity of his focus on earning money was matched only by his compulsion to drive himself mercilessly. Up at 6 a.m., constantly on the phone, and working late into the night, Chris was obsessed with expanding his business and amassing a fortune. His persistence and confidence that he could drive a deal kept him constantly busy. But as he made more and more money, his goal became a moving target. Whenever he increased his earnings, he would allocate a higher percentage to savings. That way, he still felt the pressure of having to earn more to meet his monthly expenses. And, of course, those expenses kept going up as his lifestyle became more lavish. He felt he had to have his "screw you" money, but the amount he needed always seemed to be just beyond what he had amassed.

~

COMMENTS FROM MY COUCH

Christopher's early anxiety was still dictating his attitude toward money. The knot he had had in his stomach since his days as a striving child had never gone away.

Clearly, Chris is a Money Amasser. Money represents security, safety, power, and sometimes revenge to him. Although he loves his wife and children and would do anything for them, he finds the most satisfaction and pleasure in making a deal.

At 50, he is well on the way to building a fortune. He paid attention to the signal of time passing in his 40s, and changed the structure of his work-life to position himself for the future. However, Chris still measures his self-worth in dollars – a measure that has limited validity, since he can always find someone who is wealthier than he is. His self-esteem also depends on the admiration he gets from his competitors. Outdoing one of them gives him particular gratification.

Although I worry that Christopher will look back and regret having been so overwhelmingly focused on making money, he has assured himself (at least externally) of being able to live well. It will take him a lot longer to adjust his feelings internally so he is not haunted by the image of his father. His compulsion to "even the score" and refusal to depend on others will not yield the safety and security he longs for.

~

A Creative Spirit: Andrea's Story

Andrea lives and breathes music. Her home is a beautiful old mansion in the middle of a city park. It's rent-free, because she takes care of the building. She was 50 a while ago, but is so in love with singing and giving voice lessons that she hardly noticed this key birthday as a trigger for self-reflection and possible change.

Andrea gets immense pleasure from finding furniture and interesting artifacts at flea markets. She sews many of her own clothes. Her excitement was contagious as she told me about sewing together 50 old T-shirts to make herself a quilt.

If she runs out of money or becomes sick and can't pay her medical bills, she still probably won't worry. She is part of a family: a community of artists who look after each other no matter what happens. The lush life will elude her, but she really doesn't care.

~

COMMENTS FROM MY COUCH

Andrea is a Money Avoider who rarely thinks about her finances. They are what they are. To the same extent that Christopher concentrates on money, Andrea concentrates on ignoring it and pursuing her art. I can imagine Chris at 65 sitting on his deck and reading his investment statements with a smile of self-satisfaction, while I see Andrea at 65 busy with rehearsals for her latest opera. Each will be happy in a different way, since they have set a direction for themselves and followed it wholeheartedly.

~

The Tipping Point

Around 50, both men and women begin to realize — not just think abstractly about — the fact that they will not live forever. Women experience menopause; parents grow frail or pass away; friends develop health problems; we all begin to experience aches and pains where there used to be none. Retirement, although still distant on the horizon, begins to recur in our thinking. Career peaks are within sight and children are leaving the nest. We wonder, "What next for me?"

Unfortunately, the future may not be that rosy. Some 25 million of today's 50-year-olds have a net worth of less than $100,000. Say you're 50 and have $50,000 put aside. If your savings grow at a compound 10 percent a year (an extremely optimistic assumption), you'll have $208,840 by age 65. That sounds pretty good, but suppose you live another 20 years afterward? Let's make another assumption, that you invest your retirement savings conservatively, just keeping pace with inflation. If you can live on about $10,000 a year plus Social Security, your money may last as long as you do — but you're not likely to have a comfortable old age. You'll probably have to work at least part-time, if your health permits, to make ends meet. (Because there are so many issues related to retirement, I have devoted a later chapter to it.)

SUMMING UP FROM THE COUCH

So far I've sketched out the developmental progression from childhood through adolescence to young adulthood and beyond, to provide an idea of the pivotal issues that surface in each developmental phase. Such issues as trust vs. mistrust, autonomy vs. self-doubt, initiative vs. inferiority, identity cohesion vs. identity confusion, and intimacy vs. isolation deeply influence how we interact with others in our world.

By midlife our roles are set: we have an ongoing relationship not just with people but also with money, expressed in both thought and action. As key issues play out, money can either help us get to a good place or lead us toward isolation, rigidity, stagnation, and ultimately despair. No matter how our lives have developed, money harmony is vital.

Chapter 11 Exercise: Aging with Grace

Consider the following questions and write down your answers:

1. If you are 50 or older now, think about physical changes you've noticed in yourself. If you're younger than 50, what changes do you think you might notice? What do they feel like? How do they alter your thinking about yourself?
2. At what point would you want to stop working? Do you know how much money you'll need to have saved by then? (If not, find a financial advisor and/or educate yourself about retirement savings.)
3. Do you want to make any changes in your career or in your family/career balance? This is the time to make any major structural changes to your life.
4. Are there any money scripts you can identify that are currently influencing your behavior?

A 50+ Person's Response to the Chapter 11 Exercise:

1. If you are 50 or older now, think about physical changes you've noticed in yourself. If you're younger than 50, what changes do you think you might notice? What do they feel like? How do they alter your thinking about yourself?

Having already reached (and passed) 50 leaves little for my imagination to ponder. Thankfully, menopause was mild. Although I have no physical symptoms that I notice, the fact that I have recently been diagnosed with osteoporosis has changed the priority I assign to the need to exercise. It is also an early reminder that my body is beginning to decline and that the physical strength and stamina of youth are no longer a given. I need to devote time and energy to the goal of maintaining my health, recognizing that I no longer bounce back so easily from the consequences of ignoring my body. The change in my sleep pattern is an additional annoying reminder of that awareness. When I was younger and had less than a restful night's sleep when one of my children was up at night, I could work an entire day and still feel that I was functioning. Now, in my 50s, I experience headaches, a foggy mind, and increased irritability that persist until I can catch up on my sleep. As far as my body is concerned, time no longer seems to be on my side.

2. Do you want to make any changes in your career or in your family/career balance? This is the time to make any major structural changes to your life.

I cannot imagine having the financial security to retire at this stage in my life. As a woman who has recently had to provide the better part of college tuitions for both of my children, I have not yet had the chance to make retirement as much of a priority as I would like. I am hoping to do so in the very near future.

3. At what point would you want to stop working? Do you know how much money you'll need to have saved by then? (If not, find a financial advisor and/or educate yourself about retirement savings).

The fact that I now need to make retirement plans a priority is a distinct challenge to the career change I would like to effect. In order to retrain and reeducate myself, I would need to stop earning an income that would contribute to making my retirement more financially secure. The conflict I am now experiencing pits the desire to work in a more satisfying way against the need to provide for the years when I am no longer able to work. The solution to this dilemma as yet remains unclear.

4. Are there any current money scripts that you can identify that are influencing your money behavior?

No Answer.

PART IV:

HOW MONEY MAY AFFECT YOUR LIFESTYLE

You may be single, coupled, divorced, and widowed at various times in your life. Each of these states will affect your relationship with money differently — as it did for some of the people you'll meet in the next few chapters.

HALF OFF!

Chapter 12:
Flying Solo

SINGLEHOOD

"Living alone makes it harder to find someone to blame." —Mason Cooley

Back when the popular norm was the nuclear family — Dad, Mom, and two or three kids — single adults used to be viewed with curiosity or pity. But by 2009, for the first time since the U.S. began keeping track of marriages, more people aged 25-34 were single than married. There are a number of reasons:

- Many young adults don't want or haven't yet found a life partner.
- An increasing number of women don't see the need to marry in order to live with a partner or have a child.
- Half of all first marriages end in divorce.
- Married women tend to outlive their husbands.

Although our cultural bias still remains strongly tilted toward couplehood, being single in one's 20s and even 30s is not that unusual in our highly competitive and work-driven society. In college, we're surrounded by like-minded peers.

The venues to meet friends and dates are clear, available, and abundant. In the working world, however, these opportunities decrease sharply. Computer dating has become popular because so many single people of all ages are too busy to go out and socialize with potential mates.

Once people in their 20s start partnering up permanently, the pool of available singles dwindles more. When you are 30, finding like-minded people becomes not only more difficult but also more expensive. Unless you work with colleagues who are suitable for dating, you may have to create social networks that provide support, friendship, and, if you choose, the possibility of finding a partner. An example of a relatively informal network is the annual Burning Man event in the Nevada desert, a temporary community of unconventional art-minded people who gather from all over the country.

By necessity, thirtysomething singles have to be willing to initiate action to develop relationships. This need is particularly compelling for women who want to have children with a partner.

Some Advantages of Singlehood

On the other hand, being single can be both satisfying and enriching. Many a philosopher has emphasized how important it is to "know thyself." Introspection, combined with interpersonal engagement with friends and colleagues, allows you to learn about yourself and your fundamental values and goals. You have the opportunity to learn who you are in relation to yourself as well as other people. Living alone for an extended period of time gives you more freedom to make changes in yourself and your environment. You can maintain a balance of independence and interdependence with others, without being completely locked in.

To varying degrees, everyone has the need to connect with other people and feel part of a community. People who live on their own learn ways of maintaining connectedness with others that sustain their independence and enhance responsibility for their own choices and life direction. (Some do it better than others, of course.) If you have trouble making good decisions, living alone can give you the chance to figure out why.

Furthermore, single living is excellent for finding out your relationship with money and developing your financial self. Since you are the only one managing your money, you can spend, save, and allocate it as you see fit. You can experiment with a variety of methods of dealing with money without influencing someone else's money behavior. And because you're on your own, you have an opportunity to really experience the value of money and learn to treat it with respect.

Along with singles who are actively seeking a partner or who choose to live alone, singlehood also includes those who are divorced or widowed. In this chapter, we'll focus on people who are on their own by chance or by choice.

Let The Music Play On: Laura's Story

At age 27, Laura landed a sought-after teaching job in the suburbs. Having graduated from a top music school with honors, she could command a solid entry salary plus benefits. After she developed a reputation as an engaging and effective teacher, she boosted her income to $60,000 a year by giving private flute lessons.

When her 30th birthday came and went, Laura realized that connection with a significant other was not happening. Although she was very capable of taking care of herself, she wanted a relationship with someone she could love and trust. As her friends paired off, she became more keenly aware of her own desire. Yet, fiercely independent, she knew she would not settle for just anyone.

In order to fill the loneliness she sometimes felt, Laura went to parties, concerts, and shows. Outgoing, fun-loving, and pretty, she had confidence that she would have a good time whether or not she met the man of her dreams. Her need to connect, of course, led her to spend money. Other people her age were doing the same thing, so why shouldn't she?

At the end of the month, her credit card bill was more than she had anticipated. She could pay most of it, but would have to let some of the balance wait until next time. She rationalized that her friends were doing the same thing, especially since she knew for a fact that many of them earned less than she did. Besides, what was the fun of being young if you had to stay home all the time? She certainly didn't want to miss meeting her ideal guy. The $50,000 she still owed on student loans would sometimes creep into her consciousness, but the interest rate was so low that taking time to pay them off didn't seem so bad.

This pattern continued for months. Why not? She was young and had a good job with health insurance. Her slowly escalating debt level was nothing special for her generation. One of these days she would catch up. Of course, being young, healthy, and employed made it difficult for her imagine a time when she might not have a job or be so carefree.

But when her car broke down and cost over $6,000 to repair, Laura became painfully aware that she had no savings for such an emergency. She didn't have a high enough credit limit to pay the bill with her credit card. Embarrassed, she ended up asking her mom, dad, and grandmother for help. She knew her family had all managed to save lots more than she had, even though they made less money. But being of a different generation, Laura assumed that carrying debt was normal, acceptable, and almost inevitable. Her view was "Do what you want to do, and figure out how to cope if something bad happens — but hope it won't."

~

COMMENTS FROM MY COUCH

It's no accident that credit card companies market to college students. Once a credit card casts its spell of convenience over a young person, it takes mammoth will power not to succumb. That's how Laura's courtship with credit cards began. After 10 years of enjoying the ease and comfort of charging purchases, it's little wonder that she and her credit card are wedded to the seduction of "buy now, pay later."

If Laura had had a live-in partner, his money type might have conflicted with hers. This contrast could have made her more aware of her money habits, potentially leading her to change how she handled money. While singlehood may make it more difficult to identify unhealthy money behavior, it does have one big advantage: since there is no one else to accommodate, it's much easier to alter one's habits.

~

Living It Up: Pete's Story

Pete heads the parts department of a foreign car dealership. He has been in love with cars for as long as he can remember, and lives for the day when he can afford his own Ferrari. Most of his weekends are spent with like-minded buddies playing music, hanging out in bars, and going to NASCAR races.

Now 40, he has been with the dealership for 12 years. He earns enough not to have to worry about money, although he doesn't save very much. He figures he can always earn more if he needs to. After all, he doesn't have to support a family.

Years ago Pete thought about marrying his steady girlfriend, but his ardor cooled as he watched his married friends split up, one after the other. It seemed to him that the ex-wife and kids got all the assets, while the ex-husband was stuck with the bills and child care payments. No, that wasn't going to happen to him! He had grown fiercely protective of his own time and interests, and wasn't about to give them up.

COMMENTS FROM MY COUCH

Pete is among a growing number of men in their 30s and 40s who have enough discretionary income to indulge their hobbies, along with a "protective selfishness" that makes them unwilling to take the risk of a long-term intimate relationship. They view women with suspicion and disdain. Their career keeps them driving hard, as does their music and their narrow focus on having fun with the guys.

As long as Pete is strong and healthy, he will likely survive in this established pattern. But were he to get sick or lose his parents or the brother with whom he is close, he could discover that he is out of step with most of his peers who have found a caring life partner. His life may well become lonely, particularly as he gets older.

Fear of getting sick and not being able to work is a major concern for singles. Without a partner's income, a lost paycheck can mean having to invade one's savings, piling more debt onto credit cards, or letting bills go unpaid. The thought of a long-term illness or injury may weigh on Pete as he gets older. Unless he does something about this concern (one possibility would be to buy long-term care insurance), it will likely loom as a larger and larger fear.

~

No One Can Control Me If I'm Alone: LeeAnn's Story

A senior scientist at a top pharmaceutical company, LeeAnn liked being around people. She just didn't want to live with any of them.

When she was growing up, her controlling mother demanded that she do exactly what was "asked." Without emotional support from her quiet, retiring engineer father, she felt forced to obey her mom. She wasn't encouraged to think for herself or manage her own money.

When LeeAnn got to college she attracted the attentions of strong men, but had too little dating experience to cope with them. Intimidated, she retreated into the world of books. Being studious allowed her to maintain her loyalty to her mother, who continued to dictate do's and don'ts to her, including how to spend her money. It never occurred to LeeAnn that she had a choice. By the time she reached graduate school, she was living out a deeply ingrained belief that she was not attractive to men and would never find a husband. As gregarious and people-loving as she appeared, on a deeper level she could not let herself long for something that she knew would never happen.

At the same time, she had begun to earn a stipend as a research assistant. Relishing the sense of independence that came from having money of her own, she secretly bought herself beautiful jewelry and perfume. Had her mother found out about these luxuries, she would have insisted that LeeAnn buy them for her. The only way LeeAnn could enjoy these pleasures was to keep them secret.

In her early 50s with a good position that paid well, LeeAnn still considered planning and managing her finances to be "boring." However, she worried constantly that she wouldn't have enough money to retire. When her father died, he had left nothing for her and only a pittance for her mother.

Thoughts of getting older began to preoccupy her. She imagined what it would be like if she couldn't get around and had to rely on other people to help her. She would have to hire caregivers, of course, because no one would be there for her. These fears were shadows in the background of her busy day-to-day life. Her efforts to avoid thinking about money left her feeling a constant low-grade uncertainty about the future.

LeeAnn was such a good avoider that she didn't even realize how much she resisted dealing with her beliefs and feelings about money. When her mother suddenly died, the crisis threw her into a tailspin of fear and depression.

COMMENTS FROM MY COUCH

Emotional isolation is a major issue for most singles. They need to work harder at reaching out to others — a real challenge for people who are shy, introverted, or have social anxiety. We all have a basic human need to share our thoughts and feelings with someone who will respond with love and affection. Without this kind of connection and support, all the difficulties of life are magnified. LeeAnn's fear of being controlled, misunderstood, and hurt was so strong that she preferred to suffer loneliness rather than risk being dominated and absorbed by someone else.

Her lack of interest in money fed her personal fears. She was unable to feel the security and peace of mind of having enough money. Claiming the same indifference to money as she did to finding a life partner, she kept working and hoped her fears would go away. It's as if part of her wanted something different to happen — a prince to ride up on a white horse, perhaps, and take away all her financial worries — but the rest of her was convinced that nothing like that would ever occur.

In therapy, LeeAnn realized that since she was the only one who knew about her money situation, only she could do something about it. Unless she confronted her avoidance and learned to understand her relationship with money, her fears might come true by default. This feedback from me and the members of her therapy group helped her overcome her fear of reviewing her finances.

To her surprise, she discovered that in addition to an inheritance her mother had left her, she had saved far more than she thought. She wasn't in bad financial shape, after all! Had she faced her money fears earlier, she wouldn't have endured such anxiety for so long.

~

The Worrier: Rob's Story

A curious and thoughtful young man, Rob loved to read, develop ideas, and teach. After many false career starts, he realized that the only thing that would really satisfy him would be to get a Ph.D. in English literature. He knew he would never make a lot of money, but reading and writing were his passion. His dad, a college professor, had "sold out" and gone to work for a bank in order to give his family financial security. Rob vowed that he wouldn't let worrying about money stop him from staying true to his passion and proceeding with his plans.

While working on his doctorate, he lived in an inexpensive garage apartment. Some modest financial support came in from an assistantship and from his family, who were ambivalent about his career path. Rob liked his no-frills existence and tried not to worry about money, but he often found himself awake at 3 a.m. wondering how he would ever get out of debt. One way to free himself from his anxieties was to go to the local bookstore, drink coffee, and look at books. This had a downside: by the time he left, he would have bought a book and spent another $6 on coffee and a pastry. The more he worried, the more coffee he drank and the more books he bought.

~

COMMENTS FROM MY COUCH

Worry plagues most of us. But by itself, worry is unproductive. It is not a plan. It simply mingles concern with wondering, "What if....?" *What if I break my leg, lose my job, and have my home burn down?* Some worries are highly unrealistic. Consider the case of a 78-year-old bachelor worth $10 million who was considering two assisted living facilities. The first one was well kept up, in a beautiful location, and cost $6,000 a month; the other was in a rundown part of town, smelled strongly of urine and disinfectant, and cost $2,800 a month. The multimillionaire was about to sign up for the cheaper place because he worried that he couldn't afford the other one!

Worry is also repetitive. That is, we go over the same thing again and again looking for an answer, but the worry never changes and the answer never comes. When we think of something repeatedly, changes in brain patterns make it more likely that we'll hark back to that thought again. In effect, we establish a hyperlink in our brain circuitry. The more we think about something tinged with a negative emotion such as worry, fear, or anxiety, the more likely we are to believe it will come true.

Most important, worry is not preparation. Preparation is thinking things through in a thoughtful, careful way in order to formulate a response. This process requires us to logically assess what the outcomes are likely to be and whether they will be good or bad. We can then make a sound judgment that leads to effective action. Both Rob and the $10 million man need to work on understanding their behavior, reorganizing how they think about themselves and their situation, and then revising their behavior and planning instead of worrying. This will help them turn their worried state into greater calm.

Infinite Degrees of Freedom: Jarrod's Story

At 38 Jarrod likes being single. At the same time, he imagines what it would be like to find a committed, long-term partner he could trust. He is well aware of his own tendency to be distrustful. Suspicion that he might be taken advantage of keeps him more distant than he might wish, yet he likes being generous. When he is interested in a man and invites him to dinner, he expects to pay the check. When he is asked out, he likes it when his date offers to pay for him, but it doesn't upset him if they decide to split the bill.

Jarrod is very aware of the power differential when he dates. He muses that with heterosexual dating, gender roles often dictate who pays. There are far fewer role conventions in the homosexual world — "no clear footsteps on the dance floor," as he puts it. When the bill comes, he thinks: *Is my date older or wealthier than I am? Is he of another race, with all the expectations and conventions that go with that?* For instance, when Jarrod invites a date who is younger and makes less money, he will offer to pay the whole bill. When Jarrod is the guest, he will wait until the bill arrives to see what his host proposes to do. It gives him a sense of excitement and anticipation to see how his date will handle the situation. He never verbalizes this dance around money and dating, preferring to live with the mystique of the unspoken.

When Jarrod thinks about living with someone, his immediate concern is that he will lose his freedom and be subject to his partner's demands. He can't stand the idea of pooling his money or sharing a credit card. What if the relationship doesn't last? Many of his gay friends are in long-term committed relationships, but he can't be sure he will be as lucky.

Contrary to his dating behavior, Jarrod is very outspoken about his finances. He readily discloses how much he makes, how much he earns, and how much he saves. Since most "gayborhoods" are in urban areas, he pays more than usual for his condo, parking, and local taxes. Although he has been employed by the same company for nine years, he's unsure whether being openly gay will affect his job security. He has been thinking about getting disability (income protection) insurance, since he would have no one to rely on if a health crisis kept him out of work.

Knowing he has to save, Jarrod has also taken advantage of his company's 401(k) plan. It has a 25% employer match, meaning that if he contributes $10,000 a year, the company will put in another $2,500. His only hangup is that whenever he speaks to a financial advisor about his savings, he always feels they are telling him, "That's not enough!"

If and when Jarrod finds a domestic partner, he wants to keep his money separate except for a joint household expenses account. If they buy a house together, it will be as "tenants in common." That way, he can bequeath his share to whomever he chooses instead of having it go automatically to his co-owner.

Jarrod's biggest fear is that his relationship with a partner won't last. He has nightmares about being alone on his deathbed.

This image reminds him that once he is in a committed relationship, he will need to draw up a legal directive allowing his partner to visit him in the hospital and take part in medical decisions.

൶

COMMENTS FROM MY COUCH

In a heterosexual marriage, there are legal conventions for dealing with property and money. For example, if a person dies without a will, his or her surviving spouse automatically receives all or a portion of the estate. Since laws vary from state to state, it's important for a single person to prepare for worst-case scenarios. You will need to have a knowledgeable attorney draw up documents that specify your desires.

Unfortunately, this means contemplating things that no one wants to think about. The "status quo" effect is active here, and it may take a crisis to bring these financial matters into focus.

Living by oneself and determining how long to live single is a very personal and individual decision that many of us struggle with at one time or another. It can be the best of times or the worst of times, depending on how well you get along with yourself and what your goals are. It's also more expensive, but the freedom it offers can be alluring. Being single challenges you to keep socially active and connected.

For most people, singlehood is most satisfying when you are forging your career path and developing close relationships. As your life plan becomes more articulated, you may happen to find a like-minded soulmate along the way. That is the optimal time to say goodbye to singlehood, embrace partnership, and often save money in the process.

൶

Chapter 12 Exercise: Being Single

If you are currently single, try answering these questions to explore how being on your own affects your attitudes and actions around money. Knowing your money type, do you feel in charge of the behavior that results? (See Chapter 7 if you're not clear on which money type(s) you are.)

1. Does it create opportunities for you that you value?
2. How do your money type and current budget influence the way you present yourself on dates or with people you are romantically interested in? Do you talk about money or disclose financial intimacies to your date?
3. Do you have an idea how long you will remain single? Are you using this timeline to make strategic financial decisions? If so, write down one or two examples.
4. If you have been single for more than 15 years, has the way you plan and use your money changed over that time? If so, how?

A Single Man's Response to the Chapter 12 Exercise:

1. Does it create opportunities for you that you value?

My money type does not fit into any of the categories from chapter 7. I am neither a binger nor a spender. I am closer to a spender because I view money as a means to an end and like to have nice things. However, I do not live extravagantly — my money mostly goes towards hobbies and things that get a lot of use. Additionally I work hard to keep credit card balances at zero and work within a budget. My strategy around money is to develop a budget that includes exact amounts for all of my regular expenses/bills and use an average amount (on the scale of months) for things that vary, like entertainment or car maintenance. This allows me to feel confident that the basics are taken care of. I feel very in charge of my money type and appreciate the fact that it allows me to enjoy my money rather than feel constantly anxious about it.

2. How do your money type and current budget influence the way you present yourself on dates or with people you are romantically interested in? Do you talk about money or disclose financial intimacies to your date?

Dating forces a change in my budgeting and often the use of my credit cards until my expenses become more predictable. I don't spend hugely more than I would regularly, but I do different things and the cost of things like dinners tend to be different. When dating someone for an extended period, my money type allows me to not appear to be a cheapskate because I have discretionary money in my budget that I can use to make up for new expenses. I tend to talk about money with my dates in terms of what my and her general view of money is, but I don't discuss the details of my budget unless I am in a committed relationship.

3. Do you have an idea how long you will remain single? Are you using this timeline to make strategic financial decisions? If so, write down one or two examples.

I will start to save when I expect to get engaged and settle down. Both of these things require a good amount of cash (for a ring, wedding, house or new apartment, etc) so I work to at least make a dent in those expenses.

4. If you have been single for more than 15 years, has the way you plan and use your money changed over that time? If so, how?

I haven't been intentionally single for that amount of time, but my money habits have basically stayed the same. My budgeting has gotten more refined and my skills have improved, though.

Chapter 13:
Two's Company

COUPLES AND THE GENTLE ART OF LYING

"Every competent counselor knows that no matter what the marriage problem, the system that sustains it is found in both people." —Anonymous marriage counselor

In the beginning, love makes a partner perfect. As they bask in their mutual good feelings, each of them knows the other can do no wrong. Since most couples avoid conflict in the early days of marriage, they don't discuss the frequently divisive topic of money. As long as there is enough to pay the bills, who cares about anything else?

But as time moves on and the reality of everyday life takes hold, things may change. According to a 2003 study by Jay Zagorsky, a research scientist at Ohio State University, money ranks as the first or second most often argued-about topic in marriage. Considering the current recession's unprecedented combination of job losses, investment losses, and losses in home value, we can assume this continues to be even more the case.

In order for their relationship to thrive, a couple needs to establish basic rules of communication based on a genuine understanding of each other's position. Each partner also needs to respect the other's position and sensitivities, without necessarily agreeing with them. These two qualities — mutual understanding and respect — make it possible to hear each other's point of view without getting into a fistfight.

When Money Types Clash

If the partners' communication skills aren't well developed, they can easily fall back on money type patterns from childhood. For example, say the husband, whom I'll call Bart, is a Spender, and his partner, Sarah, is a Hoarder. When they married they put their money in a joint account. Sarah notices that big withdrawals are appearing on the bank statement. Mystified, she wants to know where all the money is going. When she asks Bart, he says he needed to get something for work. "No big deal," he assures her. This upsets Sarah but she doesn't want to admit how she feels to Bart, especially since he seems to have a good reason for the withdrawal. Bart gets uneasy, realizing that Sarah may monitor their bank statements. He doesn't want to upset her, but he really wants a zoom lens for his new camera. So instead of having his paycheck direct-deposited, he cashes it, pockets the money for the purchases he wants to make, and banks the rest. This way, he thinks, his spending won't be as noticeable. He's right — for a while. Then Sarah catches on. She is disappointed and hurt that he didn't trust her. Bart feels guilty, but is secretly glad he bought the camera and the lens.

~

COMMENTS FROM MY COUCH

This is how the gentle art of lying creeps into a relationship. Not only is Bart lying to Sarah, but he thinks he has found a way to get what he wants without upsetting her, which means he's lying to himself.

This deceit came about because they didn't make a point of sitting down to discuss how they felt about money. Like most couples, they began to react to each other's money behavior and acted out their feelings instead of talking about them. Neither of them wanted to cause any friction in their relationship. Now, however, negative feelings of disappointment, shame, and betrayal have entered their world of affection and trust. The serpent has slithered into the Garden of Eden.

Not only do Sarah and Bart have to talk through their emotions about money, but now they have to confront each other about the bad feelings that have cropped up between them. They may be able to reverse the downward spiral if they can catch it before it picks up momentum, but this will take effort and commitment. If they don't address the issue, their negative feelings will end up undermining their relationship.

How can they start such a difficult conversation with each other? Let's pretend we can read their minds and listen in on what they say:

Sarah might begin, "Bart, have you got a few minutes? I need to talk with you about something important." (Easily said — but in her gut Sarah worries that this confrontation might break up their relationship, because Bart can be defensive and stubborn.)

Sensing this is serious, Bart temporizes, "Honey, let's talk later. I just got home from work and I need a beer. And then I want to go out for a run."

Though disappointed, Sarah had thought he might react like that. "OK, but when can we talk?"

"How about this weekend, when we're not so pressured?"

Sarah refuses to back down. "No, I don't want to wait that long. How about after you come back from your run? I'll cook dinner and we can talk while we eat."

Nice way to ruin a good dinner, Bart thinks to himself. *But she's getting anxious, so I'd better go along with this.*

Over dinner, Sarah says, "I really want us to work this out, Bart, but I'm concerned that you are hiding something from me. Your paycheck is short and you don't seem to mind."

"To be honest, I needed to get a lens for my camera. It will really help me take better pictures. If I get good enough, I can earn some extra income for us."

"So you see the lens as an investment, not just part of your hobby?" she asks.

"Yes, exactly! But I was afraid to tell you because you worry about money so much. I didn't want to upset you, although obviously I have."

"Well, I wasn't thinking of the lens as an investment, but that makes sense to me. Maybe we should talk about our money differences so we don't hurt each other again."

Bart agrees. Opening another beer, he heaves a sigh of relief.

~

Love and Marriage: Jane and Patrick's Story

When a couple lives together without being married, they can maintain the illusion of separateness, knowing they can always leave the relationship. This allows them to act more like two people who care for each other and are sharing a common space, without feeling the emotional intensity of a long-term commitment.

Consider Jane and Patrick. After living together for eight years, they had many mutual interests and loved to spend time with each other, with or without friends. They were content with their jobs and with the direction of their lives. As their friends settled down and began to have children, they felt pressured to get married, although they didn't plan to have kids. Each had spent a long time getting over a rocky childhood. Moreover, they didn't think they earned enough to support a child.

As time passed, Jane felt she needed the security of marriage. She couldn't explain why. After much discussion she finally convinced Patrick to go through with a simple civil ceremony, followed by a casual celebration with close friends.

Two months after their wedding, their relationship started to unravel. Patrick felt the walls closing in on him. Jane didn't feel the closeness to him that she had expected. Yet nothing had really changed, except a 20-minute marriage ceremony at Town Hall.

Jane and Patrick had always had separate money, aside from a household expense account to which they contributed equally. They kept the same system after their marriage, but it no longer worked as well. For the first time, Patrick began to notice how much money Jane spent on music CDs and gadgets for her guitar. If she spent too much and didn't have enough to cover their rent and utilities, would she expect him to make up the shortfall?

He began to make little offhand comments like "You're really getting into your guitar these days. Are you sure you have time to do that?" Feeling picked on, Jane started to make her music purchases on the sly. She opened a new credit card in her name and took care not to leave receipts lying around. When she went grocery shopping, she asked for cash back. The more carefully she hid her expenses, the more suspicious Patrick became and the more annoying questions he asked.

Jane's Spender habits and Patrick's Hoarder tendencies hadn't been much of a problem while they were only living together. But after marriage, their individual financial decisions affected them as a couple. Unless they learn to talk about what is happening between them, they will become locked in a downward-spiraling struggle. They may say, "It's not about the money" — but when people say that, it usually *is* about the money.

~

COMMENTS FROM MY COUCH

The emotional impact of marriage often blows open a closed door, allowing unresolved issues of the past to intrude into the relationship. The marriage commitment itself tends to increase a couple's expectations of each other, while unconscious needs evoked by its personal meaning can worm themselves into the relationship in troublesome ways.

A couple's interactions are dynamic: they react to and play off each other. The more flexible their interplay, the greater their chances are of being able to talk out their differences. If that's impossible, their reactions may become a repetitive pattern, sometimes locking them into impasses and stalemates.

When partners have a difference of opinion about money, shading the truth is a common way of trying to avoid outright conflict. Although this may seem to be an attempt to protect the relationship, it can actually have the opposite effect. Money becomes a magnet for negative emotions such as shame, anxiety, desire for control, and revenge.

Patrick wanted to control Jane's spending because he was afraid she would overspend, forcing him to make up the difference. He felt insecure and incompetent for not earning more money. Being monitored by Patrick made Jane feel controlled and distrusted. She saw no reason she shouldn't spend her hard-earned money on what she wanted. Both partners felt threatened in a way they hadn't foreseen when they committed to a future together.

If this pattern becomes entrenched, simple questions about spending can turn into accusations of thoughtlessness or selfishness, while quiet concealing of receipts will turn into outright lying. Jane's Spender and Patrick's Hoarder money types are polar opposites, pushing them apart and tearing the fabric of their relationship. They need to sit down and be clear with each other about how they want to spend their money — both separately and as a couple.

These discussions are difficult because money often becomes entwined with other aspects of a couple's relationship. Patrick and Jane have to listen with empathy to how they are affecting each other emotionally. He is feeling worried, insecure, and inadequate, while she feels controlled and stifled. What started out as Patrick's worry about having enough money has turned into an emotional battle for control that is starting to constrict and poison their interaction. They need to learn to talk about money openly and develop a budget that includes saving for the future.

Once partners are locked into this sort of battle, communication ceases and the opportunity for cooperative planning and mutual understanding fades. Goodwill gives way to emotional distance. Collateral damage often occurs to children who are hurt or confused by their parents' rift.

It doesn't have to be this way. Partners can learn to understand each other's perspective and empathically listen to each other's views. Just repeating to your partner what they are trying to say even though you might not agree with it knocks down barriers of defensiveness and distance. The hard part is coming to a compromise that each of you can live with and enjoy, despite having to give something up.

As Comfortable As an Old Shoe: My Story

With more than 30 years behind us, my husband and I are a good example of a couple that has been married for a while. I'm a Money Worrier/Hoarder/Amasser; he's a Money Avoider. I hate to waste money and get anxious when I do. He spends money, but not recklessly. Together we have enough money as long as we spend thoughtfully.

During the early phases of our marriage, we didn't talk about money because we were both riding on our childhood assumptions about it. I believed that he was smart and would take care of all things financial. His parents presented a united front that there would always be enough for what he and his brother needed, so he didn't worry about money. Our childhood money scripts were in full flourish!

When we go into a store together, his artistic eye will be caught by a beautifully packaged item. I come along and ask how much it is and whether we really need it. His face dims and the joy is taken out of his planned purchase. He may still buy it but he hates upsetting me, so it doesn't give him as much pleasure as he thought it would. I don't mean to ruin his fun; I just want to protect our money. If my voice gets too harsh, he feels controlled. If he wants something that doesn't make sense to me, I feel we are wasting a precious resource. Neither of us is wrong, but we create unwanted tension in our relationship.

Another conflict can occur when we have dinner at a really nice restaurant. He has two or three glasses of wine, while I hardly ever finish one. Since I'm a vegetarian, his food is usually pricier than mine. Of course he is entitled to have what he wants, but the difference can easily be $40 or even more. This annoys me. Should I start ordering more food to make up the difference? That would be silly. How about if I flip his plate when he isn't looking? That might be fun, but probably wouldn't accomplish anything. Or should I just swallow my discomfort and watch what my Scotch heritage considers to be near-gluttony? Yet neither of us really wants tension.

Once, in my own "crazy about money" way, I suggested that he pay me $40 every time we go out for a really nice dinner. I would then take that money and put it in my "pleasure bank" for something I really want. He was not thrilled with my suggestion but went along with it, at first grudgingly. When he saw how much more relaxed I was when we went out to dinner and how much his contribution meant to me, it stopped bothering him. I put the money he gave me toward something I really wanted – more investments!

After discovering how well this experiment worked, we decided to separate our money. That way he could spend his income exactly the way he wanted and I could do the same. At first he was insulted by this idea, but as we lived it and he experienced the greater emotional freedom it gave us both, he was fine with it. No one is complaining now.

COMMENTS FROM MY COUCH

Everyone drags childhood issues into their relationships, and my husband and I are no exception. His money script is that there will be enough money as long as he doesn't buy $100 bottles of wine every time we go to dinner, while my knee-jerk reaction money script is that any luxury will ultimately lead to impoverishment.

The point is that our differences became more and more encrusted with anger and resentment until we learned to talk openly about them. We've had to work hard at it (particularly since he believes he is more right and I believe I am more right), but we keep talking to each other because nothing else works. Sometimes we can even laugh at ourselves during these discussions, which represents a lot of progress for us.

Money issues don't exist in a vacuum. Your money type, your money scripts and how you deal with money, what value you give it, and how comfortable you are talking about it will influence many aspects of your relationship with an intimate partner.

Soul Mates Or Sparring Partners: Martha and Devon's Story

Martha and Devon are another example of how past attitudes are tightly woven into the fabric of everyday life. Devon's scientist father had made a good living in academia, and his mother managed their money skillfully. Any shortfalls were made up for through a trust that Devon's grandfather had established. Following in his dad's footsteps as a scientist, Devon never worried about money. Somehow there would always be enough, even if the monthly bills said otherwise.

Martha, a Money Worrier, came from a family that pinched pennies. Her father ran a small print shop, and money was chronically scarce. When she asked for a glass of milk, he would scream that she was wasting money. Early on, Martha internalized the money script message that no one would ever be there to support her, understand her needs, or care how she felt. She became used to the idea that she had to earn her own money to buy what she wanted, and she found creative ways to do it. For example, when her father complained that skiing was too expensive a sport, she learned to embroider ski jackets and sold enough of them to pay for ski lessons.

Now, as a wife and mother of three small children, Martha thinks about money all the time. She is acutely aware that she and Devon don't earn enough to pay the monthly bills.

Meanwhile, Devon feels he is above worrying about money. As a Money Monk, he believes it's a necessary part of life, but not something to strive for in and of itself.

Martha earns much less as a massage therapist than Devon does as a tenured professor. She has pointed out to him that by consulting just one day a week he could earn enough extra income to meet their needs, but it's like talking to a brick wall.

When he refused to take their mounting debt seriously, she felt alone with her worry. Deeply afraid that they would end up defeated and broke, she didn't believe any promises Devon made about improving their financial situation. If he spent more than the bare minimum on food, clothes, or entertainment, she slipped into uncontrollable anxiety that led to frustration and occasionally even to rage. She became increasingly negative toward Devon, and eventually he moved out. This temporary solution only made their money problems worse.

The more she fretted, the more he avoided; the more he avoided, the angrier and more insulting she became. They grew so polarized that neither of them heard a word the other was saying. Eventually the tension exploded in a knockdown, drag-out fight that left them both shaken and scared. They realized they had to change their relationship.

~

COMMENTS FROM MY COUCH

After many therapy sessions of miserable fighting and blaming, this couple's dynamic has begun to shift. Martha realized her anger was getting her nowhere. She talked about her despair: after giving up her career to move to the college town where Devon wanted to teach, she could not get his attention about their money problems and was unable to earn much on her own. He could go to work and be buoyed up by his students' admiration and his department's support, but she was left alone with their three children, the dog, and her worries.

Martha's experience of Devon was that he was lying to himself and to her about money. Devon, however, simply believed he had an optimistic attitude about getting control of their finances. He was good at dreaming up pure science proposals that would increase his stature in the academic world. Since these ideas were also potential sources of income, he believed he was doing his part in financial planning. His two blind spots were a refusal to address Martha's worry and an inability to recognize that at least some of their money problems were real and required action.

It became clear in our continuing sessions that Devon's Money Monk attitude interfered with getting consulting work that could make up their financial shortfall. Consulting would have forced him into applied science, which conflicted with his father's and his college's affirmation and approval of "pure" science. To Devon, science was its own reward; working for filthy lucre would have tainted this noble pursuit.

For the two of them to move forward as a couple, Devon will have to become more comfortable with consulting work. Once he develops this additional source of income, Martha will believe that he is not lying or avoiding and will feel that she has an equal and reliable partner. In the meantime, just as she learned to embroider ski jackets as a teenager, she has started doing website design in addition to her massage work.

Their dynamic puts more focus on Devon changing first. He is the one avoiding money issues, so his change by necessity has to come first. Martha's major work will come when Devon has successfully completed his part. Can she accept the good news that he is bringing in more money? Or will their spending expand and the money worries continue? Only time will tell.

~

Parenthood and Planning: Beth and Sue's Story

When Beth and Sue's children were two and four, the couple moved to the suburbs. They couldn't afford private school in the city, and the suburban schools had an excellent reputation. Still, they were a little nervous about living in a community that might be much more conservative than their diverse urban neighborhood.

They merge their money even though Beth, an Avon salesperson, earns only half as much as Sue does. Both are satisfied with this arrangement because Beth spends more time with the children and takes on other household responsibilities, including managing their money. Beth is a Money Amasser and Sue is a Hoarder, which are compatible styles that lead to little conflict. They plan and are careful with their money. The only big expenses they allow themselves are for their children's education and development.

Because they are such good planners, they have drawn up wills naming each other as beneficiary. They each have a living will and have completed health care directives.

They do have some concern about whether Beth would have enough money if something happened to Sue. Beth would not receive Sue's Social Security benefit, as a heterosexual spouse would. Sue has designated Beth as the beneficiary of her 401(k). However, if Beth inherits it, she would have to start taking distributions immediately and pay tax on those distributions. In a heterosexual marriage, a spousal beneficiary could inherit the 401(k) without having to take taxable distributions until age 70½. Sue has bought a substantial life insurance policy to help pay these taxes and support Beth and the kids in case anything happens to her.

Lately they have been on a savings campaign, not for the kids, but for Sue. She has struggled all her life feeling that she is a man in a woman's body. As a math whiz working in a male-dominated company, she believes she could do even better were she a man. Not only would she feel more at peace, but she and Beth think it would be better for their youngsters to have a female and a male parent. What finally cemented her decision was her bosses' support. She is such a highly valued software engineer that the company will back whatever decision she makes.

~

COMMENTS FROM MY COUCH

Beth and Sue have been together as a couple for 10 years, and have little fear their relationship will break up. They are devoted to each other and their children. They have both vowed that they will always try to work out their differences, even if they have to go to therapy to do it.

On the financial side, they manage their money well. They are keenly aware of the need to teach their children about money and are setting a very good example for them. Because Sue and Beth are so strategically minded and financially fit, they (and I) have confidence that they will do well over the long term.

~

Murky Mental Accounting: Joel and Layla's Story

In Chapter 7, we examined the story of Joel, a Risk Avoider who had a hard time borrowing money because of his parents' Depression-scarred mindset. His mother used to tell him about saving up for weeks just to buy an ice cream sundae. As adults, they continued to live frugally. They never talked about what they wanted or could afford, only whether they could justify buying necessities.

This upbringing left Joel with a fear of taking financial risks, even reasonable ones. When he wanted to expand his music business, he couldn't decide whether it made sense to borrow money. When he thought about developing an international presence for his business, he fought making a commitment to it.

On the other hand, Joel did feel comfortable managing his and his wife Layla's day-to-day expenses. He had little interest in anything but music and teaching, so his material desires were minimal. They had enough money to live comfortably but not extravagantly.

However, Layla views their financial position with great anxiety. She thinks she and Joel have less money than most people. Nothing Joel can say reassures her. She is an unusual combination of a Worrier and a Spender, with mental accounting habits that perplex him. For instance, she believes she has plenty of money in the bank as long as there are blank checks in her checkbook. Or she will go to a department store and make ten $30 purchases, then tell Joel she has no idea what the $300 charge is for. It might seem to him that she is lying, but it's perfectly clear to Layla that she bought some things for $30, not one item for $300. Another habit she has perfected is avoiding Joel's displeasure when she spends. She will buy two similar dresses and show one to him. If he likes it, she will keep it and, unbeknownst to him, take the second one back. If he doesn't like it, she will keep the one she didn't show him and take the other back!

As long as Layla sticks to her mental accounting techniques, she delights in her moments of spending. When she steps back and compares herself to other people, she sees everyone else having more money. She wants Joel to work harder or even go into a different business to earn more. He hasn't been able to make a difference in her mental accounting or her experiencing their situation as just this side of poverty. To Layla, money is an illusion and these are times of scarcity and deprivation.

൴

COMMENTS FROM MY COUCH

It's little wonder that Layla treats money as an illusion. She grew up feeling that money was scarce. Her father, brought up in the Depression like Joel's parents, never earned much money until he lucked into real estate at age 50. Although his income skyrocketed into the millions, he refused to spend money on himself or on his family. He remained as stingy with his children as he had been when they were growing up. No loving Christmas presents; nothing but penny-pinching.

With a money personality shaped by poverty and want, Layla's father then shaped her personality by depriving her and her brothers and sister of financial security. Layla now carries these childhood attitudes about money (her own and her dad's) into her relationship with Joel.

In some ways, her belief that they are in a rocky financial position may be her way of putting brakes on the spending she would allow herself if she believed they were well-off. Joel has given up on trying to persuade her otherwise. Their respective quirks may limit their trust in each other and the comfort of mutual understanding; but as long as Joel holds the purse strings, the balance in their relationship will most likely stay as is.

൴

CONCLUSIONS FROM MY COUCH

A couple can complement each other in a healthy way, or they can aggravate and polarize one another. In fact, since the two partners profoundly influence each other all the time, it doesn't make psychological sense to think of each of them as completely independent entities. Even the two words imply an interwovenness: "wife" implies that there is a husband, while "husband" implies that there is a wife.

Couples learn to adjust to each other's money type over time, although some do better than others. The most important factor is the ability to listen empathically to your partner. (Actually, this is the key to working on any problem in a relationship.) Empathic listening means putting yourself in your partner's shoes so you can see things from their perspective. If the two of you are in conflict and you are emotionally invested in your own position, understanding your partner's stance can be very hard when you really want to scream and cast blame. You may need to cool off a bit first. That doesn't mean "forget about it"; it means thoughtfully returning to the subject at a better, calmer time.

Remind yourself that if and when you do understand your partner's point of view, you are still free not to agree with it. When your partner has the experience of hearing their position repeated to them, they will know you get what they are saying even if you disagree. Through empathic listening and responding, you may be able to help your partner find a way out of a childhood belief or "truth" that he or she couldn't discover alone. You may also succeed in finding some truth in your partner's perspective.

Learning how to listen, compromise, and modify behavior patterns isn't easy. In fact, it's extremely difficult. But if you can grasp how the other person feels and trust that they can grasp what you are experiencing, there is a good chance to have a productive exchange. One way to help the listening process is to have your discussion in chairs that are placed back to back. This way, you hear each other's words without seeing expressions. It helps break old patterns of reading physical cues and getting revved up by what you think you are seeing in your partner's body language and facial expressions.

You and your partner share responsibilities and dreams. The constant, sustaining presence of this person can provide you a sense of connectedness and investment in someone who knows you well and loves you. There may be conflicts to work out and compromises to make; but your "other half" can serve as a sounding board and a source of affirmation and support — and once in a while as a sparring partner — as you work your way together toward money harmony.

~

Chapter 13 Exercise: Exploring Your Partner Relationship

The goal of this exercise is to help you understand your partner better, so the two of you can work together with money more harmoniously. (If you already did #1 as part of the Chapter 10 exercise, go straight to #2.)

1. What money type do you think your partner is? What type does your partner say he or she is? (You may want to refer to the money type descriptions in Chapter 7.) Ask your partner what money type you are, and compare that with your own self-assessment. Use these findings to discuss what you like and dislike about your own and your partner's money behavior. Do your types complement or conflict with each other?
2. For one weekend, exchange money types with your partner. Become his or her money type so you can

see how it feels and how different the world appears. Does it help you to better understand your partner's perspective?

3. Do you or your partner indulge in mental accounting (treating money differently even though a dollar is a dollar), together or separately? If so, write down one or two examples.
4. How often do you "shade the truth" in order to minimize conflict with your partner? If so, write down one or two examples. Then, if you feel brave enough, talk to your partner about why you do it and see what happens.
5. Are you aware of any of your own or your partner's childhood money scripts that affect your relationship and your own sense of well being?

A Married Person's Response to the Chapter 13 Exercise:

1. What money type do you think your partner is? What type does your partner say he or she is? (You may want to refer to the money type descriptions in Chapter 7.) Ask your partner what money type you are, and compare that with your own self-assessment. Use these findings to discuss what you like and dislike about your own and your partner's money behavior. Do your types complement or conflict with each other?

My money type is a Money Avoider and my Partner's money type is a Hoarder. We both agree as to each others money type.

My partner hates that I avoid almost everything when it comes to the use or planning of money. I hate my partner's refusal to spend money creating the impression that we don't earn enough money because there's never enough of it available. Like most things there is a degree of complementary and a degree of conflict. I would prefer that both of our attitudes would be less extreme than they are.

2. For one weekend, exchange money types with your partner. Become his or her money type so you can see how it feels and how different the world appears. Does it help you to better understand your partner's perspective?

Role playing has not been a successful strategy. I avoid it like the plague!

3. Do you or your partner indulge in mental accounting (treating money differently even though a dollar is a dollar), together or separately? If so, write down one or two examples.

Mental accounting is a topic of interest. My partner does excessive mental accounting. I do no mental accounting (or physical accounting for that matter). I calculate what's in my pocket but that's about it. My partner is aware of every penny in every account.

4. How often do you "shade the truth" in order to minimize conflict with your partner? If so, write down one or two examples. Then, if you feel brave enough, talk to your partner about why you do it and see what happens.

I don't think we "shade" the truth. We have pretty consistent behaviors. My truth is "shaded" in avoidance. My partners approach is transparent and is very straight forward. My approach to me is optimistic. My partners approach seems to be shrouded in the pessimism of reality.

5. Are you aware of any of your own or your partner's childhood money scripts that affect your relationship and your own sense of well being?

Yes, the biggest one is that "borrowing money is weak and bad—you're a fool if you do it." "Investing in yourself or your business is akin to showing off and that is selfish."

My spouse's come from growing up with wealth and a very stingy father and silent mother. Hers are: "there will never be enough." This made her angry so she developed the belief that "No spending opportunity should be missed."

Chapter 14:
Suddenly Single

DIVORCE AND WIDOWHOOD

We could never learn to be brave and patient,
if there were only joy in the world. —Helen Keller

Losing a partner to divorce or death brings about a restless churning of the soul. The disruption of familiar life patterns begets grief, uncertainty, conflicts, and tarnished hopes for the future. Only with the passage of time will a clear path emerge again.

Whatever the economics of the situation may be, social support is vital to well-being. Friends and family can help a suddenly single individual to contain his or her anxiety, hurt, and anger. When you review the stories in this chapter, think about each person's relationship with money and how it might change in order for them to be happier with it and with themselves.

Divorce: Separate But Unequal

You've probably heard the dismal statistic that half the marriages in the United States end in divorce. While money is a major cause of marital conflict and at least some divorces, it can also be a reason for couples to stay together, since living separately is a lot more expensive.

When people contemplate getting a divorce, they are usually in a state of emotional turmoil that keeps them from thinking straight about money. But before starting proceedings, it's essential to determine how divorce would affect your financial situation. This is as simple as creating a "before" and "after" comparison of your monthly expenses and income. If you don't know what these numbers are, find out and write them down. Without the facts, you're at an extreme disadvantage.

Also, don't forget to take into account the costs of the divorce. After getting an estimate from your attorney, double that number. If you think you and your spouse can work out a separation by yourselves, you can save a lot of money by consulting a divorce mediator instead of going to court.

When a husband and wife do break up, the woman tends to be put at a cultural, social, and financial disadvantage. Often she knows less about money than he does. Amid the emotional upheaval of divorce, she may not fully participate in the negotiations over lawyers' fees, living expenses, child support, or alimony. When the assets are split up, she may cling to what she is familiar with — the family home — instead of insisting on a share of her husband's retirement portfolio. The result: he gets the cash, she gets a high-maintenance money pit.

After a divorce, women also tend to remain single much longer than men. This can mean an extended period of living (and possibly raising children) on a limited income, including the humiliation of having to move from a nice home to a more modest place in a less attractive neighborhood. Changed financial realities can be terrifying for both women and men, forcing them to reexamine their relationship with money.

~

When Fury Rules: Pam's Story

When Pam's husband had an affair, it blew their marriage apart. She was hurt, angry, and appalled by his selfish refusal to work on their shattered relationship. Bitterness on each side fueled a stormy separation.

Stunned and confused during most of the divorce proceedings, Pam couldn't act in her best interest despite having a lawyer. As a result, she ended up legally bound to contribute as much as her ex-husband toward the expenses of raising their teenage sons, even though he earned three times as much as she did.

Afterward, Pam was furious at the terrible financial position she was in. She couldn't give her two boys the extras that her ex-husband could afford. Her resentment was so intense that it paralyzed her and prevented her from asking him for more reasonable support. She knew her anger hurt her sons, but she couldn't contain it.

~

COMMENTS FROM MY COUCH

Pam's dreams of being loved and taken care of have been dashed. Money is tight, and her standard of living has declined. She had always counted on her husband to be the primary earner and manage their money. Now that they have split up, her teaching job won't provide enough income to keep her and her children afloat, especially once the boys reach 18 and child support ends.

Pam's attitude and money script had been "Someone else will provide for me." Now she has to learn how to provide for herself, but her learning curve is hampered by resentment, pain, and anger that she has so little money. This muddies her thinking and discourages her from moving forward.

Clearly, Pam needs to reconstruct her money belief to something more positive and proactive, like "Money will come to me if I regard it with seriousness and respect, the way I regard the students I teach," or "I'm great at solving other people's problems; now I'm going to do that for myself."

Picking up the pieces of her life will be the challenge of a lifetime for Pam. After reestablishing her relationship with money, she will need to continue building a network of friends she can depend on for support and encouragement. She must grow away from her blind rage at her ex-husband for abandoning her, and become a stronger advocate for herself with him and others as she learns to deal with her finances.

It will take years of hard work for Pam to attain the responsibility and maturity to evolve a new life for herself, particularly after her sons go off to college. That's a tall order for someone who feels overwhelmed and abandoned. But to her credit, Pam has taken responsibility for her future and is working hard to forge her own way.

~

Buying a Way Out: Anna's Story

After an unpleasant divorce, Anna felt constantly lonely despite her challenging job and dozens of business associates. Whenever she went home to an empty house, she was reminded of her 15-year-old daughter, who had told the divorce court judge that she wanted to live with her dad because her mother worked all the time. Anna was devastated when the judge awarded custody to her now ex-husband.

No matter how high-powered everyone else thought she was, Anna didn't experience anything right about herself. All she knew how to do was work. How in the world was she going to meet anyone new? She tried computer dating, but hated to put her picture in her profile. Even though people told her she was attractive, she no longer believed it. She saw other women as far more appealing and doubted that she would ever find another husband. As the months went by, she began to feel more isolated and desperate. Living the rest of her life alone terrified her.

She began to obsess about changing the way she looked. A tuck here, a few less wrinkles there… did she dare have a total body remake? *No, that's crazy,* she would tell herself. *Besides, it would cost a fortune. But, darn it, life owes me something!*

Anna couldn't put the idea of a body makeover out of her mind, even though the cost would be about $100,000 — much more than she could afford. Then, without warning, she disappeared for a month-long vacation. Her return to work was a shock to her co-workers: slim, proportioned, with a different nose and less wrinkled face, she looked like a different person, not just a younger version of herself. She was so pleased with everyone's positive response that she almost believed how good she looked. She started dating. Although she didn't find anyone who quite suited her, she felt happier and not so alone.

Then Anna's boss confronted her, and her new life took a turn for the worse. In her loneliness and resentment, she had financed her makeover by writing $100,000 in phony checks on the business account. Before she could absorb what was happening, she was arrested for embezzlement.

~

COMMENTS FROM MY COUCH

Anna's story makes it clear how money is a magnet for needs and emotions. Lacking a sense of self-worth and driven by desperation, she rationalized that she had a right to steal the cash that would enable her to become more attractive, find a partner, and relieve her loneliness. Had she taken the time to examine herself from within, she might have discovered that it was not her looks that were holding her back but her negative attitude toward herself.

This failure to respect her own authenticity poisoned her relationship with money, with others, and with herself. Moving forward, she must focus on learning to value herself as a person and understanding that attractiveness is more than skin deep. Unfortunately, it will not be the easiest thing in the world for her to build a true sense of self-regard and worth while she serves out her sentence in prison.

Of course, not all divorces have as traumatic outcomes as Anna's and Pam's. If there is mutual agreement to split up, parenting responsibilities continue to be shared, and financial resources are adequate on both sides, it's possible for the ex-spouses to maintain a more stable sense of self as well as optimism that the future will hold something better.

Another problem does require attention, though. When a divorced person remarries, the new wife or husband may resent support payments to the former spouse. If the new mate feels that his or her lifestyle is being sacrificed for the sake of "that greedy bitch" (or "bastard"), it can complicate relationships with stepchildren and natural children. As we have already seen, it's next to impossible to make effective financial decisions when one is consumed by negative feelings. If there is no attempt to examine or revise one's relationship with money, the unhappiness that results will create yet another impediment to problem-solving.

~

Painful Times: Widows and Widowers

After losing a spouse to illness or accident, widows and widowers must confront many of the same difficulties as divorced people. If theirs was a loving relationship, grief at losing their partner may be much more intense. Sadness, a sense of unfairness, and remorse for not having enjoyed their time together to the fullest may cause depression, depletion, and helplessness. There is a strong tendency to live in the past and not move forward with rebuilding one's life.

If the departed spouse handled all the finances, the result is double trouble. The survivor may be left with a mortgage, insurance, household expenses, and investments to manage. Dazed with grief and loss and overwhelmed by a multitude of financial choices, she or he is vulnerable to dishonest professionals and rapacious family members.

If you have recently lost a spouse to death, you need time to grieve and rebuild your life. The tendency is to either live in the past with one's lost spouse or charge ahead too quickly and prematurely start another relationship. Isolating yourself is the wrong thing to do, and jumping in to an intimate relationship too soon is the worst thing you can do. Hold back on immediate intimacy until you have mourned and "let go " of your late spouse.

~

A Match Made in Heaven: Clara's Story

Bernie had been Clara's idol from the day they met in college. Married soon after they graduated, they were very happy together. Bernie was a first-rate teacher and mentor at the local college. Clara started her own decorating business after the children entered school. Her idealization of Bernie was total; he did everything brilliantly. Since he was willing to take care of the finances, she let him do it without a second thought.

When he was 52 and she 51, Bernie was killed in an automobile accident. By then both children had graduated from college and moved to the other side of the country. Clara felt her life was over. Although she had many women friends and acquaintances, Bernie had been her best friend. She went into a protracted depression, unable to work or speak. Thin to begin with, she lost 20 pounds. For months she didn't touch the growing stacks of bills and notes from friends.

When her depression finally ebbed, Clara realized that she could hardly take care of the bills, much less handle everything else that bewildered her. She had no idea what Bernie's neatly kept records meant. What made it worse was that every time she looked at them, images of him flooded back. Weeping, she wanted to die. What was the point of living without him and with her children far away?

COMMENTS FROM MY COUCH

There are really two issues here. In most cases, the first would be relatively easy to resolve. Clara had no knowledge or skill in managing money, but she could fix that by hiring someone to teach her. The second issue was tougher to grapple with: her emotional reaction to having to deal with financial matters.

Money, she believed, was something Bernie ought to be taking care of. Her feelings of loss and abandonment were so profound that she could not absorb any coaching about money management. It took three years for her to admit to herself that he was no longer with her and that it was up to her to look after her money. Only after another two years did she feel strong enough to take his voice off her answering machine. Then she could at last begin to query her relationship with money and assess how it needed to change in order for her to take better care of herself.

For instance, her old belief might have been "Bernie is brilliant at everything he does; what I do won't be as good," or "Why should I take time to learn something that I'm not interested in?" I encouraged her to reframe her relationship with money to something like "If I learn about money, I'll not only know what I have, but I may be able to plan a trip I didn't think I could afford." Even if she found she had less money than she thought, the certainty of knowing what she did have would be deeply calming, especially in such disruptive circumstances.

It would have been a mistake to try to push Clara into decision-making before she had healed enough to accept it. It can easily take a year or more before a widow or widower is able to start actively moving forward. Meetings with a grief counselor or grief group may help the survivor work through the pain of his or her loss.

Not surprisingly, the better the marriage the greater the pain when a cherished spouse dies. Careful planning and teaching each other skills during a happy marriage can prevent confusion and fear from adding to the anguish if calamity strikes.

Once Married, Now Single

The breakup of a marriage, for whatever reason, forces survivors to exercise muscles that may have grown weak through disuse. Whenever you'd like to do something with a friend, it takes advance planning. Since nothing is going to happen unless you reach out, you have to develop initiative that may have been dormant when you were half of a couple.

On the other hand, singlehood offers constant opportunities to do what you want without having to compromise. You can test your judgment more easily, since the effects of financial decisions are clearer when there is only one person responsible for making them. It will be up to you to find an advisor, develop a financial strategy, and think about what you want to achieve with your money.

There are real difficulties in singlehood as one ages, especially without children or other family members close by. Having a circle of dependable and supportive friends can make all the difference between an uneasy future and a "Third Chapter" of life that is rich and rewarding.

Chapter 14 Exercise: Letting Go

Imagine the situation you would be in if your spouse suddenly died or asked for a divorce:

- How well would you know the state of your joint finances?
- Do you know where your investments are?
- What if you die first and your spouse is left the family money manager? How much of an effort have you

made to educate your spouse or keep him/her informed?
- How are you going to remedy the situation?

If you are going through (or have recently been through) a divorce or the death of a partner, also do whichever of the following exercises is appropriate.

DIVORCE. Self-esteem takes a nosedive no matter how much someone may have wanted a divorce. Write down what makes you feel good about yourself right now, and put it on a index card on your refrigerator. Since it takes three positive events (things like receiving a windfall, getting a compliment, having a great time with a friend) to balance out one negative event, you will have to work extra hard to focus on good things in a time of turmoil.

WIDOWHOOD. It's important to reach out to others who can help you grieve before you start a new intimate relationship. Create a social calendar for yourself and make sure you reach out to other people even if you don't want to. There is no specific timetable here; just understand you are going through a process that deserves time to unfold and resolve.

A Suddenly Single Person's Response to the Chapter 14 Exercise:

Comments and Exercises:

Divorce Comments:

When many people think about getting a divorce they are in emotional turmoil and have difficulty thinking straight about money, even if they are aware that it is important.

This is one time when it is important to think through what a divorce would mean to your money supply BEFORE you start proceedings. In that spirit, write down all your expenses and income before you see a lawyer. Then write down the expenses and income that would change as a result of a divorce. How does that affect your present numbers?

Remember to ask the lawyer for his/her fee structure and what they think the divorce will cost. Then double that number and use that as an estimate of what you will have to pay a lawyer (If you think you can work a separation out yourself, consult a divorce mediator. It will save lots of money.) If you don't know what your income/expenses are, take the time to learn and then write them down. Without the facts you are at an extreme disadvantage!

Self-esteem takes a nosedive no matter how much someone may have wanted a divorce. Write down what makes you feel good about yourself right now, and put it on a 5' X 7' card on your refrigerator. Since it takes three positive events (things like receiving a windfall, getting a compliment, having a great time with a friend) to balance out one negative event you will have to work extra hard to focus on good things in a time of turmoil.

Divorce Questions:

1. If you had known before you contemplated divorce what you know now, would you still have done it? If so why and if not why?

I have to preface this answer with the explanation that I don't make decisions in my life based on how difficult it will be to carry out those decisions, but rather based on what is best for me or the situation. I never would have had kids if I had known how hard it would be, but at the same time, I never would have understood how rewarding it is. I really believe that there is never a "right time" to have kids, or to get divorced for that matter, it's a matter of what I want in my life and how I want my life to be. I don't know if I would have made the same decision at the time I did if I had known how traumatic it was going to be (I had NO idea how horrific it would be), but at the same time, I didn't make my decision based on how difficult the divorce would be. I made the decision based upon how I wanted to live my life and how my life at the time was hugely unsatisfactory for me. I felt like I was capable of being in a much more fulfilling relationship and that I was not where I was supposed to be, given my strengths and emotional capacity. I was not with someone who fully appreciated me, or who appreciated me at all, and certainly did not care or even consider my emotional needs. That was no longer acceptable to me. I realized that I had a plan in the back of my head to wait until the kids were finished with high school (10 years from now). That realization made me see how illogical it was to waste 10 years of my life and that of my husband. I had been thinking about leaving him for years, but the decision all of a sudden was unavoidable to me.

I had just turned 40 and was having something of a midlife crisis I suppose, realizing that we are only on this planet once. I looked back at my life the way it was at the time and sort of panicked, realizing it was nothing like I felt I deserved or that it even approached the possibilities that life and relationships had to offer. I also thought, and still do, that my kids were of an age that they would be able to make some sense out of it. They had friends (very few) with divorced parents and would still understand that they were loved. When they were younger, I just had the sense that they would fall apart and their reality would be completely upside down if we split.

I would certainly not do it the same way I did it, but hindsight is 20/20. I became emotionally attached to someone online because I was emotionally neglected and vulnerable. It was impulsive and stupid, however, and I never would have crossed that boundary if I had to do it over. It was purely emotional. I also would hope that I would divorce in a more mature way, fighting with him less during the process. I have to say, though, that much of the fighting was out of my hands because I haven't been fighting for months and he's still taking me to court and trying to engage me in conflict at least once a week, and it's been almost 2 years since he left and 5 months since the divorce was finalized. I don't know if anyone getting divorced can avoid the emotional trauma of breaking a family apart and dashing all of your expectations in life to pieces, however, so I don't know if I could do it better if I had a do-over.

2. What are the three most important things for someone to consider who is contemplating divorce

a. Definitely whether or not they have tried counseling or working through their problems. Especially if there are children involved, there should be AT LEAST one attempt at counseling, preferably more, depending on the fit between the couple and therapist. Both partners should also be in individual counseling, too. If there are still shared activities, a friendship, love, then there are parts of the relationship that can be salvaged. If a divorce is still the decision, at least it could be done with careful consideration, insight, and planning.

b. A divorcing couple should have a survival plan for how they will bring in income, how they will live, how they will care for the children. If they are in danger in the relationship, meaning if it is abusive, they should have an emergency plan for safety should the partner become violent.

c. Have a support plan in place and understand that it will be hard and emotional, no matter how prepared you are. Get a therapist.

3. What helped you the most healing form the experience of divorce?

Really allowing myself to grieve and experience the emotional trauma as it was happening, rather than avoid it. That way it didn't bite me in the ass later and I was able to use the affect in the moment to explore what was driving my emotional reaction. Still working on it.

Therapy, group and individual. Two therapeutic contacts weekly, in between family and friends. Sometimes I felt like a puppet on a string and everyone around me just kept picking me up and pushing me along when I had trouble doing it myself.

Definitely being able to support myself financially.

Support of friends and family. My parents and sister and so many friends were really present when I needed them. My mother comes almost weekly to do laundry, straighten up and cook. My sister came to court with me several times. They all tolerated my moods. My friends didn't let me stay in bed sometimes. They listened. And listened.

I was surprised by how mature people were, how they didn't judge me harshly. I was surprised by how understanding his family was (cousins) and saw me based on our relationship that had developed rather than the drama of what was unraveling.

Having to take care of my children, so I had to wake up and get going every day. Had to go to work to pay the bills.

As I went through the divorcing process, I gained more self confidence because I handled it. Realizing that nobody would be there for me 24/7, so I had to rely on myself and stop expecting others to make me feel better.

Once the paperwork was finalized and I was able to pay a couple of bills, I felt more stable.

Exercise helps me feel much, much calmer.

Widowhood

If you have lost a spouse to death, you need time to grieve and rebuild your life. The tendency is to either live in the past with one's lost spouse or charge ahead too quickly and prematurely start another relationship. It is important to reach out to others, many others, to help you grieve before you start a new intimate relationship. Isolating yourself is the worst thing you can do and jumping in to an intimate relationship too soon is the worst thing you can do. Create a social calendar for yourself and make sure you reach out to other people even if you don't want to. Hold back on immediate intimacy until you have mourned and "let go " of your late spouse. There is no formula time table here. Just understand you are going through a process that deserves time to unfold and resolve.

4. After the initial shock of your loss, describe what it felt like to be left without your spouse. Were you inclined to withdraw or reach out to others? What acted as the main ways to soothe yourself through the loss?

In my case, my wife was diagnosed with lung cancer and given less than a year to live. She died 13 months to the day after her diagnosis, so we had more than a year to spend together and prepare for what was coming. It still was a terrible shock, because our focus, naturally, was on her needs and those of our two daughters. On her death, I found myself in a maelstrom of feelings, with little real preparation. As her primary caregiver, I felt terrible to realize I was relieved of an almost all-consuming burden. Of course, my wife was ready for death as a release from suffering and was cheerful and unafraid on the day she died. But I was still wracked with guilt. I also was very surprised to find how so much of our mutual history died that day—little inside jokes, nicknames we had for people, silly memories. I would never use my nicknames for her again, nor would anyone use hers for me. As for reaching out to others, we had family support, nurses, caring neighbors and friends, but I found myself exhausted and in no mood for company for a week, at least. The reaction I got from even close friends was that of a leper—uh-oh, there he is, his wife just died! No one knew what to say, yet a few people did manage to say unimaginably stupid things. As for money, luckily, I had the kind of job and enough seniority that I could do a lot of work from home. I did experience a terribly hollow feeling when a month after she died, having worked very long hours as a distraction/way of coping, I was recognized as the firm leader in sales with a record month. I remember coming home to an empty house and tossing the plaque on her side of the bed. I began to realize how much grief saps the satisfaction and pleasure you might otherwise get. The money, a shocking amount for me, meant nothing at all. I had plenty of reasons to go on, two daughters who were leaning on me for support, who had always been very close to me, a career, good friends, a belief in God, and a desire to live up to my promises to my wife. I did find, and still find, that I feel bound to be two parents in one, to try to make up for the void. It doesn't really work, of course, as nothing can replace a lost parent.

5. Did you or your partner's relationship to money become an issue after their death? If so, how?

One thing that was striking in my case was the irony of it all—my wife's biggest fear was to be poor in retirement. I remember the letter she got from Social Security: "Congratulations! Your application for disability income has been approved. Reason: You are not expected to live 6 months or more. "She had private disability insurance but the insurance company forces one to apply for Social Security disability and then deduct that amount from what they must pay out.... something you don't realize unless you read the fine print. What events or interactions helped to rebuild your confidence that your life could go on and eventually improve? I love my family and love my job, and of course, living a year with someone who is dying will certainly focus one's attention on what matters in life, and what a privilege it is to be alive. I lost some of my tendency to worry—how bad could anything else seem after this blow? And it helped my confidence in a strange way. Two years later, marrying a beautiful young woman, and helping raise her children gave me ample reason to feel that life was good, and it is.

PART V:

MAKING MONEY WORK FOR OR AGAINST YOU

Now we are going to move on to some of the ways people use money, for better or worse. If you have learned your money lessons well, you will see results in the way you invest, the kind of debt you carry, and how much money you are willing to put at risk. The consequences of these lessons will be realized during retirement, including the opportunity to leave a legacy you are proud of.

INVESTMENTS
$
+
–
RINO

Chapter 15:

Taming the Bulls and Bears

INVESTING

"Look at market fluctuations as your friend rather than your enemy; profit from folly rather than participate in it." —Warren Buffett

January 3, 2000 (NASDAQ: 3,901.69): This market is on fire — might break through 5,000. Unbelievably, our portfolio has grown 50% in three years. The paradigm shift is real, the market *is* different. Lucky to have gotten in when we did – those tech gorillas just keep going up.

March 1, 2000 (NASDAQ: 4,784.08): Listened to grouchy bear analyst today, forecasting a big bump in the road here, maybe like we've never seen before. But others say more to go on the upside, maybe breaking 5,000. Put a call into my broker, Val. He says nothing to worry about, full steam ahead. My financial advisor, Debra, agrees, but not so wildly enthusiastic. They both need to agree with each stock trade. That is my method, the discipline I'm sticking with. I'm not trying to be the Lone Ranger here.

March 15, 2000 (NASDAQ: 4,582.62): Just got a call from Zach who recommended Val in 1997. He's furious. One big position, a gorilla tech, just lost 15 points. He had $200,000 in that position. He just lost $75,000. Thank God I only had $20,000 invested, but that is still $7,500 gone. What the hell is going on here? Better call Val. Sunny as ever, Val helps me see this is just a temporary loss. If the market goes up too much too fast, a market drop or a correction is healthy if the underlying stock fundamentals are sound. I shouldn't worry, we still made money on that stock — $10,000 originally invested, so still ahead $2,500. Debra doesn't like what just happened. The size and suddenness of the drop worry her. I'm confused and want to believe Val. My rule is to act when there is agreement between Val and Debra; otherwise, no action until there is agreement.

May 1, 2000 (NASDAQ: 3,958.08): Val keeps telling me to look for a summer rally and we are down now to 3,958 from 4,784. 826 points down from March 1 and he thinks a summer rally is coming. Debra is getting scared. Don't know what to do but wait. I couldn't look at the last statement. How did I get into this? Val knew what he was doing and he is still so optimistic. Debra worries me and I don't know who to believe. Thank God I've got a job and can work. I'm thinking about this all the time anyway, but not so bad when I'm focused in on something else.

June 1, 2000 (NASDAQ: 3,582.50): We are down 376 from last month. Val is right; we are getting back on track. I can't look at the monthly statements. I can't stand to see how much we have lost. Debra keeps telling me we have to look for a bottom. She is holding her stock positions, but she's not happy. Val thinks we will recover. When they disagree I do nothing, not like me but I've never been here before. It is all my fault. Thought I knew what I was doing, but now this, oh, God.

September 1, 2000 (NASDAQ: 4,234.33): We are back up 652 points this quarter, maybe Val is right, we will recover. Debra is looking for a bottom around 3000. Just hold on until then and try to recover losses. I can't stand to look at the statements. This can't be happening. Just hold until the bottom comes. Maybe we should just get out. Zach left Val and is watching his stocks on his own. He is really pissed and he acts.

I can't leave Val or Debra, who else would I go to? Oh, my God how can this be happening?

December 1, 2000 (NASDAQ: 2,645.29): We have crashed through Debra's 3000 bottom, 1589 points down from September. Is this what they mean by blood on the streets? There is no way I can open those statements now. The losses are bloody. My husband says we ought to get out, just cut our losses, but that's not what Val and Debra are saying. They keep saying hold on and eventually things will get better. Why didn't I see this coming, I don't know anything about this damn market, but now I don't want to think about it and I'm thinking about it all the time. Why am I so loyal to Val? He got me into this and now I can't get away from him, or should I?

February 1, 2001 (NASDAQ: 2,782.79): You'd think a new year would bring something good. Talked to my friend Jim last night. He's been in the market for years and feels bad but not sick. He mentioned joining an investment club. They analyze stocks technically. Maybe I should join, but all guys and just one other woman. Later, not now, the NASDAQ is up just less than 1%. I should find out what the investment club is like.

April 2, 2001 (NASDAQ: 1,782.97): At the Profits Investment Club meeting we all talked about our losses. In the members' personal accounts, not the pooled club account, everyone was overinvested in tech. That's consoling, but I'm embarrassed to tell them how much I've lost, I don't even know. I've got to get more skill. I rely too much on Val and Debra, but they are the experts, I'm not, and how come they didn't know better? 1782 is the lowest the NASDAQ has gone and my neighbor Joe sold out at 2000 — he wanted to protect capital. He does all his investing on his own. At least he has cash, but then he has no hope this market will turn around. He will miss the upside if it does. What upside? I'm crazy to think that, but what is wrong? Why do I keep holding on?

July 2, 2001 (NASDAQ: 2,148.72): The NASDAQ has lost over half of its value in a little more than a year. Is 2000 the bottom?

August 1, 2001 (NASDAQ: 2,068.38): Oh, God here we go again, down the slide. Val is not saying much these days, and Debra is just looking for the damn bottom. It's my fault we loaded up on tech, glutton that I was and now I understand why we are supposed to diversify, have a range of stocks in all different industries so if one goes bad, we have the others that keep plugging along. I have lost hundreds of thousands of dollars and I keep sitting here watching what we have melt down to less and less, when is this going to end? Joe sold and that's what we need to do, get in cash, none of this waiting for the bottom anymore. If we have cash, after the bottom has been reached, then take the money and diversify and watch it build up.

August 17, 2001 (NASDAQ: 1,867.01): Tears, this is the first time I have cried, it's like selling our soul to the devil, he promises and then he doesn't deliver. We are screwed by greed we didn't know we had, just let go — more tears, just let go — get in the shower — let the waterfall of tiny water droplets massage my shame away. Act, no more waiting to see it get worse. I'll call Val in the morning and tell him to sell, just get rid of it all and hold the cash....

October 1, 2001 (NASDAQ: 1,480.46)

December 1, 2001 (NASDAQ 1,400 and going down): But we are in cash, and we are not going down, that solid cash is staying. Thank God Joe sold! It broke me out of the daze. My system didn't work; I'm going to have to become the expert myself.

Why Investing Pushes Our Buttons

Most modern humans, no matter what their money type may be, are hardwired to like making money. Anticipation of big gains lights up our nucleus accumbens, the spot in our brain that indicates pleasure. On the downside, our desire to feel this pleasure often leads us to act on our emotions instead of thinking rationally. Several of the behaviors we discussed in earlier chapters may come into play:

- **The herd instinct:** Everybody says tech stocks are booming — better jump in before it's too late!
- **Anchoring:** Your investments have fallen far below their purchase price, but you won't abandon them until you've recouped your losses.
- **The endowment effect:** You buy lots of stock in the company where you work, because you know it best.
- **Status quo bias:** You don't bother to read the account statements for the mutual funds you bought eight years ago.
- **Mental accounting:** You contribute faithfully to your 401(k) through a deduction from your paycheck, but consider your tax refund to be "play money."
- **Loss aversion:** The investments in your child's college fund have nosedived, but you hate to sell them and realize your losses. (It's interesting that "realize" has both a monetary and an emotional meaning, isn't it?)
- **The "sunk hole" fallacy:** A once-great stock is going down, but you keep buying it because it's a better and better deal.

Remember, you're the only one who has control over you. If investing makes you crazy, you need to step back and take stock — as I did.

Hitting Bottom — and Climbing Out

As the excerpts from my 2000-01 investing diary show, I was immobilized and unable to process the market downturn. Not only am I personally sensitive to losing money, but we humans feel a financial loss more than twice as intensely as a gain. Remember, too, that we are hardwired to experience twice as many negative emotions as positive, which helps serve as an early warning system so we can ward off danger. I experienced fear, anxiety, shame, and embarrassment, but still failed to act in my best interest. I could not accept the monetary loss or the magnitude of it, so I did nothing, hoping the market would recover and all would be well again. Loss aversion and status quo bias locked me into the position to "decide not to decide."

I pride myself on being in touch with my feelings and the feelings of others. After all, that's how I make my living. But how can I explain my paralysis to myself or to anyone else? What impeded a more rational response was, first, the shame I felt at my apparent greed, a greed that supported an aggressive approach to the market. Second, I had a now naïve-sounding idea that a broker had an expertise I did not possess. By necessity I had to rely on the broker's "better judgment." Any gut sense I had that he was taking too much risk was muted by his enthusiasm, knowledge, and experience of the market. Third, I figured I had a well-thought-out approach. I'd listen to the broker's recommendations and then talk them over with my financial advisor, Debra, who was not a broker but an MBA who had spent her career watching the market. They both had to agree on a trade before I made a final decision.

Throughout the crisis, their consistent advice was to wait out the market correction and to get a sense of where it was going to bottom out — i.e., at what point it would stop going down. At points during the decline, Val wanted me to sell some high-flying stocks. But Debra advised holding on to see where the bottom was before selling. I had to make a decision without their mutual agreement, thus breaking my own rule of only acting when there was agreement. I could not rise above my fear, shame, and anger. If I sold, it would be an admission that I was wrong and that my financial loss was real.

Not until I processed my negative emotions did acceptance of the financial loss free me to act. It took over a year and a half of turmoil before I was brought to my knees to surrender to the reality of what had happened. This surrender, and a vow to recoup as much of the loss as I could, gave me the impetus to sell all our tech holdings and invest the proceeds in diverse market sectors.

What further intensified my struggle was that I lost faith in my so-called system and didn't believe anyone any more. From embarrassment, I didn't talk about my losses, which left me alone and isolated.

I became determined to never again let such craziness happen. Even though I value sound professional investment advice, I knew I needed to be able to evaluate stocks myself. So one of the first things I did was join an investment club affiliated with the NAIC (National Association of Investors Corporation). The members meet in the basement of a Mennonite church once a month. Following NAIC guidelines, they use a detailed quantitative system of evaluating a company before they consider buying its stock. This system, which emphasizes knowledge of fundamentals critical to good investing, has served the club very well since its launch 10 years earlier.

Now I have a way of evaluating a company's worth without relying solely on anyone else's opinion or advice. I can form my own opinion about a stock, which allowed me to better assess suggestions made by my investment team.

Speaking of teams, this is a good place to raise an important question: is it important for an investor to have a financial advisor or broker?

Do You Need Help to Invest?

Many people invest successfully on their own through mutual fund companies or discount brokerages. And if you have a 401(k), the choice of where to invest your money is probably left up to you. Do you need an investment professional to help you with these decisions?

In making this determination, a couple of factors come into play:

1. **How much time do you have?** If you're young and just starting to build wealth, you have time to learn how to do it yourself — and don't have a lot to lose if you make mistakes early on. Or you can find a competent financial advisor and form a lifelong partnership with them. On the other hand, if you're beginning to invest later in life, and/or have accumulated money that will be vital for your financial security, I would strongly suggest looking for an advisor you can trust. (In the next section, you'll find ideas on how to identify someone who is right for you.)
2. **What arrangement would be the best fit with your personality?** Are you the kind of person who doesn't trust anyone else? Or are you a Risk Avoider who isn't sure what kind of portfolio would help you safely reach your goals?

To me, the core issue isn't so much whether or not you seek help as how engaged in the investing process you want to be. I'm a strong believer in active investment management, because I know nobody will look out for my money with as much care as I will.

So while the ultimate choice is "whatever floats your boat," I would caution against non-engagement in either of its extremes:

- The first extreme is turning your money over to someone else because you don't want any responsibility for it. Sure, it may be a relief to hand off this burden, especially if you have Money Avoider tendencies. But if you fail to participate in important decisions about your money, you're not taking the best care of yourself that you can.
- The second extreme is making investments by yourself and then ignoring them. If you're going to invest on your own, you can't just "buy and forget." I think it's fair to say that nobody ever got rich by ignoring their money.

If there were a magic box you could simply drop your cash into that would automatically produce big returns, all the people who turned their money over to Bernie Madoff would be rich and happy. Whether or not you're working with an advisor or broker, I believe you need to know what you're investing in and why you're doing it.

So however you invest — by yourself or through an intermediary — you need to educate yourself. Subscribe to personal-finance magazines like *Money*, *Kiplinger's Personal Finance*, and *SmartMoney*; read books; go online to investment-related websites (see "Recommended Resources" at the end of this book); join an investment club, or seek a money mentor who's willing to help you learn. Even then, I'd be cautious about going it completely alone. You can inadvertently take too much risk and not realize it until the market turns sour. My investment club experience persuades me that talking with others has a balancing effect. I truly believe that do-it-yourselfers should have other people they can talk to, such as fellow investment club members or an advisor.

When investing on your own, you'll also want to make sure you have time to keep up with all your holdings. If you buy individual securities, I'd allocate an hour a week to each one. You'll need to learn how to read an annual report, spend time listening to conference calls with company executives, and keep up with current company news. In short, managing a 20-stock portfolio can be the equivalent of a part-time job.

The most important decision is whether you can carry the emotional responsibility of investing on your own. When it's your money, or yours and your partner's, you'll feel the losses and gains much more acutely because you made the buying decisions.

That's why a one-time consultation with a planner may be valuable for do-it-yourself investors who want a professional assessment of their financial situation. You can also ask the planner to prepare a strategy, then implement it yourself. Since life is full of changes, I would suggest hedging your independence by checking in with your advisor once or twice a year to see if your plan needs to be updated.

If you decide to invest through an advisor or broker, you will benefit from his or her expertise and exposure to information about securities. You can determine the level of input you want to have, from being very involved to giving up most of the responsibility for portfolio decision-making. In any case, you'll have someone to share the emotional responsibility for your money.

Either way to invest — on your own, or through an advisor — is fine, as long as you're aware of the consequences. What works best for me is to invest through an investment club, manage a small portfolio of my own, and work with a trusted broker whom I consider my investment advisor. Each method of investing counterbalances the others, so this diversified approach gives me the best of all worlds.

Again, I'm not saying this is the way for you to go. My goal is simply to guide you in making choices that will help you take better care of yourself. Even if you turn over day-to-day control of your money to an advisor or broker, I don't believe it's in your best interest to forget about it. It's your money, and nobody cares more about it than you.

~

Broker? Advisor? Planner? The Financial Name Game

There are two main kinds of investment professionals: brokers and financial advisors. A **broker**'s main business is buying and selling securities for clients. Anyone who sells mutual funds must pass a test to obtain a Series 6 license from FINRA, the Financial Industry Regulatory Authority. If they sell stocks, bonds, and options, they must pass the more difficult Series 7 test as well. Generally paid on commission, brokers are governed by the "suitability rule" (non-fiduciary), which requires them to have "reasonable grounds for believing that [a] recommendation is suitable" for a particular client, according to FINRA.

A **financial advisor** not only advises clients on investments but also has broader expertise, often including insurance and sometimes tax planning. Usually working for a fee or a fee/commission combination, they typically search for the best solutions for clients from among stocks, bonds, mutual funds, life insurance, fixed or variable annuities, certificates of deposit, preferred stocks, options, and/or long-term care insurance. In addition to Series 6 and 7 licenses, financial advisors must be licensed **Registered Investment Advisers** (RIAs). If they sell insurance, they also need to have a state insurance license. Regardless of title, the underlying issue is whether the advisor or planner has fiduciary responsibility, i. e. is contractually bound to act in their client's best interest, regardless of the consequences to the advisor/planner.

Some RIAs are **financial planners**, which means they take a more holistic view of a client's finances, including (but not limited to) cash flow management, education planning, retirement planning, investment planning, risk management and insurance planning, tax planning, estate planning, and succession planning (for business owners). They're typically compensated with fees rather than commissions. "Certified Financial Planner" is a well-respected professional designation indicating that an advisor has passed a rigorous series of tests on various aspects of financial planning.

My bias is that life moves so fast that any long-term plan can quickly become obsolete. For example, if you lose your spouse or your job, get a pay cut, or have an accident and can't work, the plan for which you've paid $500 to $2,500 could become tomorrow's birdcage liner. Thus it is important that you find a financial planner that is well trained and that fits your personality. Developing a long term relationship with a trusted advisor who know you and your situation will help if and when you hit financial bumps in the road.

You may come across many other titles such as Wealth Advisor, Retirement Advisor, Retirement Specialist, and Senior Advisor, which mean that some certifying organization or association attests to the holder's expertise in a particular area. Some designations are the result of training and testing; others are not. Before you sign on the dotted line with one of these apparent experts, be sure to find out who issued the designation and how it is regarded within the financial community.

What's Behind the Names?

Another important consideration is that investment professionals each have their own "brand," compounded of the way they relate to people, the kinds of investments they handle or favor, and the type of clients they prefer or specialize in. In my experience, they can be sorted into the following eight categories. (Although many advisors and brokers are women, I'll use "he" for the sake of simplicity.)

The Cowboy: Yahoo! Take a chance; that's the only way to make money! Caution is for those who aren't smart enough to beat the system.

The Churner: You'll hear from a Churner quite often, since he needs your permission to buy or sell an investment. If the Churner is compensated by a commission on each trade, beware: his interests may not be the same as yours.

The Authoritarian: He isn't interested in educating you or even paying attention to your opinion. He's the expert; you're supposed to go away and let him do his thing.

The Listener: He wants to know your goals and risk tolerance, and will help you identify them if you aren't sure. Intuitive and thoughtful, he enjoys building relationships.

The Teacher: He's willing to teach you what he knows about investments and the markets in general. Although he values your relationship, he tends not to put as much emphasis on getting to know you and your needs as the Listener.

The Technician: He tends to make investment decisions based on performance charts and software programs. You may find him less people-related and less sensitive to your needs.

The Phantom: He doesn't call you back, or lets his administrative assistant do it. You hardly ever hear from him except for a quarterly call to review your assets.

The Holistic Advisor: He is interested in every aspect of your financial health, not just your investment goals. Although this approach takes more of his (and your) time, it pays off in the long run because he can give you better advice.

~

Finding an Investment Advisor or Broker

If you've decided you'd like to look for a suitable investment professional, I would suggest following these three steps:

Step 1: Self-Assessment

Define what you're looking for. How engaged do you want to be in developing and executing an investment strategy? If you intend to be actively involved, you might focus on a Listener, Teacher, or Holistic Advisor. If you're fine with letting your investment professional operate more autonomously, an Authoritarian or Technician might suit you better.

Seek investment professionals who concentrate on clients with your level of wealth and/or in your particular career field (for example, doctors, lawyers, teachers, or CEOs). An advisor who primarily serves clients like you is more likely to be familiar with investment, tax, and other financial strategies that you can benefit from.

Step 2: Interviews

You'll want to interview several different advisors or brokers (I would suggest four or five). Begin by asking friends for referrals to investment professionals they trust. To expand your slate, you might search an online directory of registered financial advisors or brokers. If you're investing shared money, be sure to include your spouse or significant other in the interviews.

It's always best to meet these interviewees in person, if you can. Ask about their philosophy – not just regarding investments, but how they like to interact with clients. How available would they be to answer your questions? Would they enjoy teaching you about investing? What are their professional qualifications, level of experience, and background? How are they compensated? How would they define their "typical" client, in terms of net worth and occupation? Tell them about yourself: your financial goals, the challenges you face. And be sure to take notes (trust me, the interviews will blur in your memory otherwise).

Also, you'll want to take into account the size and nature of the company where the interviewee works. Is it a one-person practice, or a national firm? It can make a difference if expanded services are available through a particular advisor, such as estate planning or risk management, that you may later want to take advantage of. A broker working for a big firm could feel pressured to sell its own investments.

Last but not least, talk to current clients. Probe their satisfaction level in depth; ask about the candidate's strengths and weaknesses.

Step 3: Decision-Making

In reviewing each of the interviews, write down your impressions or discuss them with a friend. Did you feel the interviewee had a grasp of what you need? Did she or he leave you feeling understood and important?

When you make the final decision, go with your instincts. You hope for a long-term relationship with this person, so be sure you feel comfortable with him or her. How will it be to deal with this individual weekly or monthly over the years? How would she or he react to a conflict or misunderstanding? You want someone who will be understanding, fair, and committed to your best interests.

Sleep on your decision. If it still feels right in the morning, go with it!

~

My Story: Finding the Right Professional

I consider myself an active investor, but I didn't want to go it alone. Yet after the technology market crash, I realized that I needed a different investment advisor. I'm embarrassed to admit how much longer it took me to act. One might expect that my hemorrhaging losses would have catapulted me away from Val into the arms of the most conservative broker on earth, but I had a sense of loyalty to Val. And maybe this mess hadn't really been all his fault. Maybe my compliance had been part of the problem. After all, unlike many investment professionals during this slow-motion train wreck, he hadn't lain low hoping clients wouldn't call. Instead, he was always available and had an optimistic take on the situation. He reassured me that many other people had lost money too (including my parents and the parents of everyone I went to college with). That was how the market was; if we stuck with it, we would eventually grab it by the horns and win.

But I wanted a more conservative broker. I interviewed three candidates referred to me by money-savvy friends. I didn't like any of them, but the alternatives of staying with Val or managing everything myself weren't acceptable. Finally a friend told me about Bob, his trusted broker of 20 years. The relationship had worked well for him, despite a temporary rift when Bob refused to go along with what became the tech bubble.

I reluctantly called Bob. Calm and low-key, he listened closely to me and picked up on my qualms. I decided to give him a small amount of money to invest. His choices proved to be well diversified, moderately profitable, and less risky than Val's had been. Eventually, I shifted everything to him.

~

How Much Risk Can You Stand?

As Bob did, your advisor or broker will ask about your risk tolerance — the ability to withstand losing money in the pursuit of making money. You may be asked to fill out a questionnaire inquiring about your goals and expectations, how long it will be before you need to cash in your investments, and your attitude toward risk (ranging from "I don't mind if I lose some money" to "I need to earn a profit, however small"). Your answers will be used to develop a risk tolerance profile that fits one of these categories:

- **A Conservative Profile** means you would feel more secure with less risky investments in your portfolio. However, these "safer" choices also have less potential for big returns.
- **A Moderate Profile** means you might prefer investments chosen to produce somewhat higher possible returns in exchange for taking somewhat more risk.
- **A Growth Profile** means you place greater emphasis on earning more with your investments and are willing to tolerate correspondingly more volatility.
- **An Aggressive Growth Profile** means you are strongly focused on earning high returns and can live with substantial risk to pursue those opportunities.

Many people think they can stand to lose money. I did too, until I actually lost a lot of it. It turned out that I was much more risk-averse than I'd thought. When times are good, especially if you have never lost a lot of money, it's easy to underestimate your risk tolerance because you can't imagine the pain you will feel.

Try this mental exercise. Suppose you have $1,000 in ten $100 bills. Lay each $100 bill on a table. Think about what you might buy with the money. The next day, take away a $100 bill so you have a total of $900. How does it feel to have lost 10% of your money? Write down what your emotions are. What can't you do, now that you have $900 instead of $1,000? The next day, take away another $100 bill. Keep taking away money until your palms begin to sweat or your heart starts to race.

In other words, you need to imagine a loss scenario in as much detail as possible before assessing your risk tolerance. The more honest you are with yourself, the better you and your money will get along and the happier you will be.

COMMENTS FROM MY COUCH

Clearly, investing evokes strong emotional reactions for many of us. Some people get a thrill from waking up in the morning wondering what has happened to their high-risk investment in Venezuelan bonds. Others feel sick worrying about moment-to-moment stock fluctuations.

By learning to identify and understand your emotional responses to investing, you will go a long way toward managing your money more effectively. The next step — how you develop and implement your investment strategy — is a very personal decision. You can choose to do it on your own, perhaps supported by an investment club; work with a financial advisor and/or a broker, or some combination of both approaches.

My own choice is to entrust most of my money to a trusted broker and financial advisor. Even though I keep learning the disciplines of investing as a member of an investment club and have a small portfolio that I manage on my own, I don't feel I have enough time to do everything by myself. Even if I did, I wouldn't feel comfortable bearing the emotional responsibility alone. My solution gives me what I feel is the best of all worlds: active input into the investing process, while someone I trust helps me make decisions and keep tabs on the overall picture. This lets me stay busy thinking about my work and other important aspects of my life.

Chapter 15 Exercise: Riding the Roller Coaster

To invest effectively, it's critical to identify and understand your emotions around risk. For example, do you avoid risk because you're not comfortable dealing with money and possible financial loss? Or do you feel you can't trust anyone else not to take too much risk, so you need to do everything on your own?

Think about the emotions you feel. Are they helping you move forward or holding you back? If they're holding you back, imagine yourself feeling that positive "moving forward" sensation.

1. What belief might you have to change to move forward?
2. What would you like to believe about yourself moving forward?

3. What actual changes in your life would you have to make to move toward your goals?

An active, practiced imagination can help you reorganize your emotional experience and attitudes in a positive direction, so you can approach investing without feeling so "crazy about money."

Maggie's Response to the Chapter 15 Exercise:

1. What belief might you have to change to move forward?
2. What would you like to believe about yourself moving forward?
3. What actual changes in your life would you have to make to move toward your goals?

I had no idea what my real relationship to risk or risk tolerance was until I lost so much money in the tech bubble of 2000. Before that, I was much more willing to take a calculated risk because I had never experienced a huge loss directly. A slow leak of a loss when you are in your 40s doesn't have the same jolting effect as a big, quick loss some years later. This "in my 50s" loss experience helped me be more realistic about what can happen when you feel euphoric and believe that what goes up will stay up forever. That said, I go back to what I suggested as an experiment to help us evaluate our risk tolerance.

<u>The $100 bill test</u>: When I remove the first $100 bill I feel a twinge of disappointment that I won't have that money to buy computer software or something else I want. After taking the second one away, I start looking at what is left. Two $100 dollar bills taken randomly out of the $1000 dollar lineup looks like someone losing their teeth. Teeth are pretty essential. What am I allowing to happen, I think to myself, and I

start to feel anxious. That is a signal to myself that I really don't like what is happening and I'm entering the worry zone that will really stay with me. In percentage terms, I'm down 20% and that is putting me close to my edge. I don't want to see any more of my hard-earned money disappear.

Right now, I still feel nervous from finishing the risk test. Anxiety is high and I'm feeling risk-averse. I don't want to lose anything. The anxiety is holding me back from any thoughts of going ahead positively. I would have to change my belief that it is easy to lose money and that it feels awful when I do. Only the certainty that I won't lose any more significant money will make me feel better.

OK, so I can imagine moving forward positively if I'm really careful about what happens to my money and don't take huge chances. If I believe that what I invest in (after doing a careful analysis of the company) has positive growth potential over a several-year period, I could chance it. I'd have to believe that if things change for the worse I could see that and alter my course of action instead of continuing on in the blind hope that things will get better.

RINO

Chapter 16:
Playing the Odds

GAMBLING, DEBT, AND RISK

"A dollar picked up in the road is more satisfaction to us than the 99 which we had to work for, and the money won at Faro or in the stock market snuggles into our hearts in the same way." —Mark Twain

Most casinos have no clocks. They don't have windows, either. They are purposely designed to foster the illusion that time stands still. Gambling is the total reality — the fun, the thrill, creating the pulsing, prodding possibility that with just one pull of a lever, just one roll of the dice, you will become the chosen one upon whom riches will be heaped. For the split second of that win you will be special, blessed by the luck of the universe, making you King or Queen of the Free Win, not like the rest of those poor losers around you. Something for nothing and being special, all in a flash. Just think: the drop of one card can begin a flood of money. And this excitement and belief can only be sustained by looking ahead, charging forward and not looking back, not remembering how many times you pulled the lever and your money was taken away. The action is brazen, the next move that might bring an even bigger windfall and make you even more special. This is free money, not earned, not taxed. *Yours.* That's the allure of gambling: the promise of free money and the thrill of taking a risk for big gains. The anticipation of excitement fulfilled and dreams expanded creates a draw that can be so intense, the person under its sway forgets gambling's realities. Probability dictates that the house always wins, that jackpots rarely occur. Most of the time gambling gains are minimal – or, like losses, are piled up amid denied memories of other disappointments. All of this magically disappears from the gambler's mind. It's as if the casino owns a fairy godmother's magic wand, and *poof,* unpleasantness vanishes. What doesn't disappear from the gambler's memory are the occasional wins scattered hither and yon, like pixie dust wafting about the casino. (Taken from a sermon by Rev. Peter Vanderveen)

It's part of human nature to want to be special, of course. When life goes wrong, the longing to be special becomes even stronger. People who are down on their luck often wish something spectacular would happen, so they can feel like someone of value. "See me, admire me, love me" is what they yearn for.

When folks have trouble feeling good, they can drift into medicating themselves with gambling, drugs, or another activity that mutes negative feelings and creates a sense of euphoria. This activity can become so captivating and enlivening that it's hard to imagine how problems could result. However, the short-term "high" of possibility, risk, and euphoria can (and usually does) lead to hangover effects, from a headache to an empty bank account.

A Moment in the Sun: Brett's Story

Brett's father was a shrewd businessman who made millions from selling his machine parts business. Brett, his only son, had no idea how to be as successful as his dad. After graduating from college, he went to work in a local business. He did all right, but had a hard time finding good friends. Computer dating didn't help. He often felt lonely and wanted more from life.

One weekend he decided to go to Atlantic City for a change of scenery, figuring he would play the slot machines. To his surprise, he won $200. Brett, who had always considered himself a loser in anything he tried, was thrilled to come home with two hundred "free" dollars in his pocket. As the weekends rolled by, he spent more and more time at the slots. The casinos began inviting him to stay in their hotels for free.

Soon enough, Brett began to live for his gambling weekends. If he'd ever added up all his losses, he would have realized that he barely broke even. But all he remembered was the incredible split-second intoxication of a win. The moment of grandeur, of specialness, was so emotionally compelling that he took bigger and bigger risks in order to experience it over and over.

After depleting his bank accounts he borrowed from credit cards to finance his gambling, disregarding their 29% interest rate. What he loved most was to "double down," increasing his bet on a promising hand in order to maximize the chances of a big win. Since the odds always favor the house, Brett ended up losing even more.

COMMENTS FROM MY COUCH

Gambling, and the financial, interpersonal, and internal debt it creates, is a misguided effort to enhance self-esteem. People who have extreme and persistent gambling habits are making their best effort to feel good about themselves. They have not been able to develop more effective ways to feel good about themselves, and probably won't until they hit rock bottom and life becomes so unbearable that they are forced by external circumstances to change.

Brett's gambling was an attempt to make up for the companionship and validation of being "special" that he lacked in real life. One of the few things he could control was his money, which he used to try and satisfy his unmet emotional needs. But the more he gambled, the more money he gambled away. Since his parents persistently rescued him from abject failure, he had never really hit bottom. It wasn't until they started therapy that the tables began to turn. They decided together to let him sink or swim.

Brett sank. He lived out of his car, with no place to take a shower and barely enough money for food. His dad became anxious that "the street would get him," and proposed that he use part of an inheritance to pay for rehab. Brett reluctantly agreed. After staying in an inpatient gambling addiction program for over a year, he got a job and found a girlfriend. To his credit, he has been living gambling-free for the last two years with no financial support from his parents.

Oh, That Restless Feeling: Hugh's Story

Hugh had a top-flight job at a law firm. Although he was sought-after professionally and his wife and daughter adored him, this satisfaction was not enough. He began to look for ways to create more intense feelings of risk and excitement.

Hugh told me about the boost he got when he walked into his favorite casino and was immediately acknowledged by the staff and crowd as a big spender, a "whale." Everyone looked at him with awe and respect. They obviously knew how successful he must be to blow $20,000 a night without blinking an eye. What they didn't know, of course, was that he had depleted his savings and hadn't paid his mortgage in months. Only when Hugh's wife threatened to leave him did he consider giving up gambling.

~

COMMENTS FROM MY COUCH

Why would someone who apparently had everything start to gamble it away? One answer could be that they need to feel constantly stimulated. Without this thrill, the normal successes of life — a good job, ample income, a contented family — seem dull and gray. There's no fun in winning unless you are slightly aroused and surprised, with that expansive feeling of being viewed by the world as important, special, and unique.

The tragic part of addiction is that over time, it takes more of whatever you are addicted to in order to feel the same thrill. This enslaves people to an intense drive for *more, more, more*. The rest of their life recedes into the background, or becomes tedium to be endured until the next exhilarating high.

Emotions underlie the addictive process. As we've discussed, emotions amplify experience. In most people, sources like family, work, recreation, or philanthropy generate the healthy pride, pleasure, and well-being that make us feel good. If our emotional needs aren't being satisfied (or we don't know what they are), we're more likely to seek intense feelings from extreme activities like high-stakes gambling or bungee-jumping. Unfortunately, the shame and guilt that also go with a gambling addiction are usually denied and buried away. It is only when the downward spirals begin that shame and guilt engulf the rapture of "big win" memories. To escape these negative emotions, gambling addicts typically start chasing the big win again.

Is there any such thing as "healthy gambling"? Yes, although in my experience it is unusual for people to have the will and discipline to resist the intoxication of excitement. If you're the type of person who can go to a casino with $100 and leave when it is gone (or when you have won up to your predetermined limit) without giving in to the many inducements to keep gambling, more power to you! While others are still chasing "the big win," you will have peace of mind.

How High Can You Fly? Tom and Stella's Story

Tom and Stella, stockbrokers in their 30s, liked to compete with each other to see who made the most money from one day to the next. The market was on an upswing, and they were poster children for irrational exuberance. Not content with the return on the stocks he already owned, Tom invested "on margin" with borrowed money, using their stocks as collateral. The future gains, he figured, would allow him to pay back the margin loan and still make money.

Instead, the market turned sour. The value of his portfolio tumbled, including the price of the stocks he had used as collateral. The brokerage firm issued a margin call, meaning that Tom needed to put up more collateral to secure his loan. To answer the margin call, he had to raise cash by selling some of his stock. The market fell further. Another margin call. He sold even more stock. When the market finally bottomed out, he had sold all his holdings and was left with only $200. Had he not borrowed on margin, he would still have owned his original stock — with big losses on paper, to be sure, but the possibility of benefiting when the market recovered.

Leveraging — investing with borrowed money as a way to amplify potential gains, at the risk of greater losses — was so popular a strategy during the late 1990s that when technology stocks weakened in 2000, the whole market collapsed like a house of cards.

Since Stella was not as highly leveraged as Tom, her losses were less severe. She became enraged at his rashness. Tom's sense of his own prowess deflated. Emotionally devastated, depressed, and defensive, he blamed his boss, the economy, and his "greedy" clients instead of examining how his emotions had led him astray. He began to comb the market for high-flying stocks, desperate for the intoxicating "wins" that used to come his way so regularly. Sadly, before long he lost his job and his marriage.

COMMENTS FROM MY COUCH

Even though Tom's addiction to the risk that promised so much was killing him financially, he felt he could not afford to give it up. This kind of addictive behavior is reminiscent of experiments where rats are given cocaine as a reward for pressing a lever. The rats become so addicted that they forget to eat and drink, continually demanding more of the drug until they die of thirst and hunger. Just like the rats, Tom craved the high he got from his early investment successes. Because he had few other sources of positive reinforcement about himself, the market downturn threatened his sense of identity.

Tom couldn't bring himself to sell his stocks at a loss early in the decline, because it would have forced him to face his misjudgments and the pain of loss. He also feared missing an opportunity to recapture gains if the market unexpectedly recovered. Unable to accept his mistakes and modify his behavior, he continued to delude himself that things would turn around. Because he couldn't foresee how bad it would get, he kept digging himself into a deeper and deeper hole. In the end, it became a psychological and financial catastrophe for him. We can hope that the market crash was a powerful learning experience for this young broker.

~

Taking Risks to Feel Better

Other forms of addiction can push people into gambling. One is the urge to be one-up on everybody else — what I would call a "chip on the shoulder" mentality. Luke is an example. Intelligent but a poor student, he was surprised to find that he was good at poker. He used his skill to symbolically defeat the other students who had thought he was a jerk. What could be better than to make money in a way that freed him from the pain of his past, fed his need for risk and excitement, and made him feel powerful? Luke keeps a careful record of his wins and losses, so he can convince himself that he is not addicted to gambling. Continued wins, he thinks, will repair painful memories of those who hurt him in the past, allowing him to finally feel good about himself.

Then there are self-loathing gamblers, who discount their talents and abilities while criticizing themselves and acting in self-defeating ways. Take the case of Gary, a professional athlete. A hero on the field, Gary is paid millions of dollars, but he gambles incessantly and is always in debt. No matter what he does right, he sabotages himself by bingeing on drugs, alcohol, food, sex, and gambling. Blind to the need to act differently, he continues his self-defeating, self-hating behavior. So what if it makes him feel bad? Real men don't dwell on their feelings!

COMMENTS FROM MY COUCH

You might think that Gary is a fabulously lucky individual whose talent has brought him well-deserved fame and other rewards. How can he throw it all away and risk his health and financial future for momentary gratification?

As he and I talked, I learned that he grew up with his parents and other adults scolding him for bad behavior. Like most children, he couldn't separate himself from the way he behaved, so his personality formed around the core belief that he was a bad person. To overcome this belief he plunged into becoming successful in his career. But even though he set records as an athlete, he never lost the conviction that he was a rotten person.

Addictions are usually an attempt to mute bad feelings in a fog of euphoria. But when the euphoria wears off, you are faced with yourself again. In Gary's case, it feels bad to have binge hangovers and face the financial losses he has piled up. Instead of learning to behave differently, he berates himself for screwing up again. The only way to get rid of that bad feeling is to anticipate a big win on the field, with a little help from dope or booze.

When people feel bad about themselves, they have three choices: to adapt, defy, or avoid. Because of his upbringing, Gary isn't able to adapt. Instead, he defies his pocketbook and his body, avoiding the opportunity to assess what is really going on.

How Addiction Changes the Brain

The stimulation of addictive behavior causes a massive release of neurotransmitter chemicals, drowning crucial brain areas. To protect itself, the brain produces less of these chemicals, thus making it harder for addicted individuals to get pleasure from ordinarily enjoyable experiences. This drives them to turn again and again to their favorite substance or behavior in order to feel good.

These self-defeating cycles can become so extreme that the brain switches off. With luck, it will recover. But as ex-smokers can attest, the memory of addiction is never forgotten. It continues to call the recovering addict, like the mythological Sirens whose call was so seductive that it drew sailors to their death.

Training the Lizard Brain

The limbic system, often referred to as our "lizard brain," houses the primitive instincts that helped our ancestors survive. Comprised of the cerebellum (at the back and bottom of the brain) and the brain stem (just above the where the spinal cord attaches to the brain), it can react ten times faster than our analytic brain to protect us in an emergency. However, its existence has drawbacks for us modern-day humans. In millennia past, for instance, people would eat voraciously and store unneeded calories as fat to help them survive a drought or long winter. Given a choice between "stuff yourself now" or "save the food until you're hungry," our ancestors chose to eat now. If they waited, the food might rot, some other animal might steal it, or they might die first.

Our much-maligned inability to defer gratification is chiefly due to the lingering influence of our lizard brain. Amid an abundant culture that overtly and covertly endorses excess, this primitive part of our brain acts like a kid in a candy store. Without conscious self-discipline, its appetite for gratification can easily lead us into addiction – not just to the usual vices but to society-disabling behaviors like overspending, embezzlement, and high-stakes speculation. Most commonly, it induces us to go into debt to acquire things and experiences we believe we must have.

~

A Short History of Debt

Adults who grew up in extreme poverty during the Great Depression never forgot the hard-earned lesson that "cash is king." They abhorred debt. Obsessed with creating financial security for their families, many took pride in being able to give their children the things they never had themselves. These children, in turn, came of age amid the "if it feels good, do it" cultural shifts of the '60s and '70s, from rock 'n' roll to the birth control pill and LSD.

This feel-good generation looked at their Depression-era parents — responsible people, respectful of authority and security-driven, who had worked their fingers to the bone to give them a better chance — and veered 180° to seek lives that let them feel happy and fulfilled. Rather than feeling intimidated by the uncertainty of the future, they were optimistic of finding meaningful pursuits as they made their own way in the world.

About this same time, credit cards sprang up. What freedom! A friend told me that when he got his first charge card (from Amoco), at last he could count on being able to fill up his car and get to work no matter what his bank balance was.

My husband and I applied for a joint credit card in the '70s, but he was the one who carried it, used it, and made the payments every month. Several years later, I looked at the bill and saw we were paying a small fortune in interest every month. Getting rid of that high-rate debt was a real effort, believe me, and took much longer than I'd expected.

Fast-forward to the early 21st century. With a credit card, you can buy anything from an analysis of your own DNA ($499) to a trip into outer space ($200,000). Almost every adult and most teenagers carry one card, if not two, three, or more. The result, as baby boomers' "I want it now" attitude converged with credit card convenience, is that American families piled on unprecedented levels of debt in the past 20 years. Until the Great Recession began in 2008, most of us weren't worried about what we owed. We had good jobs and figured we'd eventually catch up.

Going back to behavioral economics, our "herd instinct" prompts us to unquestioningly follow the majority. For instance, the average college student graduates with nearly $4,138 in credit card debt, according to *USA Today*. Some don't understand that making only the minimum payment may increase their debt as interest is added to the balance. One student told me that when he opened his credit card bill he would find the minimum payment box, squinting so he couldn't see the other details, and pay that amount with the satisfaction of a job well done.

Once you are caught in a downward spiral, it is hard to reverse. Your credit rating goes down because you can't pay your bills on time, interest rates go up because you become a greater credit risk, and your morale sinks because you feel helpless to reverse the process. The best way out of this dilemma is not to get into this situation, but that is often not possible, even for hard-working, well-intentioned people.

"Easy credit" can be a dangerous trap. The national average credit card debt is $4,951, according to the credit information firm TransUnion. In April 2010, credit card balances made up 98% of the $838 billion in U.S. revolving debt, the Federal Reserve says. In turn, that revolving debt was part of $2.44 *trillion* in total consumer debt. Whew!

~

Debt Wars: The Continuing Story of Devon and Martha

Credit card debt was the straw that broke the camel's back, as far as Devon and Martha were concerned. If you remember this couple from Chapter 13, Devon, a Money Monk, was a tenured professor. Martha, a Money Worrier, was a massage therapist who gave up her practice to follow him to his new job. Soon, however, she realized that his college salary was inadequate to support themselves and their three small children. Devon became so frustrated with her complaining about money that he lost his temper one night and struck her. The remorse and shock they experienced after this explosion led first to a separation, then brought them to my office months later for help.

When I saw them, they could barely speak to each other without starting a yelling match. Listening to them was like hearing two completely different, contradictory accounts of the same event. They could not agree on how much money they had, how much they spent, or anything else. All Martha could see was their monthly credit card statement for $27,000, on which they could barely make the minimum payment. She was convinced that Devon would never be able to earn enough to pay off this or any other bill. Devon was so ashamed of not being a better provider that he felt demoralized and emasculated whenever Martha talked about money. To avoid experiencing his shame, he would become defensive and mock her anxiety. Their discussions would end abruptly when one of them stormed out. Then they would avoid each other for days, each waiting sullenly for the other to apologize.

~

COMMENTS FROM MY COUCH

Martha's fear and Devon's unprocessed shame (along with the rage it could generate) had been dominating their interactions for a long time. They were taking chances not just with their economic security, but with their sanity and even their lives. They had to become more aware of the emotions that were so disruptive to meaningful communication. Since they had argued with each other for so long, they needed a third party in the room to help them undo their deeply knotted emotional patterns.

I suggested that before Devon and Martha could make any headway in their relationship, they had to put the facts of their financial situation on the table and agree on them. They also had to change what those facts said about them. Their indebtedness didn't have to mean that Devon was bad. After all, he was a well-regarded professor, a loving father, and a husband who longed for a marriage filled with mutual love. He and Martha needed to decide together on what their spending priorities should be, as well as whether to keep their incomes separate. Since at that point Devon was the only one working outside the home, it was fairer and more balanced to pool their money. Once Martha went back to work full-time, they might decide to have separate personal accounts and a joint one for shared expenses.

Even though their situation was difficult, they both wanted to change it. With their children all in school or preschool, Martha saw that she had more of an opportunity to find a part-time job. Devon, recently diagnosed with depression, began to understand why he had so much difficulty getting organized and facing the financial facts of life without shading them to fit his comfort level. This self-knowledge made him more optimistic about getting ahead in his work and finding ways to bring in more income.

~

Secret Addiction: Althea's Story

Althea's children are both teenagers, so she could return to the workforce if she wished. But although she was trained as a librarian, Althea is so unsure of her competence that she has chosen to stay at home. To all appearances, her husband, Paul, is a smart, successful pharmacist. For the last year, however, he has been working late but bringing home less and less money. Althea worries that his denials and defensive behavior mean he is gambling or doing drugs, or maybe both. She has no proof, though.

No matter how much I try to help her see that she needs to share her fears with him, Althea can't do it. She lives in her own world of denial, unwilling to find out what her husband is doing to himself. Her conviction that she is helpless and her fear that Paul is an addict, with its personal and financial consequences, hold the family hostage. Credit cards keep them afloat, but their debts are mounting up.

As is often the case with addictions, the situation will have to become catastrophic before it can change. Paul's job performance may become impaired; Althea may decide she has had enough and move out, or more likely one of their children will get in trouble and the school will recommend family therapy. Whatever the catalyst, until Althea takes responsibility for her negative self-image and the helplessness it causes, and until Paul confronts his addiction (or whatever is going on), very little is bound to change.

~

COMMENTS FROM MY COUCH

What makes you feel good about yourself? Is it your work, your friends, your skill at tennis or golf, or your ability to make someone laugh? Whatever makes you feel good about yourself is like putting money in your self-esteem bank. The more experiences generating these good self-feelings, the more potential you will have to act in your own best interest.

Self-interest is not selfishness. It's simply taking care of yourself so that you can (as the Army says) be all you can be. If you value yourself and act accordingly, the positive feelings you generate will help you make solid decisions and act in ways that bring you a sense of purpose, comfort, and fun.

Debt and gambling don't have to be extreme. Getting a mortgage and car loan, or sitting in on a Friday night poker game, are a normal part of many people's lives. It's only when this behavior veers out of control that it drains authentic good feeling from our self-esteem bank. While the overspending or excessive gambling can become a pressure relief valve or create a momentary high, repeated withdrawals may burgeon into an emotional disaster.

Just as it takes time and hard work to develop and act from an internal core of authentic self-esteem, it takes the same kind of time and slow, steady effort to deal productively with your finances. The most important thing is to get started. The first move doesn't have to be a radical hardship, like giving up a much-valued daily visit to Starbucks or trying to pay off your credit cards in a month. Just make a commitment to act in your own best interest over time, and make small, incremental changes.

Set little goals and then larger ones, and follow through with some action every day. Focus on how good it feels when you have taken a step forward, even a tiny step. Then reward yourself with something that makes you feel great, or share your success with friends on Twitter or Facebook. You'll have a right to feel proud of yourself. Small stones build grand castles.

~

Chapter 16 Exercise: Assessing your attitudes

1. What do you consider "good debt?" What might you consider "bad debt?" Write down your good and bad debt in two columns, side by side. Write down how you decided which was good and which was bad debt. Write out a plan about how you are going to reduce the bad debt. Think of a reward for yourself if your good debt outweighs your bad debt. Check this list every month and note your progress toward you goal of minimizing your bad debt. At the end of the year asses whether this exercise has helped you reduce your bad debt. Note the thoughts and emotions you have each month about the good and bad debt and write them down in your money journal.

2. Write down what you do that you consider a risk with money. Is it going to the casino, playing the numbers or not being thoughtful about how you spend money? Is it over trusting others to manage your money? When you engage with any money activity that you define as risky, write down what thoughts, emotions and bodily sensations accompany the activity or transaction.
3. For a week (or a month for those of you who want a real challenge) use cash only for money transactions. Write down what this evokes for you. Does it help you realize how much you spend and on what and whether what you are doing is worth the money you are spending on it? Or are you playing Russian roulette with your hard earned cash?
4. Taking more risk than you really want when you think it through means that you are out of control and not acting in your best interest. As you engage in your money risky behavior, rate on a 1 to 5 scale how out of control you feel at the time of the transaction. If most of your money risk activities are rated consistently over 3.5, you are definitely not acting in your own best interest. Use this scale as a guide to slowly change your money risky patterns.

1. What do you consider "good debt?" What might you consider "bad debt?"

I consider examples of "good debt" being a mortgage, reasonable car note, or student loans. A mortgage is good debt because you are building equity in your home and are able to deduct your interest from your income taxes.

I said the word reasonable in front of car note because I think if you buy a car outside of your means then it would be classified as bad debt. I have a car note on my reasonable Mazda 3, which I consider good debt. If I were driving around in a 100k Mercedes then that car note would be bad debt. "Bad debt" to me is credit card debt or any high interest debt. When you have debt that you are only making minimum payments on and the principal is not getting eaten away, then that debt is toxic.

The rest of the question doesn't really apply to me because I don't have any bad debt. I am a "debtaphobe". I think I just invented that term. I am aggressively paying off my car note because I can't stand the fact that I pay 5% interest on my loan.

2. Write down what you do that you consider a risk with money.

Things that I do that I consider to be a risk with money is sports gambling and casino gambling (not including poker). I only risk what I can comfortably afford to lose and look at as an entertainment expense. If I make a bet on a football game, it will never be more than $50 or $100. If I am at a casino and want to play blackjack, I will only bring a set amount of money in cash that I can afford to lose. I go into it thinking that I am going to lose, so if I come out with the same or more when the night is done then that is a positive. I don't beat myself up mentally if I lose. There is definitely a "high" that I and others who gamble feel when they place bets. Watching a football game that I have money on makes me feel different emotionally. There is that rush of adrenaline when I'm playing blackjack and I'm waiting for the next card that comes out to either make my hand or bust me or the dealer. If there wasn't that feeling then there would be no point to placing wagers.

When I play poker, which is a game of skill with luck involved, I am able to separate the emotional ups and downs with winning and losing. In poker you can not get too emotional or you won't be able to play your "A" game. The only thing in poker you can do is try to make the right decisions and get your money in "good". Whatever happens after that is luck and you shouldn't get mad at things you can't control. In poker, you can get all of your chips or money in the middle with the best hand and still lose. I've had instances where I've gotten all of my money in the pot with a 98% chance to win the hand and have lost. Did I play the hand wrong? No. I just got unlucky. I could get mad at my luck but what good would that do. If I did all the right things and got my money in good, what more can I do? The luck evens itself out in the long run so as long as I continue to make the right decisions I will be a winner in the long run.

One of the biggest pitfalls for a poker player is what is called "tilt". Tilt is the emotion that everyone gets when they lose a big hand where they were the favorite, or go on a long streak of bad luck, or make a series of poor decisions that cost you to lose chips/money. Tilt affects poker players negatively in future hands because they play different with a cloud of negative emotions in their head. The truly great poker players are ones that can block out these emotions and don't let it affect them in future hands. It is also important to control your emotions when things are going well in poker. If I am winning big or win a big hand, I try to stay even keeled. This helps me so if I am going through an equally bad streak I can try to act the same way.

When I first started playing poker I used to get very emotional and go on tilt a lot. Since I have learned to control my emotions when I play, I have become a much better player.

I feel that I am not risky with money when it comes to purchases. I think things through every time I make a purchase that isn't an everyday purchase. For example, this summer when I was walking through the mall I wandered into Sunglass Hut and found a pair of $180 sunglasses that I really liked. Did I need new sunglasses? No, but I wanted them. I don't like to give into my immediate impulses and wants, so I made myself not purchase the glasses and take a day to sleep on it to see if I really wanted it. Since the next day the impulses didn't go away and I realized I truly wanted the glasses I went ahead and bought them.

I recently purchased a new Apple laptop. This purchase came after several months of research and making sure I wasn't giving into an impulsive want. I try to let the impulses die down before I let myself make a rational decision. Many people don't do this and just let their impulses and wants make their purchasing decisions. That is why many people are in credit card debt because they are buying things that they want and don't need or can't afford. I'm glad that I have this will power, because I get shopping impulses all the time. I just don't give into them. I'd definitely be in credit card debt like most Americans if I just spent without thinking.

Chapter 17:
In the Third Chapter of Life

RETIREMENT

"The question isn't at what age I want to retire, it's at what income." —George Foreman

Like Camelot, there was one brief shining moment when retirees had it made.

Until the late 1970s, most of them could look forward to being supported by a lifetime pension in addition to Social Security benefits. Now, instead of providing a company-paid pension, most large and mid-sized employers offer workers the less generous opportunity to invest their own money in 401(k)s or similar retirement savings plans. These accounts let employees shelter their contributions from income tax, although the IRS will recoup this tax on the other end (including tax on interest earned). Most importantly, the switch from pensions to savings plans shifted the risk for bad investment decisions to plan participants — i.e., inexperienced and often clueless investors.

Worse yet (financially, that is), people are living longer than they used to as a result of improved health and sophisticated medical care. That means most of us have 20, 30, or even more years to keep going without a paycheck. The convergence of these two trends leaves only a few options, most of them unsatisfying or unlikely: work longer and retire later, save more earlier, become a financial and investment superstar, win the lottery, pray never to get sick, or live monastically to stretch every dollar. Most Americans seem to be counting on the lottery: 54% of workers have less than $25,000 saved for retirement, according to the Employee Benefit Research Institute. McKinsey & Company says that when it's time to retire, most of us will be short of what we need by $250,000.

At the same time that money issues become tremendously important, so do the normal developmental changes of aging. When these intersect, our patterns of managing money and spending are often altered. The following stories from my practice illustrate some of the results.

When Dreams Are Not Enough: Ian and Rosa's Story

Ian and Rosa had romantic ideas of retirement. They looked forward to reading together, traveling, and puttering around the house.

Ian's job as a criminal court judge was absorbing and stressful, while Rosa often worked 60 hours a week as an editor. In preparation for retirement, Rosa cut her work back to part-time. Combined with Ian's pension, which was 80% of his full-time salary, they figured they would be able to stay afloat if they were careful with their money.

They approached the retirement date with feverish desire, like a second honeymoon. Finally they would be free of all those nagging pressures, those difficult people you couldn't scream at, and the endless commute. They dreamed of being in their neat, cozy house, reading, doing chores, taking long walks, and making love without fighting fatigue. What a paradise it would be!

After a round of celebratory retirement dinners, they started living out their dream. Everything was idyllic. They rested, they walked, they canoodled.

This dream state continued for several months. Then I noticed Ian becoming a little "drifty." He kept saying everything was fine, but he didn't sound enthusiastic. Something had changed. His and Rosa's interaction with other people had dropped from frequent and intense to practically nil. And because they were watching their money so carefully, they had become hyper-aware of how much everything cost. To save, they ate at home more often. A big splurge was dinner at Wendy's.

After several months of not having to get up early or do anything all day, Ian was depressed. As much as he loved spending time with Rosa, he had underestimated how much he would miss the stimulation of work. Once the most sought-after criminal judge in the county, he no longer had the opportunity to talk authoritatively about the law and feel that his work was important. Now he would go for days speaking only to Rosa and his twin grandsons.

Rosa too was restless, but in a different way. After retiring from her part-time editorial position, she had been ready for something really different. Running a bed and breakfast was an old dream of hers, so she got a job at one. "Different" might have been an understatement: from being a high-profile, high-status editor to cooking meals and making beds for total strangers! The owner of the inn was not a very bright bulb, and after a month or so Rosa began to chafe under the woman's immaturity. She discovered how boring making beds and cleaning up after other people could be, and how irritating it was to have a boss who made bad decisions for her to carry out. Still, she felt compelled to put as much effort into the inn keeping job as she had to her more responsible professional position.

Moreover, it had been a source of pride to Rosa that working allowed her to make an equal contribution to their household finances. But for the first time in her life, she was not making enough money to support herself. Although this loss of independence troubled her, her drive to please her boss would not let her quit.

~

COMMENTS FROM THE COUCH

Rosa and Ian's devotion to each other was a vital characteristic of their relationship. They were interested in the same activities, held similar values, and had enough money to live simply. If they needed more, they were healthy enough to earn additional income.

However, they had not really focused on what each of them wanted on a personal level. Both had obtained affirmation and self-esteem through their work. In retirement they worked harder to respond sensitively to each other's emotional needs, but it did not occur to them to look inside themselves and figure out what they wanted individually.

Ian's "driftiness" was related in part to not knowing what to do with himself. His work, with the emotional support it had provided, had been the linchpin for his concept of himself as a productive, competent, and highly valued professional. Reading, doing fix-it projects around the house, and being with Rosa hardly constituted meaningful achievements. After six months of leisure, he felt himself losing touch with who he was. He had been accustomed to put on a suit every day and leave for an important destination: his courtroom. Now he could stay in his pajamas all day; and if he went out, jeans and a work shirt would do.

To overcome his depression, Ian succeeded in signing on to assist a lawyer friend with cases in litigation. This meant suiting up every morning, going to a law office, and doing tasks usually assigned to a new law graduate for about a third of a judge's salary. This drop in status didn't bother Ian. He enjoyed drawing on his knowledge of the law and helping his friend. More importantly, he found himself making a positive difference in other people's lives. To Rosa, his smile at the end of the day more than compensated for his absence as her daily companion.

As for Rosa herself, she persuaded herself that she could give notice at the B&B anytime. Either of her two alternatives — switching to a less responsible job with a more reasonable boss, or developing a part-time business so she would be accountable to no one but herself — would ease the pressure she felt to set the world on fire.

As we discovered in our conversations, Rosa was struggling to gain control over her constant striving for excellence, which masked a need to garner praise from others. She had unconsciously hoped that lowering her level of responsibility would release her from the pressure to excel. However, it didn't solve the problem of what to do with the rest of her life.

I encouraged Rosa to work with a career counselor. When she forgot about other people and focused on herself, she discovered that she wanted to be a travel writer. Since she and Ian were planning a trip to Italy, she could take her first crack at writing.

Although she didn't have any luck when she sent her article to travel magazines, she kept writing in hopes that her amusing stories would pique an editor's interest. With Ian back at work, she felt less haunted by the pressure to make money. Ultimately, she decided that she would rather spend carefully to stretch the income he earned and give herself the time to do what she wanted.

~

Generativity vs. Stagnation

Developmental psychologist Erik Erikson, who studied the stages of the human life cycle, noted that people in their 60s and 70s struggle with issues he categorizes as "generativity vs. stagnation." In this age bracket, we have less time left than we have already lived. This pushes us to reflect on what our life means now and what it has meant to us in the past. In other words, it's mental accounting time. The challenge is to recognize patterns that have shaped our life and to determine where we have been, where we are going, what we want to do with the rest of our life, and what legacy we wish to leave behind.

Clearly, none of us knows how long we have to live. Financial planners use actuarial charts and fancy software to estimate how large a nest egg will be needed to provide X amount of annual income in retirement. This is basically the high-tech equivalent of reading sheep entrails, since there is no way to accurately predict future market returns and interest rates, health problems, financial emergencies, or (of course) lifespans.

What we can control, though, is how we want to live. Financial projections have their place, but it may be as meaningful, if not more so, for a financial planner to help clients engage in a thoughtful life review.

The Emotional Jolt of a Life Review

A life review often stimulates strong emotions. It's not easy to look back on work that filled so much of our time (happily or not) and accept that it is over. Almost inevitably, we think about what we could have done or done differently. The *"if onlys*" may cast a shadow over the once-sunny prospect of retirement.

Whether the past is filled with satisfaction or deep regrets, we need to recognize that it is done, concluded, finished. There are no do-overs in real life. Instead, we need to ask ourselves how to create a new life that is meaningful, happy, interesting, and fun, while acknowledging the loss of what went before. Will retirement be a fulfilling extension of our earlier experiences, or will it mean disappointment and unhappiness?

Of course, money can either broaden or limit your options. Someone who has saved and invested diligently, or is fortunate enough to have a substantial pension like Ian's, has an opportunity to make genuine choices. Those in a less enviable situation may have to continue working much longer than they expected, and live with greater uncertainty about their financial security.

However, I firmly believe that with directed effort and understanding, people can improve their lot, even late in life. The first step is to use whatever regrets you have about your past as a prompt to do something different in the future. No habit patterns are so rooted that they can't be replaced, or at least modified, with effort and direction. Second, the way you have lived and worked has formed a foundation of some sort. Even though your job may not have been a perfect fit, you learned something from it that may be useful and applicable. Think of creating a resume. What's important going forward is not the specific jobs you've held, but the strengths and skills you have acquired or improved. Building on these assets will help reduce the "if only..." regrets you may feel.

∾

"My God, What Happened?": Ken and Judy's Story

Ken and Judy wanted to retire at 65, but forces beyond their control conspired to keep them working much longer. They both had good jobs at a big company we'll call Hallitine, and had saved religiously for years. Although they both worked hard, what they did at Hallitine was not their passion. Judy was crazy about singing. She sparkled inside whenever she imagined a retirement that would let her sing to her heart's content all day, every day, if she wished. Ken loved woodworking. Sitting at the computer in his office cubicle, he would dream of being home making chairs, tables, and cabinets instead of crunching numbers.

When the market tanked in 2008-09, their 401(k)s shrank and pensions were frozen. Even though they had done nothing wrong, this calamity frustrated them and made them feel like failures. To be sure, they had raised children who turned out well, and they had maintained good friendships and close family ties over the years. However, this financial blow damaged their sense of themselves as whole human beings. Self-doubts like "Where did we go wrong?" turned to severe criticism like "How stupid could we have been not to see the market collapse coming?" A cloud descended over their future, made darker by the humiliation they felt. Clearly, their retirement was not going to look as pretty as the ads showing couples strolling on the beach!

~

Blaming Ourselves for a "Bad" Life

It's very human to blame ourselves for circumstances out of our control. Our emotional desire for something often amplifies and heightens our desire for it, so our disappointment is all the more acute when we can't have it. Ken and Judy had done everything right, and yet forces beyond their control hit them and hurt them badly. Instead of recognizing and blaming the outside forces that had caused their financial loss, they turned their anger and rage inward on themselves. They experienced a sense of shame from their inability to have controlled their fate.

Children believe that if something happens, it happens because of them. If a parent or teacher is in a bad mood, they think it must be because of something they did. It takes a long time to realize that Mom, Dad, and other friendly authorities act based on an internal state that may have no relation to the child. Children also believe that things must be fair at all times. As they mature, they realize that their own point of view is not the only perspective, and that other people have different agendas and motivations, some of which are neither fair nor honorable. People can more effectively act in their own best interest when they value what they want and need, while understanding that their desires may be different and in conflict with others'.

If Ken and Judy had foreseen the market plunge and the pension freeze, could they have acted differently? This is a shaky premise since many experienced investment professionals were caught flat-footed by the crash; and not being senior executives at Hallitine, they would not have had much luck protesting an impending pension decision. Of course, they might have tried to prepare for a worst-case scenario instead of assuming the status quo would continue.

Ultimately, the couple might conclude that they were simply blindsided by unpredictable events, and get on with revising plans for the rest of their lives. Downsizing in retirement is unappealing to most people; it feels too much like deprivation. But because Ken and Judy derived such deep satisfaction from pursuing relatively affordable passions, they might not have such a hard time cutting back. They might even succeed in reclaiming their originally planned standard of living, if Ken can sell his hand-crafted furniture and Judy becomes proficient enough to work as a singing teacher or performer.

This brings up an important point. All your working life, you have traded your human capital — your education, skills, and knowledge — to earn money. In many cases, you'll still have some of this capital left when you retire. How can you profit from it? Do you need further training or experience, and if so, how can you acquire it? It's like having a diversified portfolio. If something in one sector doesn't perform well (such as a frozen company pension), you want to have others — investments, Social Security, work income — that are doing just fine.

A New Retirement Vision

Speaking for myself, I can't imagine retiring. I love my work, and I love being a part of the working community. I can see myself at 80 still experiencing the thrill of connecting with someone and helping them sort themselves out. In the meantime, I have an uncanny feeling of not being as old as I am. I feel energetic, enthusiastic, and even expansive (on good days). I'm doing the same things I did 20 years ago, and more. Only when I look carefully in the mirror am I shocked into the awareness that I'm just not as young as I used to be.

Although I want to deny it, a time may come when I will have to accept that I can no longer contribute to helping others. I can't quite imagine it yet. As far as I can go right now is to envision reducing my office hours and making more time for music, family, friends, and travel. When I hear that someone I know is ill or dying, a chill comes over me. If I were told I had a month to live, what would I change? I have no idea.

Once the time comes that I have to stop working, my main concern is whether my husband and I will have enough money to live on. Fortunately, the things we love most are free or cost very little. For example, we prefer more modest hotels when we travel. Our fellow guests are usually like-minded folks who prefer good conversation to being pampered in some snooty five-star hostelry.

Here is my wisdom about retirement planning: Find what works for you — and pursue it as if there were no tomorrow.

~

Chasing the "Number"

What money you have when you retire will probably be all there is, unless you happen to win the lottery or inherit a bundle. If you have enough so you can do what you want, your savings will be a source of pride, stability, and security. If you don't, there won't be much you can do about it except rely on your children or Medicaid, either of which may be a source of embarrassment and perhaps a feeling of failure.

I'm reminded again of Christopher, who worked 80 hours a week for years in order to be able to say "Screw you" to anyone who told him to do something he didn't want to do. He would be his own person, as free as a bird. He envisioned having total freedom to stay in bed all day, make love all night, take off to Morocco for a weekend — anything his heart desired, anytime. He has a specific number in mind ($15 million) that he believes will enable this freedom. However, setting goals and blasting past them is what he does, and he may not be able to stop. I worry that when he achieves his "number" he will feel compelled to ratchet it up to $20 million, then $30 million and more, without making time to enjoy what he already has.

His powerful drive isn't really about money. For Christopher, money equals power and more money means more power. He believes this power will protect him from being controlled by others, allowing him to do precisely what he wants. Like Rosa, who gave up her editorship for a less "responsible" job at a B&B, he doesn't see that having control of one's life comes from the inside, not from outside forces like money or work.

~

I Married You for Love, Not Lunch: Tom and Kathy's Story

Tom, a senior corporate executive, had an unusual reason for consulting me: he was anxious to retire, but worried that his wife, Kathy, would want to be with him all the time. A stay-at-home mom, Kathy claimed to be bored but had never done anything to resolve her boredom. When she met and married Tom, he asked her to abandon her master's degree program so she could devote her time to raising their children. Kathy had gone along willingly, but now that their last child was about to leave the nest, her new "joblessness" was making them both anxious.

Tom made feverish suggestions that Kathy start a business, take courses, volunteer for a community organization — anything that might fulfill her. They didn't need the money; Tom was highly paid and had invested wisely. In fact, the ease with which he had created wealth made Kathy less eager to find work. How could she compete with the couple of million dollars he had already made? It didn't occur to her that what she needed to find was a sense of meaning that was authentically hers and had nothing to do with the financial yardstick that measured Tom's career.

Instead of reflecting on how to make her life more meaningful, Kathy discovered eBay. She was immediately enthralled by everything she could buy so cheaply and so cleverly. But there was neither rhyme nor reason to what she bought: desks, antique lamps, odd assortments of jewelry, even a stuffed owl. When her purchases arrived, she would excitedly open the boxes and then stash them in the basement. Eventually Tom could no longer ignore the packages that had begun to line the basement steps. He tried to be reasonable, hoping to stop Kathy's buying binges, but she would become defensive and stomp out of the house. Furious that Tom was "threatening" her, she would drive around at breakneck speed for hours, a menace to other drivers. When Tom found a whisky flask in her car, he bristled with frustration and rage. He waited for an explanation and apology from Kathy, but she was determined not to give him one. Sullen and withdrawn, they spent days without speaking to one another.

~

COMMENTS FROM MY COUCH

With all Tom's dedication to business matters, he had not devoted enough time or emotional energy to keep engaged with Kathy. He thought that as long as he was earning a good salary, he was taking care of her. He fully expected that their retirement relationship would just fall into place in the cradle of his financial prowess.

In truth, Kathy was proud of his scientific and business success. For a long time her husband's standing in the business world and her children's achievements in school had sufficed to make her feel good about herself. But every time she thought of doing something on her own, she compared herself to Tom and felt inadequate. How could she accomplish even a fraction of what he had done? Unaware of her dissatisfaction, Tom kept expecting her to greet him with open arms at the end of the workday — her hero, home from battle to reap his rewards of relaxation and fun.

The missing ingredient was a dialogue about their relationship and their life goals. Had they had more money pressures, Kathy might have been motivated to get a job or find another way of developing her talents into genuine skills. Then, as her children needed her less and less, she might not have hesitated to do something of value.

Instead, confronted with her empty nest, she didn't know what to do. Sinking into what Erik Erikson called "stagnation," she became obsessed with buying. The satisfaction this gave her did not last, which made her spend more frantically. A whole aviary of stuffed owls would not have been able to make her feel useful.

Tom was not empathic enough to respond sensitively to her dilemma. On the contrary, his efforts inflamed her anger. Her furious response to his overtures discouraged him from reevaluating her behavior more compassionately, which in turn gave Kathy an excuse to avoid developing a more genuine source of satisfaction.

The gulf between Tom and Kathy became so wide that it would require a serious commitment from both of them to move to a better place. Their downfall was making assumptions without talking about them. Kathy in particular is between a rock and a hard place, at loose ends without skills that take effort to develop. I can only hope that in therapy she will be able to find direction and the persistence to pursue it. The curse of capability is that you have to use it. The more you have, the greater the challenge.

~

Regrets and Fear of Loss

Have you heard people say things like "If only I had done that 20 years ago, my life would be so different now," or "I should have married Jane when I had the chance"? One of the biggest downers in later life is this kind of regret, because it diminishes the opportunity to enjoy life now.

Regrets take on even larger proportions when combined with uncertainty about one's future health — the primary concern (along with money) for most older people. These things never crossed your mind when you were in your 20s. Now, though, you can't help wondering if you will continue to be strong and healthy enough to enjoy retirement activities you have been waiting for. If you need to keep working, how long will you be able to handle the stress? How can you plan if you don't know how long you will live?

Given all this uncertainty, it might be supposed that we become more apprehensive as we get older. Granted, the prospect of loss of money, loss of competence and power, and loss of independence culminate in fear of losing one's sense of self and ceasing to be. This ultimate fear, identified by psychoanalyst Heinz Kohut as "annihilation anxiety," makes us start dreading loss of all sorts.

Yet researchers find that for many people, older age does bring wisdom, maturity, and peace of mind. As a matter of fact, Stone, Schwartz, Broderick and Deaton's 2010 study found that well-being and happiness increase and worry decreases after the age of 50. This pattern holds true for both men and women, despite life circumstances that could cause stress. We all have — or can develop — tools to cope with whatever lies ahead. Indeed, a well-stocked psychic tool box is as essential for 21st-century survival as financial savvy.

~

No Fairy Tale: The Story of Jill and Hank

Jill and Hank had been together for decades. She was lucky enough to have inherited a well-funded trust that generated enough interest for them to live on. The only condition was that when she died, all the money would go to a charity her parents had chosen. This eventuality was inconceivable to both Jill and Hank, since she was quite healthy and was younger than he was. In the meantime, they were happy spending time together. Hank had some mild interest in working, but not enough to get a job.

Suddenly Jill was diagnosed with a degenerative disease. As her condition grew worse, Hank deluded himself into thinking she would recover. As long as he kept her happy, he rationalized, their life would continue unchanged. Unfortunately, Jill developed pneumonia that she was too weak to combat. Within a few short days Hank was alone.

COMMENTS FROM MY COUCH

Hank had always figured that Jill would outlive him. He had been pretty clever, he thought, to find her. He even bragged to his friends that love had provided well for him, as if having a rich partner who loved him meant that destiny had singled him out as someone special.

What Hank forgot about was his responsibility to himself. Had he imagined that he would have to support himself someday, he might have found work that rewarded him with personal development as well as income. Unfortunately, he lacked the core sense of self from which ambition could have sprung. He could only experience himself through Jill's admiring eyes. As long as she affirmed him by appreciating his wit and charm, he felt happy and animated. Jill truly loved him, but she shared his fantasy of endless safety and contentment. When her illness struck she needed him all the more, so she did not urge him to go out and find work.

Only months after her death, following many meetings with lawyers as he sought a way out of his predicament, did Hank realize that he had been left with nothing — no money, skills, or ambition? Even knowing that Jill's income would end if she predeceased him, they had been oblivious to the need to buy life insurance for her. The cost of premiums would have been negligible compared to the payout when she died.

When I last heard of Hank, he was working at Starbucks, feeling demoralized and powerless. He will remain stuck until he can recognize that his own lack of drive for independence and accountability led him down the primrose path of illusion. It remains to be seen whether he will be able to start building a life of his own.

MORE COMMENTS FROM MY COUCH

When the way we experience ourselves is blocked by anxiety, self-doubt, or depression, we risk becoming alienated from ourselves and our power to change. Unlike rape or other sudden and unexpected traumas, the aging process doesn't usually strip people of their identity. Sometimes, though, aging can provoke acute and unbearable anxiety — thus the term "annihilation" anxiety. Milder forms of losing oneself happen during major transitions like retirement, and may trigger concerns about actually dying.

I remember a radio interview with a 90-year-old poet. The interviewer kept referring to the man's age and asking what it was like to be 90 years old. Finally the interviewee spoke up. "I am not a 90-year-old," he snapped. "I am a poet who happens to be 90!" Clearly, he was not about to be overcome with annihilation anxiety!

Like that poet, we all need a sense of self in order to feel good about ourselves. With that in place, we have the potential to keep growing as long as we can draw breath.

~

The Difficulty of Looking Out for Ourselves

As the baby boomer generation moves into their 60s, they bring with them the attitude that through the modern miracles of medicine and nutrition, combined with an iron will, they will stay young and active well into their 70s and even beyond. There is a degree of possibility in this belief, but few boomers are prepared for the inevitable crises that may occur, like an accident, sickness, high inflation, or a prolonged down market. Such hardship can beat people down and wear them out — even if they do embody the American dream of youthfulness, ambition, and success.

It's a particular concern that this huge generation has saved so little for retirement. Having growing up with credit cards, boomers believe they can easily borrow if they can't pay now. After all, they can work as long as necessary to earn money, right? Thus there's a temptation to raid the 401(k) to help put their children through college — never mind what that will do to Mom and Dad's retirement savings.

I am reminded of Paula's parents, who were thrilled when their daughter was accepted at a big-name Ivy League college. (The fact that its fees exceeded $45,000 a year certainly did not detract from its luster.) So intoxicating were their pride and excitement that they thought nothing of sacrificing some of their retirement savings to spare her the pain of graduating with $200,000 in student loans. Since they had always been protective of Paula, she knew little about money management and figured they always knew best. This time, though, she was old enough to realize that they were prepared to borrow so she wouldn't have to.

The transition from high school to college is normally a leap of independence: from living by parental rules to being responsible for one's own time, money, and behavior. However, the rising cost of tuition makes it harder for college-age children to break away from their parents. Grants, scholarships, and loans notwithstanding, they most likely will need some financial support from home. Besides, the job market is tight, even for college graduates. Are you going to tell your excited teenage daughter that she will have to start her career with a huge amount of debt, because you can't afford to pay for her education as well as your own retirement?

It's a flinty-hearted parent who can pull that off. More likely, you rationalize that you can work late into your 70s, so why scrimp now? Besides, the neighbors are completely funding *their* child's college education.

What's missing here is the recognition of what you and your child truly need. As generous as it is to pay for a good education for your daughter, you would be shortsighted not to consider your own future needs more seriously. If you have a strong sense of yourself and sincere concern for your child, you will try to figure out how best to protect your financial security while providing limited funding for her. If money is a real issue, you might suggest a "gap year" during which your daughter would work to save money for college herself. If she resists deferring her education, you can help her realize that not depleting your 401(k) now may spare her from having to support you later on. After all, if you can't pay your expenses in retirement, who else will?

Telling your child that you, too, have needs that must be considered sends a strong message that she must begin taking on more responsibility for herself. Many parents are afraid to do this for fear of hurting a child's feelings, appearing selfish, or having to admit to themselves that they can't do everything. Yet nothing fosters self-mastery faster than challenging someone to rise above their current level of capability. Including your college-bound student in these discussions will go a long way toward helping him or her gain accountability and independence.

Creatively Speaking, The Choice Is Yours

You may well decide to continue working as long as you can. Only then will you need to face making radical changes in your familiar lifestyle: perhaps moving to a smaller house or a condo, spending time with grandchildren, traveling, and reflecting on how you have lived your life. Downsizing is definite evidence of getting older, of recognizing that you're on the front lines now and that sometime in the foreseeable future, your number will come up. But until that happens, stay creative. Use your ideas, memories, emotions, and knowledge to make a difference. That's generativity.

As I mentioned earlier, no one can be sure what the future will be like; all we can do is make educated guesses. Intense, often conflicting feelings are involved in thinking about retirement: the desire to be less constrained by responsibilities and obligations, to enjoy the success of our children and grandchildren, and to do something different with our lives, along with fear of becoming less important and less valued by others. The conflict between positive and negative emotions may be at their height just when you are trying to imagine giving up what you have always done.

Because this is such an anxious time, it's easy to obsess about how much money you are going to need and how much you actually have. It's more beneficial instead to think about what you look forward to, what you still want to achieve, and what would give your life meaning. Plan the future with broad brushstrokes, and trust your resilience to deal with whatever you can't foresee. This attitude will foster hope and optimism, enabling you to live productively and creatively while leaving room for serendipity and the freedom to be yourself.

∾

Chapter 17 Exercise: Rehearsing for Retirement

How would you respond to the following questions? Write down your answers.

1. When you retire, what will you be retiring from? Your particular job, your boss, your burn-out? What will you be moving toward?
2. Imagine a typical retirement week. Write down your day-to-day activities and rate your level of imagined satisfaction for each activity on a 1-5 scale, where 1 = low and 5 = high.
3. How do your retirement ideas mesh with your partner's? Write down areas of agreement and disagreement, then discuss how to resolve areas of conflict.
4. Have you estimated the money you will need for retirement? If not, make a date with yourself to use an online retirement program like myPlan Snapshot at www.fidelity.com, or set up an appointment with a financial planner.

Maggie's Response to the Chapter 17 Exercise:

1. When you retire, what will you be retiring from? Your particular job, your boss, your burn-out? What will you be moving toward?

I can imagine reducing my workload as I get older, but unless I lose my hearing and sight I'd like to cut back gradually and keep working until I'm unable to. Since I've almost always worked on my own, I can set my own schedule. At some point I won't have as much energy as I had and will need to respect growing limitations, probably with less grace than I might wish. If I were not to have much physical or mental decline as I age, I'd be fine working at least part-time up until the end. I would have to limit the number of people I saw who want long-term psychotherapy, because they will need someone around for the long haul.

I imagine I'd want to move toward spending more time with friends, family, and music and do more traveling. It is more a matter of shifting the balance of my present activities rather than completely changing how I spend my time.

2. Imagine a typical retirement week. Write down your day-to-day activities and rate your level of imagined satisfaction for each activity on a 1-5 scale, where 1 = low and 5 = high.

A typical retirement week for me would be to work for three to four hours in the morning or late afternoon, have lunch with a friend, play music, and take a walk or work out. Evenings would be filled with walking to a restaurant for dinner with my family or friends or eating in and taking a long walk after dinner. It's a very comforting feeling knowing that my grandfather always took an evening stroll and that I'm sharing that habit now that I'm inching closer to the age he was when he and I would walk together. I would rate all my activities as highly satisfactory because at this age I plan on only doing what I really like.

3. How do your retirement ideas mesh with your partner's? Write down areas of agreement and disagreement, then discuss how to resolve areas of conflict.

My husband may want to spend more of his time writing and taking classes than working. If our money holds up, he can do that without conflict with me. We may run into trouble if he wants to travel more than I do, but we will talk about it and come to some compromise. For example, he might travel on his own for a longer period and I would join him partway through his trip. The good news here is that we have been talking out issues for a long time and have a fundamental understanding of each other.

4. Have you estimated the money you will need for retirement? If not, make a date with yourself to use an online retirement program like myPlan Snapshot at www.fidelity.com, or set up an appointment with a financial planner.

We keep saving as much as we can, knowing we can never be completely sure we will have enough until the end. Most important to me is that I will be flexible and adapt to whatever our circumstances turn out to be. My money helps fund my interests and engagement in activities I love. Whether I live in a big house or a small house, go out to dinner five times a week or not at all, doesn't make a critical difference. It's the activity and people I love that will determine the quality of my life, now and going forward.

RINO

Chapter 18:
How Will They Remember You?

LEAVING A LEGACY (OR NOT)

"Those not busy being born are busy dying."
—Bob Dylan

Death usually creates a crisis of some sort. At a minimum, it stimulates intense emotional reactions and memories of the person who has died. If it's someone we genuinely loved, our sorrow can be profound and uncomplicated. When my grandfather passed away, I grieved for a long time. I had loved him, knew he loved me, and was sorry that he had suffered through his son's tirades and didn't die with the satisfaction of a life well lived. I didn't think about the money he might have left me. What was money when I had just lost a soulmate?

On the other hand, there are situations like the one I heard about where a wealthy old man died without a will. His estranged daughter and her husband had been waiting impatiently for him to pass away so they could get at the cash he had stashed in his house. They refused to have his depression evaluated by a psychiatrist, for fear that it might make him feel better and delay his dying!

Waiting for God

Why should a person's older years be filled with the shadow of others who hang around waiting, like vultures in the desert? The unfortunate truth is that we usually reap what we have sown earlier in life.

I am reminded of the summer when I was about to leave for a much-needed Colorado vacation when the phone rang. It was my brother, informing me that our 93-year-old mother had just fallen and fractured her kneecap. My immediate reaction was "Oh, God, why does this have to happen now?" In the next breath my brother told me that she would need more at-home care or maybe a transfer to a nursing home. I could hear the cash register in my head start ringing up the dollar signs. Her long-term care insurance policy wouldn't cover the extra hours she might need.

My brother, sister, and I are all beneficiaries of a trust my grandfather set up. My mother lives on the trust income, but has the right to tap into the principal if needed for health reasons. The tradeoff is that with less principal she would have less interest income in the future, and my siblings and I would inherit less after she is gone.

My mother is sweet and can converse politely, but I always sense that she's somewhere else, in a different world. She has no idea that her injury will cause financial strain. Her knee hurts so much, she says emphatically, that she wants to go to a nursing home even if it means using up the principal in our family trust.

My stomach burns. She'll feel the pain wherever she is, I mutter to myself, and it would be a lot cheaper to feel it at home. I feel callous thinking of all this money stuff when my mother is suffering with her leg immobilized in a cast.

Our family does not age well. My mother's brother started out as a Harvard Law graduate and decorated Korean War hero, but went downhill from there. He ended up having furious arguments with Grandfather, and died in a house fire. My grandfather, 89 at the time and a widower, was fiercely independent. Facing the prospect of living out his days in a nursing home, he took the .38 caliber pistol he had taught me to fire as a youngster and shot himself.

In comparison, my mother's broken kneecap seems like a mosquito bite. Rage and disgust rush through me. All of a sudden I want to make sure I get every penny my grandfather wanted me to have. I ask myself (guiltily) if it really matters how much longer my mother lives. What about my brother? He has a college-bound son and ideas for starting what could become a productive new business, but the money he needs just stagnates in a trust, generating income for an elderly woman who wants to spend it lying in pain at a nursing home.

It bothers me to have these thoughts about my mother. When we talk on the phone she has a hard time starting a conversation or sustaining one, although she can beat my sister at Scrabble and do the *New York Times* crossword puzzle. The best part of our conversation is when I suggest that we sing. I plunk out Broadway tunes on the piano and howl into the telephone as she howls back at me. We have a good laugh at the end and say good night.

As she gets older day by day, she sits more and does less. This feels like the slow coming of death, where nothing can get better, where passing through the last tunnel to the other side is inevitable but just hasn't happened yet. The waiting goes on and on. I wish I knew what she is feeling, but when I ask she changes the subject or starts to hum. I find myself imagining what I would feel being in her shoes.

Waiting is an ever-present element in my family. My father waited for his father to die, and then his father-in-law so he could get another stream of income. He never made any real effort to take care of himself. I'm proud to be different. I intend to take care of myself. I'll never put my life on hold to wait for a windfall.

~

Life or Death: Terri's Story

Terri's mother, in enormous pain from a rare and deadly cancer, wanted Terri to help her die. Terri was stunned and appalled. How could her mother put her in that position? If Terri obeyed, she would end up in prison and forever live with guilt and remorse. If she didn't, she would be denying her mother's last request.

As I sat with Terri, her mood veered wildly from one minute to the next. First she was overcome with so much fear and shame that she could hardly breathe. A moment later she imagined herself sitting in front of a huge pot of gold, counting coin after coin with the glee of a four-year-old collecting shells on the beach. Next she saw herself as a demented devil with clawed hands reaching around her mother's neck to strangle her. Amid tearful sobs, she looked at me with terror and sadness in her eyes.

I reassured her that I understood how tortured she felt. Anyone in her position would be desperately conflicted. At first Terri couldn't absorb my acceptance, sympathy, and solace. It took many sessions of listening quietly and connecting with her pain before she felt I understood the depth of her confusion and suffering. She told me she and her mother had become good friends as adults. There were hard times, too, when her mother seemed too needy and Terri had had to struggle to stay independent.

Another part of Terri's ambivalence centered on the money she would inherit. Her mother, a successful engineer, had worked to build wealth and now would not live to enjoy it. Terri's career as a visual artist was satisfying in all but the financial aspects. The inheritance would definitely improve her quality of life… but her mother had to die first.

With my assistance Terri was able to identify her mixed feelings, which gave her confidence that she would eventually mend. Her involvement with her work, and the friendship of her strong social network, helped her realize how many people loved and believed in her.

~

A Loveless Legacy: Patty's Story

Net worth is usually the deepest, darkest secret in any family. Guesswork about how much wealth a person has typically persists until the end. You probably recall the classic scene in countless movies: after the family member in question has shuffled off his or her mortal coil, the family gathers in a lawyer's office where the will is read and the camera pans across expressions of relief, consternation, dismay, or rage.

Patty's story was much like that. Her mother, Irene, had just died — a censorious woman who had lived comfortably but not extravagantly, giving Patty no idea how much money she had. Every time Patty tried to ask, her mother would shut off the discussion, accusing her of being greedy.

When Irene was dying, she insisted on taking her last breaths alone. With her final hope of closeness to her mother rejected, Patty supposed that she would be equally disappointed with whatever Irene had left her. To her enormous surprise, she was to share a $1 million legacy 50/50 with an animal shelter. How odd to feel that her mother's gift in death was more generous than anything she had provided in life!

~

It's Your Life, So Choose Well

It's normal to be intimidated by the whole idea of contemplating what will happen after you are gone. I don't expect to die soon, but I know putting one's affairs in order is part of sensible money management. A few Sundays ago, I asked the church administrator about buying a burial plot for my husband and me. In a businesslike way he asked, "Full body or cremation?" I was reeling from this bluntness when he continued, "The memorial garden is six hundred dollars and the main graveyard is eight hundred. Frankly, it's the best real estate deal on the Main Line." Choking, I managed to say that I would have to get back to him. Chances are, it will be a while before I'm ready!

Nevertheless, the passing years encourage many of us to pause and review how we want to be remembered — a process that is accelerated if we suspect death may soon be knocking at the door. One way to continue on after death is to make financial bequests that help others. Many people are guided in this process by what they value. If they love music or animals or liberal politics, they may choose to perpetuate their affinity by means of a generous gift to the symphony or the ASPCA or the Democratic Party.

People who don't have extra money for philanthropy sometimes try to assess who in the family holds the values they espouse. But when these choices are introduced, things get sticky. Suppose you have two daughters. One is living a fulfilled, productive life, grateful for your assistance in helping her reach her full potential. Your other daughter never made anything of herself, despite all you did for her. In fact, she has caused nothing but frustration and heartache. Naturally, you'd prefer to leave your money to the daughter you are proud of. But then guilt creeps in about shortchanging the other girl. Could you really be so heartless to your own flesh and blood? And how would that affect her relationship with her sister?

This dilemma, repeated again and again over the centuries, is based on uncertainty about what a legacy means. Is it a way to approve and affirm your heirs' values, a means of helping those loved ones who can benefit most from the money, a simple transfer of assets to those you have begotten, or a duty based on the sacred trust your ancestors reposed in you?

It's your money and your choice, but you're pulled back and forth by the consciousness of family blood (thicker than water, as you know). Conflicting emotions muddle your thinking and shred your decision-making abilities. The conflict is even greater if you have never established firm boundaries and expectations with your family. One thing is certain: your decision affects how you will be remembered.

If you put off this difficult choice, I can predict that you will have an even harder time making it when you are at death's door. It's awful to think of splitting your estate equally between someone you love and admire, and someone you love but have grown to distrust and disrespect. Should you be true to your own values and feelings, or is it more important to consider the long-term consequences of your decisions? There is no easy answer, except to share your concerns openly with your family from the outset.

Don't Wait Too Long to Inform Your Family

For an example of what can happen when a parent's unequal legacy is not explained to his heirs, consider the story of two sons. One son, a doctor, had earned their father's approval, while his actor brother, Russ, was viewed with skepticism. Fighting down his jealousy of his more conformist brother, Russ tried without success to please their dad. When the father died, he left two-thirds of his money to the "good" son and only a third to the son whose lifestyle he frowned on.

I suspect that Russ will never get over his hurt, anger, and resentment at this rejection from the grave. It ended his relationship with his only brother, and its scars may affect his relationship with his own children.

Could the father have remained true to himself without leaving this disaster in his wake? One obvious step would have been to inform his sons early on about the financial consequences of their career choices. Had Russ known that their dad would punish him for following his own muse instead of living a more conventional life, he would have been prepared for the lopsided legacy. Alternatively, he could have made a case to his father about the decision's unfairness and tried to work out another solution. On the father's side, such an open discussion might have shown him clearly what painful conditions he was attaching to his love.

The point is that an early conversation about your intentions gives everyone a chance to prepare. They have an opportunity to speak their minds honestly and directly before it's too late, perhaps giving you new food for thought in return.

How Old Is Your Money? Makal's Story

Another factor in planning your legacy is how long money has been in your family. Makal grew up in a family that had been wealthy for generations. Her parents had been well off before the Holocaust, but after surviving the concentration camps, they were penniless when they arrived in New York. They worked hard and made another fortune, starting with used car parts and progressing to high-revenue parking lots.

Makal grew up wrapped in financial security, expecting that she not only would get a high-paying job but also would find a husband dedicated to building a fortune at least the size of her family's. However, the fellow she married in college had different ideas. Bright, capable, and hard-working, Aaron came from a background that was comfortable but not wealthy.

When Makal brought him with her to therapy, she complained that he spent too much time playing in his beloved rock band. What was wrong with her husband that he wasn't striving hard to earn more money? Where were the new couch and the new car?

Aaron made it clear that he wasn't interested in killing himself to possess more material goods. He wanted to enjoy himself and have fun. It didn't take long for Makal to say goodbye, leave her job as a college administrator, and sign up for business school. After she and Aaron were divorced, she took up with one of their best friends, a man who had no qualms about doing whatever it took to make money.

Despite the breakup of her marriage, Makal was pleased with the way their two children had turned out. Their son, a hard worker, was just finishing law school. Their daughter had lost 20 pounds in college, which thrilled Makal because the girl now fit the role of a privileged princess scouting for her Prince Charming. She would be the fifth generation to land a rich husband, following the script written decades ago by Makal's family. Wealth has become such an aphrodisiac for the two children that they will almost certainly carry out their mother's will.

Once money has been in a family for several generations, a sense of security and identity with wealth develops, with an expectation that it will continue. As the "new money" of three generations ago matures into "old money" (or at least middle-aged money), well-established traditions are carried on. Children are coached and groomed for a life where they will lack nothing. What sometimes happens, however, is that the new generation is so far away from their enterprising, striving great-grandparents that they don't learn to make anything of their own lives.

I'll never forget one teenager I saw from such a family. He was a quirky kid, used to getting and doing whatever he wanted. Though smart, he goofed off in school, relying on his lazy charm to get out of anything he didn't want to do. He seemed to have no goals in life and drifted along from one fleeting relationship or passion to the next. His parents' warning that he had to work hard simply didn't register. What he saw from day to day was the ease of living that his family wealth made possible. Expecting to be taken care of for the rest of his life, he felt no need to push himself.

In a situation like this, I might suggest that the parents consider letting the child know that he will not be receiving most of their estate. Of course, they can set aside an amount for him — "Enough so that he can do anything, but not so much that he can do nothing," in Warren Buffett's words — but he needs to know that he is expected to live a productive life of his own.

Contrast this young man's lack of initiative with Christopher's situation. Chris is the fellow we have followed through several chapters whose late father's bankruptcy propelled him into a dogged effort to become financially secure. Brought up to be competitive, he worked hard to accomplish what his father couldn't: to become wealthy. And that he is. He still panics, though, when he thinks he doesn't have enough work lined up to keep money pouring in. Yet he once told me that if he didn't earn another nickel, he would be able to sustain his affluent lifestyle for at least 10 more years.

If Christopher's net worth keeps growing, he will have a hefty fortune to leave to his children. Having struggled up the income ladder from lower middle class to upper class, he will want to ensure that they and their families continue to enjoy this status while living out his values of hard work and personal achievement. In the end, he is going to want recognition as the one who broke the family chain of subsistence living, so it will be hard for him not to be very controlling in how he bequeaths his money.

Defining a Legacy with Grace and Dignity

There is no "approved" way to leave a legacy. It's up to you to decide what you want to do with your money and how you want to do it. Some people believe it's essential to please or accommodate members of their family. At the other extreme are self-centered people who use money as a weapon to control their heirs. Between these undesirable extremes are people who know the principles they believe in, and have a long, sustained relationship with their children or other beneficiaries. They are able to talk openly about the eventual inheritance with these heirs, ideally starting in their teenage years.

The rule of thumb (for those who could afford to follow it) was that during retirement one would live off the income from one's investments, leaving the principal as an inheritance for the kids. These days, fewer people subscribe to this rule. Rather, they plan to spend a good part of their money and leave less to their heirs. This might once have appeared selfish, but it's no longer considered selfish to spend your own money on yourself. The key, as the Greeks said, is "moderation in all things." First live the life you worked for; if anything remains, leave it to those you love. The message this legacy sends is that hard work and focus throughout life produces rewards for *you*, not just for those who live on after you — a good example for your children to follow with their own kids.

Can you bring yourself to think about leaving your assets to others? Contemplating your own death is difficult at best, and may seem impossible once you are old enough to doubt your immortality. It's easier if you have had a satisfying life and are clear about what, and whom, you believe in.

If you haven't been able to talk to your heirs because of a rift in the relationship, I urge you to make the effort anyway. Should you have developed misperceptions about them, you will not be able to correct your thinking unless you reestablish a dialogue.

The exception might be an instance where the heir is unreasonable and unwilling to talk honestly with you. This was true in Constance and Al's situation. One of their five children, Ellen, kept getting into legal and financial trouble. She would lie or tell half-truths about what was going on, seeming to get satisfaction from distressing her parents. Every time they thought she had turned over a new leaf, they were disappointed.

I urged them to keep trying to talk to her, but they were too worn down to follow my advice. Without telling Ellen, they set up a spendthrift trust for her (one whose rules strictly limit the release of trust assets) with a bank and lawyer as trustee.

Although I was upset at first with their decision, I soon realized that the struggle to talk some sense into her was hurting them and their relationship to each other. Their pain showed me how important it is for someone leaving a legacy to believe their choices are justified and to feel good about themselves. In my eagerness for Ellen's parents to work everything out with her, I had become blinded to this cardinal rule of mine.

If there's a moral here, it is this: Do what feels right at the time. If you can sleep at night, you will have done well for yourself and your family.

∾

Chapter 18 Exercise: Life After You

Does difficulty in imagining your mortality prevent you from intuiting your thoughts and feelings about it? Here's an exercise that may prove helpful:

1. Imagine your funeral in every detail, exactly as you would like it.
2. Write your eulogy. What would you wish your family and friends to say about you?
3. What would you say about yourself? What did you believe in? What did you achieve? How would you like to be remembered?

Your answers will help you see what you value and what you wish to leave behind.

Maggie's Response to the Chapter 18 Exercise:

1. Imagine your funeral in every detail, exactly as you would like it.

In a Quaker meeting I attended a while back, a striking-looking, white-haired man stood up and said, "What good is it if, at my funeral, people say what they really think of me when I'm not there to hear it? Why don't people tell me now?" That question has stayed with me and made me think that our own funeral is really for other people to gather and mourn the loss of what they knew us to be. If we design our own funeral, we can use self-knowledge to convey a picture of our lives to others so they hear directly from us what we loved and valued and want to leave behind.

I would like a non-traditional church service with lots of music, both classical and folk, and plenty of opportunity for everyone to share their thoughts about me. I would want my love of connecting and participating with other people, be it singing in the choir, working on projects, or just hanging out, to be expressed through the prayers and structure of the service.

2. Write your eulogy. What would you wish your family and friends to say about you?

My eulogy might go something like this: "Maggie worked hard and played hard. Her growing up was not easy. As a matter of fact, it took fortitude and persistence at a young age to overcome the unintended roadblocks that stood in her path early on. But through that persistence and focus, she was able to carve out a meaningful and sustainable life course that included a cherished husband and two sons, a career committed to helping others as she had been helped in her teen years, close friends, and enough money to do what she valued with her time. Her greatest wish would be to pass on to her family and friends the spirit to accomplish whatever dreams they may wish to fulfill as she watches and cheers everyone on."

3. What would you say about yourself? What did you believe in? What did you achieve? How would you like to be remembered?

I would most wish my family and friends to say that they really knew me, that I was spontaneous and fun to be with and that I was thoughtful, perceptive, and smart and that I made something out of my life.

In addition to what is in my eulogy, I would say that my aliveness came from being present in the moment with whatever I was doing and pushing as many moments as possible to the edge of discovery and authenticity. I most achieved being myself and using myself as an instrument of my interests, desires, and caring about other people. I would like to be remembered as uniquely me, a person who made a difference to others.

PART VI:

BECOMING A MONEY MASTER

If you are productive and harmonious with your money, you may need to change very little about your relationship with it. However, most of us learn the hard way, which means that it may take a big loss to prompt us to examine and improve our attitude and beliefs about money. The more you work on applying the lessons in *Crazy About Money* to your own situation, the closer you will come to the goal of becoming a Money Master.

RINO

Chapter 19:
Mission Accomplished!

NO MORE CRAZINESS ABOUT MONEY

"If you know how to spend less than you get, you have the philosopher's stone." —Benjamin Franklin

I hope the stories you've read in *Crazy About Money* have helped you realize that whatever money issues you're dealing with, you're not alone. At one time or another we all struggle to clarify our financial values. You now recognize a financial self as being part of your personality and life progress, which makes it easier to think about money and manage it well.

Still, you are part of a big crowd if you have trouble with self-esteem and wriggle out of looking at yourself, or if you struggle to be fully accountable for your thoughts, feelings, and actions. Almost everyone finds learning to respect and love themselves to be a long, slow process. As you've seen, it's a process that evolves throughout your life.

I've shown you how positive, productive thoughts and behavior can be impeded by powerful negative emotions about money. Negative emotions were bestowed on us to signal danger and help us protect ourselves, but they must be kept in their place so they don't dominate our lives. Try to regard fear and other negative emotions as red flags for trouble that you can resolve, allowing you to go on and develop positive, sustaining experiences. Of course, excessive optimism can cloud and paralyze your thinking as well. It's best to focus on your thoughts and feelings, identify what they are, and then ask yourself what you really want. If you practice this discipline regularly, it will help free you up to set goals and work toward them more effectively.

Your Financial Self

Who is your financial self? What does money mean to you, and what is your relationship to it? Have you determined whether you are a Spender, Hoarder, or some other money type? Have you identified old childhood money scripts, challenged them and thrown out the parts that don't work and enhanced the parts that do?

No matter who you are now, the roots of this identity started forming in your childhood and evolved during each subsequent stage of psychological development. Like most children, you were probably introduced to money at a very early age. You may have noticed funny pieces of paper in Mom's handbag or heard coins jingle in Dad's pocket. Eventually you realized that at the store, they had to hand over some of the paper, the coins, or a little plastic card in order to take things home.

You probably didn't feel a sense of ownership about money until you were given an allowance or payment for doing chores. I believe allowances are most meaningful when they are received as a reward for doing assigned tasks, thus linking the concepts of work and pay. Ownership develops further once a child is old enough to do jobs outside the home, like managing a paper route or doing yard work for neighbors.

Adolescence is a crucial time in the development of a financial self. It's healthy for teenagers to earn money to pay for clothes, a cell phone, etc., or to save for a big-ticket expense like a car and car insurance. Some parents insist on a total commitment to schoolwork, and discourage their teen from working during the school year. However, adolescence is an important time not just to establish independence and identity, but also to lay the foundation of a healthy relationship with money. The attitudes you develop in these early years will affect how you think about money and how you manage it for the rest of your life.

The next tipping point in establishing a financial self is getting a job. If it doesn't pay enough to fund your preferred lifestyle, you'll have to decide whether to work harder to earn more, live on less, or (the worst option) borrow on your credit card in order to keep going. Settling down, often with a partner, speaks eloquently of your success in managing money so far. Can you qualify for a mortgage? Will you finance the purchase by yourself, or will your parents help you?

Your financial independence and strategic ability to manage money will set the stage for further accomplishments as you develop your career and/or raise children. If you have been able to develop a cohesive sense of your money self, it will pay off in the later stages of life, allowing you to reap the rewards of fulfilled needs and values.

Where Are They Now?

Do any of the people you've met in my stories impress you as heading toward money mastery? Let's check in on a few of them.

TERRI

You may recall that when her pain-wracked mother, Irene, asked Terri to help her die, Terri became tremendously distraught. Grief overcame her when her mother finally passed away. Irene's request had stirred up such a maelstrom of love and hate that Terri was immobilized for several months after her mother's death. She tried to return to painting, but found she had no heart for it. When Irene's estate was distributed and Terri learned that she had inherited hundreds of thousands of dollars, her feelings of guilt and depression impelled her to consider donating the money to medical research.

Fortunately for her own future, she continued therapy before acting on this impulse. She began to understand that she was punishing herself for having negative feelings toward her mother, whom she fundamentally had loved. Irene's request to help her die had put Terri in a horrible bind that her mother didn't comprehend. It was not the first time Irene had failed to understand Terri's point of view. Terri remembered wanting to wear a dress to the junior prom like the ones the other girls had, but her mother picked a dress that was to her own taste and insisted that Terri wear it. Similar incidents echoed in her mind as she tried to deal with what she was learning in therapy: that she had a right to her own feelings, that it was important to nurture and protect these feelings, and that she was not responsible for the way her mother behaved.

Terri's growing belief in herself aroused positive ideas and feelings that combated the negative self-perceptions she had felt earlier. Instead of giving the money away, she found someone to help her invest it wisely. Occasionally it occurred to her that she would be punished for acting so boldly in her own behalf, but when nothing bad happened, her relief and optimism about the future were restored.

SYLVIA

Sylvia, the CEO of a nonprofit organization, came to therapy for "an exorcism" because she couldn't get rid of anxiety about her money, on and off the job. When she came to understand that her parents' expectations of her were their ideas, not her own, she began to wriggle free of their perceptions. As she found her own voice and learned to like it, Sylvia experienced the excitement of trusting her own ideas. She became brave enough to create a new company division, even though it meant raising capital. Her fear of managing her own and her company's money diminished as she sought active advice from financial specialists whom she chose herself.

Another worry Sylvia shared in therapy was that she would have no one to care for her if she fell ill, because she had too little money to hire nursing assistance. But as her confidence in managing her savings grew, her mental images of being a bag lady on the street faded.

In the end, this Money Worrier didn't exactly get an exorcism, but she did learn to keep her money devils at bay. By putting money in perspective, Silvia was able to look to the future with less worry and learn to set constructive goals for herself.

JOEL

The Depression-era mentality of Joel's parents no longer dictates his financial choices. Instead of being shackled to the idea of waiting until he can pay with cash, he is planning to borrow money to expand his business. Lately, though, he has begun to worry about keeping up with his wife's spending. I would like him to talk with her and reach an agreement about limiting her purchases.

Unfortunately, Joel isn't able to put his foot down. Instead he has tried to resolve his money anxiety by earning more income. He's an expert on several money-making schemes, from buying tax-acquired property for the cost of its tax lien to collecting interest on credit card debt he has bought. Why is he doing this, when he has become more comfortable with risk-taking and intends to invest borrowed money in his company? Shouldn't he be cured of his obsession with financial security by now?

Well, yes and no. Joel is better in many respects, but he still wants the ultimate security of many income streams besides his core business. One day, he hopes, he will find the "perfect" scheme: profitable enough to be worthwhile, yet completely risk-free.

CHRISTOPHER

Christopher continues to make buckets of money. His "thrill of the deal" is as fresh and new as ever, and he is sure he is on the right road for himself and his family. Although his wife and children no doubt enjoy their financial ease, they don't appreciate conversations with him being fitted in around his cell phone calls, or the weariness that makes him a zombie when he comes home from work.

Christopher cares about them, but he can't quit his addiction to fast-breaking deals. Even when he shuts off his cell phone and computer to make time for himself and his wife, his mind inevitably wanders back to business and new ideas for more deals.

Christopher feels he hasn't yet reached the "screw you" stage that will allow him to say no to any demand that comes his way. To his credit, he is now able to laugh at himself because he realizes he will not end up like his father with only $30,000 to his name. However, the amount he needs for living expenses keeps climbing, and he may never feel as if he has attained his deeply desired state of financial nirvana. I hope he will keep working to set a firm goal, and will adjust his mental math at that point to accept that he has "enough" and can finally relax.

DEVON AND MARTHA

The most exciting development for Devon and Martha is their growing ability to listen to each other. They may not like what the other person is saying, but instead of firing back in anger, they wait their turn and try to address each other's concerns. Martha is learning to accept that Devon did not become disorganized simply to make her life more difficult, but because depression robbed him of his organizational abilities. Devon is working hard to understand why he settles for short-term gratification, when delaying might produce a more satisfying outcome. He is learning not to blame others for his own lack of follow-through.

Martha still worries about their debt, but she sees they are making progress and is more optimistic that one day they will catch up. She is pleased at Devon's success in finding low-interest credit cards. Instead of focusing all her energy on him, she has begun to take her own achievements more seriously and recently launched a computer business on her own. The most satisfying improvement in their relationship is that they've recently started saying what they appreciate in each other.

~

HEATHER

Heather, the English professor who fell apart when her husband left her for another man, ended up many thousands of dollars in debt after ignoring her bills. Because of her rapid improvement in therapy, Heather recovered enough to ask her family to help her pay off her debts. They agreed to do this by selling a family business that was no longer providing much income. When Heather heard that she would receive $90,000 from the sale – more than she needed to take care of her bills — she was so elated that she abruptly ended therapy. I can understand how she must feel at having been relieved of her shame and confusion, but it concerns me that she may repeat the mistakes that got her into trouble.

I gave her the name of an investment advisor who could help her establish a basic budget and invest her newfound money sensibly. However, she did not follow through on this recommendation and refused to answer my follow-up phone calls. I worry that she will ride the blissful wave of her windfall and, having failed to change her money attitudes, will end up in debt just as she was before seeing me. Heather is an example of someone who found temporary relief to be so intense and gratifying that she mistook it for a solution to her ongoing money avoidance. Only time will tell whether she is still "crazy about money."

~

MY OWN STORY

I have never been in a better place with money. Writing and teaching about my own and my clients' experiences and vulnerability, I have gained deep appreciation for the complexity of money matters. Every time I do something wrong, I struggle to master my own misperceptions and mistakes.

I am our family's primary money manager now, with input from my husband and direction from our trusted broker and financial advisor. Although I miss the excitement of higher-risk investments, we have learned to celebrate our gains. Wisdom may feel boring in the short term, like moving at turtle speed, but I know it pays off over the long term.

I can still wake up in the morning wondering in panic if we will have enough, but at this point I'm not sure what "enough" really means. In any case the feeling passes as I get into the day, taking advantage of my signature strengths and focusing on current pleasures and pursuits.

One of my deepest satisfactions is seeing what my sons have learned about money from witnessing my pain and eventual mastery of it. Now in their 20s, they understand the hard work involved in earning money and are conscious of how they spend it. My younger son, who helped me edit this book, has given me insight into how his generation views money and emotions. He takes advantage of our financial advisor's counsel, creates spreadsheets for his budget, contributes regularly to his 401(k), and enjoys having money left over for fun because he plans so well. I may never be as financially confident as he has learned to be, but I will certainly give him a run for his money!

∾

The Money Master

We've reviewed various money types in earlier chapters — for example, the Amasser and the Money Monk — but there's one I've saved for last: the Money Master. This term was popularized by pioneer financial psychologist Dr. Kathleen Gurney, whose research in the early 1980s identified nine different groups with characteristic attitudes and feelings about money, money management, and investments. The members of one particular group were wise financial decision makers, successful in accumulating assets, and likely to be very involved in managing their money. Confident of their future financial security, they were generally content with their financial achievements. Interestingly, they were also likely to trust the honesty of other people when dealing with their money. Dr. Gurney dubbed this group the "Money Masters."

It takes time and lots of practice to become a Money Master. According to Dr. Gurney's study, 38% of them are 60 or older. They are likely to be college graduates, but their attitudes are more important than their years of education:

- Money Masters are in control; their emotions don't control them.
- They have developed a secure sense of themselves, both financially and personally.
- They are good at setting goals and executing them.
- They are actively engaged in managing their money, but are willing to consult with financial professionals whose judgment they trust.
- They have a strong work ethic and take pride in what they have accomplished.
- They have found the optimum balance between mastery of money and the self-satisfaction, contentment, and sense of security it creates.

In other words, Money Masters work hard and enjoy to the utmost what they have achieved. They epitomize Lao-Tzu's adage: "He who knows much about others may be learned, but he who understands himself is more intelligent. He who controls others may be powerful, but he who has mastered himself is mightier still." I'd broaden this epigram to include both genders — and support it wholeheartedly.

~

A Psychologist's Take on Money Masters

Having read this far, you know that my basic message is the importance of understanding your emotional reactions to money so you can make it work for you. One reason why Money Masters are successful is because they score low in emotionality — the degree of positive or negative emotions felt. They consider money rationally, as a tool to buy security, happiness, and peace of mind. They have worked hard to experience and understand their emotions (not just deny them), so emotions no longer impede their ability to use money effectively. In addition, Money Masters score low in anxiety when making financial decisions. A mistake does not cause them to doubt their judgment. If they discover they've made a bad investment decision, for example, their sense of self remains intact.

Money Masters don't really have a money-making secret. What they do have are attitudes that foster financial success. They have developed a strong financial self and are high in feelings of self-esteem and personal worth. They feel contented and secure. They believe they can accomplish their goals and trust others they deem trustworthy. It's worth noting that they also believe their self-confidence gives them more security than the money they have accumulated.

It's Not 'Only Money'

When someone says, "It's only money," it usually isn't. When they say, "It's not about the money," it usually is. That's how reluctant most people are to be frank about what money means. We all carry around emotions and thought patterns from years ago that are now embedded in our money attitudes and behavior. We may think we're simply dealing with the facts, but emotions are always a part of how we understand the facts.

If you actively try to identify these feelings and thoughts, you will be much closer to managing your money rationally and effectively. Keep an open dialogue going with your spouse or partner, and focus on using your signature strengths as much as you can through the day. These qualities, honed through use, will help you clarify other important values. For example, if you are a doer and like helping people, using these strengths daily in your job and/or personal life will make you feel good about yourself.

As you glow with pleasure, you may imagine doing something else that will lead you to new, interesting pursuits. If you are spending your time doing things you don't like or feel bad about yourself for other reasons, there will not be the time or energy to imagine all the good and pleasurable things you could be doing and achieving. In other words, positivity brings more good feelings, while beating yourself up takes time and energy away from taking really good care of yourself.

Where Do You Go from Here?

Right now, I hope you feel excited and motivated to take charge of your money and put it to work for you. At the same time you may hesitate, scratch your head, and wonder exactly what your first step is. I want *you* to think of your first step. Maybe it means being more honest with yourself, or speaking more honestly and directly to a partner or spouse, or perhaps finding the right financial advisor. Once you have committed yourself to that first step, I can suggest things to do next.

Let's say you decide your first step is finding out exactly where all your money goes. You have committed to writing down all your daily expenses so you can view your entire financial picture at the end of the month. OK, so you accomplish that and you see that you need to be more careful about making money choices that reflect your most cherished values. Good step! Next, you might decide what you want to do about saving and investing. Is it something you want to do by yourself? Rereading the chapter on investing will remind you of your choices. Then decide what you want to do. The main thing is not to put off decision-making. DO IT NOW. You can always change your mind later, if need be.

When you reflect on what it takes to be a Money Master, you may think, "How can I ever get there? I'm so far away from money mastery that I'll never catch up." But through persistent small steps that lead to small changes that build up into big changes, you can grow toward money mastery. Rome was not built in a day, and neither is wisdom about money. Remember, 38% of Money Masters are 60 or older. Mastering money may take months of changing your beliefs, attitudes, emotions, and behavior, but the result is worth it!

Final Exercise: Changing Your Life

1. What is the most important lesson you have learned from reading *Crazy About Money*?
2. What are some of the other lessons?
3. As you put this book down, what changes are you willing to commit to and work on?
4. What would you tell a friend about your experience with *Crazy About Money*?

No Longer Crazy (After All This Time!)

When people are crazy about money, it's because their emotions have become tangled with their thinking and their thinking has grains of truth but not the whole truth, something I might call "truthiness." Since we're all emotional beings, you may not be able to avoid slipping into occasional craziness about money. But the more mindfully you can apply what you've learned from my comments and the exercises you have done, the more balanced you will feel. Be compassionate toward yourself when you make mistakes, and learn from them. Even Zen masters never give up striving to improve.

Once your money devils are quelled, you will be free to enjoy yourself without emotions confusing your decisions. You will find you have more energy to enjoy what is most important in your life... because you're no longer crazy about money.

References

Akerlof, George A. and Robert J. Shiller, 2009. *Animal Spirits: How Human Psychology Drive the Economy, and Why It Matters for Global Capitalism*. Princeton, NJ: Princeton University Press.

Ariely, Dan, 2008. *Predictably Irrational: The Hidden Forces That Shape Our Decisions.* New Your: Harper Collins.

Azar-Rucquoi, Adele, 2002. *Money As Sacrament: Finding the Sacred in Money.* Berkeley, CA: Celestial Arts.

Beebe, Beatrice and Lachmann, Frank, 2004. *Infant Research and Adult Treatment*. New York: Routledge, Talyor and Frances Group.

Benson, April, 2000. Ed., *I Shop, Therefore I Am.* Lanham MD: Rowman & Little Publishers, Inc.

Belsky, Gary and Thomas Gilovich, 1999. *Why Smart People Make Big Money Mistakes And How To Correct Them.* New York: Simon and Schuster Paperbacks.

Bernstein, Peter L., 1996. Against The Odds: *The Remarkable Story of Risk*. New York: John Wiley & Sons, Inc.

Bodnar, Janet, 2005. *Raising Money Smart Kids.* Chicago, IL: Kaplan Publishing.

Budge, Scott G., 2008. *The New Financial Advisor: Strategies for Successful Family Wealth Management*. New York: John Wiley & Sons, Inc.

Brafman, Ori and Brafman, Rom, 2008. *Sway: The Irresistible Pull of Irrational Behavior.* New York: Broadway Books.

Condon, Gerald M. and Condon, Jeffrey L., 2001. *Beyond the Grave: The Right Way and the Wrong Way of Leaving Money to Your Children (and Others).* New York: HarperCollins Publishers, Inc.

Diener, Ed and Biswas-Diener, Robert, 2008. *Happiness: Unlocking the Mysteries of Psychological Wealth.* Victoria, Australia: Blackwell Publishing.

Domini, Amy L. with Pearne, Dennis & Rich, Sharon L., 1998. *The Challenges of Wealth: Mastering the Personal and Financial Conflicts.* Homewood, Ill: Dow Jones-Irwin.

Frank, Robert, 2007. *Richistan: A Journey Through the American Wealth Boom and the Lives of the New Rich.* New York: Crown Publishers.

Frey, Bruno and Stutzer, Alois, eds., 2007. *Economic and Psychology: A Promising New Cross-Disciplinary Field.* Boston: The MIT Press.

Gallo, Eileen and Gallo, Jon, 2002. *Silver Spoon Kids: How Successful Parents Raise Responsible Children.* New York: McGraw-Hill.

Geist, Richard, 2003. *Investor Therapy.* New York: Crown Business.

Gilbert, Daniel, 2006. *Stumbling on Happiness.* New York: Alfred A. Knopf.

Glassman. Saly A., 2010. *It's About More Than the Money: Investment Wisdom for Building a Better Life.* Upper Saddle River, NJ: Pearson Education, Inc.

Gurney, Kathleen, 1988. *Your Money Personality: What It Is and How You Can Profit from It.* New York: Doubleday.

Harman, Hollis Page, 1999. *Money Sense for Kids.* New York: Barron's Educational Series, Inc.

Kahler, Rick and Fox, Kathleen, 2005. *Conscious Finance: Uncover Your Hidden Money Beliefs and Transform the Role of Money in Your Life.* Rapid City, SD: Foxcraft, Inc.

Kahneman, D., & Tversky, A.,1984. Choices, values and frames. *American Psychologist, 39,* 341–350.

Kahneman, D., & Tversky, A. (Eds.). (2000). *Choices, values and frames.* New York: Cambridge University Press.

Kansas, Dave, 2005. *The Wall Street Journal: Complete Money & Investing Guidebook.* New York: Three Rivers Press.

Kenneth M. and Morris, Virginia B. *The Wall Street Journal Guide to Understanding Personal Finance,* 1997. Morris, New York: Lightbulb Press.

Kessel, Brent, 2008. *it's not about the money: unlock your money type to achieve spiritual and financial abundance.* New York: HarperCollins.

Kinder, George, 1999. *Seven Stages of Money Maturity.* New York: Dell Publishing.

Mellan, Olivia and Christie, Sherry. *The Client Connection: Helping Advisors Build Bridges That Last,* 2009. The National Underwriting Company.

Klein, Stefan, 2002. *The Science of Happiness: How Our Brains Make Us Happy—and What We Can Do to Get Happier.* New York: Marlowe and Company.

Klontz, Ted, Kahler, Rick and Klontz, Brad, 2006. *The Financial Wisdom of Ebenezer Scrooge: Transforming Your Relationship with Money.* Deerfield Beach, FL: Health Communications.

Klontz, Brad and Klontz, Ted, 2009. *Mind Over Money: Overcoming the Money Disorders That Threaten Our Financial Health.* New York: Broadway Books.

Lawrence-Lightfoot, Sara, 2009. *The Third Chapter: Passion, Risk and Adventure in the 25 Years After 50.* New York: Farrar, Strauss and Giroux.

Lifson, Lawrence E. and Geist, Richard, 1999. *The Psychology of Investing.* New York: John Wiley & Sons, Inc.

Malkiel, Burton G., 1996. *A Random Walk Down Wall Street.* 1996. W. W. Norton & Company, Inc.

Mellan, Olivia, 1994. *Money Harmony: Resolving Money Conflicts in Your Life and Relationships.* New York: Walker & Company.

Mellan, Olivia with Sherry Christie, 1995. *Overcoming Overspending: A Winning Plan for Spenders and Their Partners.* New York: Walker & Company

Mellan, Olivia and Christie, Sherry, 2001. *Money Shy to Money Sure: A Woman's Roadmap to Financial Well-Being.* New York: Walker Publishing Company.

Mellan, Olivia and Christie, Sherry, 2009. *The Client Connection: Building Bridges That Last.* Erlanger, KY: The National Underwriter Company.

Needleman, Jacob, 1991. *Money and the Meaning of Life.* New York: Doubleday.

Nemeth, Maria, 1997. *The Energy of Money.* New York: The Ballantine Publishing Group.

Opdyke, Jeff D. *The Wall Street Journal: Personal Finance Workbook.* New York: Three Rivers Press.

Perle, Liz, 2006. *Money, A Memoir: Women, Emotions and Cash.* New York: Henry Holt and Company, LLC.

Politser, Peter, 2008. *Neuroeconomics: A Guide to the New Science of Making Choices.* New York: Oxford University Press.

Reed, Audrey, 2002. *Money Toolbox for Women: Simple Solutions for Mastering Your Money.* Minden, Nevada: Works In Progress, Inc.

Ruffenach, Glenn & Greene, Kelly, 2007. *The Wall Street Journal: Complete Retirement Guidebook: How to Plan It, Live It and Enjoy It.* New York: Three Rivers Press.

Schott, John W. with Jean Arbeiter, 1998. *Mind Over Money: Match Your Personality to a Winning Financial Strategy.* New York: Little Brown and Company.

Seligman, Martin, 2004. *Authentic Happiness.* New York: Simon & Schuster Adult Publishing Group

Shefrin, Hersh, 2000. *Beyond Greed and Fear.* Boston: Harvard Business School Press.

Siegel, Daniel, 1999. *The Developing Mind: How Relationships and the Brain Interact to Shape Who We Are.* New York: The Guilford Press.

Stiles, Paul, 2005. *Is the American Dream Killing You?* New York: HarperCollins Publishers, Inc.

Stone, Arthur A., Schwartz, Joseph E., Broderick, Joan E. and Deaton, Angus. Kahneman, Daniel, ed. "A snapshot of the age distribution of psychological well-being in the United States." *PNAS*, vol. 107, no. 22, June 1, 2010.

Thaler, Richard and Sunstein, Cass R. 2008. *Nudge:* Improving Decisions About Health, Wealth and Happiness. New Haven: Yale University Press.

Tisdale, Stacey and Kennedy, Paula Boyer, 2007. *The True Cost of Happiness: The Real Story Behind Managing Your Money.* New York: John Wiley and Sons, Inc.

Tversky, A., & Kahneman, D., 1981. "The framing of decisions and the psychology of choice." *Science, 211*, 453–458.

Nouwen, Henri, et. al., Schut, Michael, ed., 2008. *Money & Faith: The Search for Enough*. Denver, CO: Morehouse Education Resources.

Stanley, Thomas J., 2001. *The Millionaire Mind.* Kansas City, KA: Andrew McMeel Publishing.

Stanley, Thomas J. and Danko, William D., 1996. *The Millionaire Next Door: The Surprising Secrets of America's Wealthy.* New York: MJF Books.

Twist, Lynne, 2003. *The Soul of Money: Reclaiming the Wealth of Our Inner Resources.* New York: W. W. Norton & Company.

Wilder, Barbara, 1998. *Money Is Love.* Boulder, CO: Wild Ox Press. Wilkov, Jennifer, 2006. *Dating Your Money: How to Build a Long-Lasting Relationship with Your Money in 8 Easy Steps.* Brooklyn, NY: ESP Press.

Zweig, Jason, 2007. Your Money and Your Brain: How the New Science of Neuroeconomics Can Help Make You Rich. New York: Simon & Schuster.

USEFUL WEBSITES

LINKS:

authentichappiness.com: interactive site about happiness

barbaramitchell.com: counseling for psychological aspects of money issues

basic.esplanner.com: offers free strategies for achieving retirement goals and more

betterinvesting.org: official National Association of Investors Corporation website

cardweb.com: everything you need to know about merchant cards

financialrecovery.com: program to undo money paralysis

kahlerfinancial.com: "cutting edge" financial planner

maggiebakerphd.com: counseling for psychological aspects of money issues

mint.com: budgeting management

moneyharmony.com: financial coaching, intergenerational retreats, teleclasses

nerdwallet.com: everything you need to know about credit cards

portfoliomonkey.com: investment guidance

rgrandy@capitolsecuritiescom: "cutting edge" financial broker/advisor/planner

shopaholicnomore.com: structured programs to overcome spending

ACKNOWLEDGMENTS

I want to thank all my clients who gave me permission to share their stories in the composite illustrations that are the heart and soul of the book. Thanks also to my family, in particular, my husband, Howard, and my son, Alec, and Abi Wolfe for all their consistent and cogent conceptual and editorial help. *Crazy About Money* grew in clarity and cohesion with the unflinching help of my editor, Sherry Christie. Thanks also to my son Nick for his marketing wisdom and to Bill Gross for his public speaking and marketing coaching.

Other consistent advise and emotional encouragement came from my developmental editors, Rev. Barbara Abbott and the Church of the Redeemer Women's Retreat, Sharon Lee, and my Telemony Financial Therapy Advisory Group: Olivia Mellan, Barbara Mitchell, LCSW and April Benson, Ph. D. and, of course, by my financial advisor, Bob Grandy. AAMS. Thanks also to Chuck Anderson and Naomi Reiskind, Ph. D. who acted as my "third ear" about book ideas and editing, marketing and general business decisions. Cartoons and the cover illustration were thankfully rendered by Christophe Pouchet and Jonathan Kirk, respectively.

A general thanks goes to all my friends and acquaintances who have generously listened to my adventures writing Crazy About Money.

INDEX

abnormal genes, 56
Ackerman, Diane, quotation, 47
Adams, Scott, quotation, 61
addiction
brain function and, 280–281
catastrophe as motivation to control, 285–286
euphoria and, 279
gambling and, 274–275
rat experiment analogy and, 277
adolescence. *See* teen years stage
adulthood stage. *See* money beliefs, and effects in life stages
advisors. *See* brokers; financial advisors
aggression, 53–54
aggressive growth risk profile, 265
aggressive self-promotion, 16
aging process, 55–57
allowance payments for children, 85, 334
Alzheimer's disease, 55, 56
the Amasser, 118–119, 178–180, 219–220
amygdala, 75
anchoring effect, 68–69, 72, 253
anger-rage, 14
annihilation anxiety, 307, 309–310
anxiety-anguish, 14
APOE-e4 gene, 56
attitudes about money. *See* money scripts; money types
the Authoritarian, 261
authority, attitudes toward, 142–143

baby boomer generation, 281–282, 310
back to back communication method, 223–224
Baker, Maggie
approach to therapy, 2, 6. *See also specific clinical stories*
money analogy of, 45
personal stories, 4–6, 50–51, 65–66, 87–89, 169–170, 177, 214–216, 249–252, 254–255, 264–265, 267, 302–303, 318–319, 341

balanced life, 13–24
  happiness and wealth, 18–19
  innate emotions and, 14–15
  money scripts and, 16–17
  perceived threats and, 13–14
  Seligman's levels of happiness, 18–22
Baldwin, James A., quotation, 83
basic needs, 17, 18
Beebe, Beatrice, 84
behavioral economics, 61–80
  anchoring effect, 68–69, 72, 253
  clinical stories, 61–62
  confirmation bias, 72
  endowment effect, 70–71, 253
  herd instinct, 71–72, 253, 282
  loss aversion, 63–64, 66, 73–74, 76–77, 253
  mental accounting, 66–70, 220–222, 253, 298
  origins of, 62–63
  practical application of, 73–74
  status quo bias, 65, 253
  sunk hole fallacy, 64, 253
beliefs, 16
  See also money beliefs, and effects in life stages; money scripts
bequests, 322–323
  See also legacies
Berchtold, Nicole C., 56–57
Billings, Josh, quotation, 177
the Binger, 116
biology and behavior, 47–59
  age-based differences, 51–52
  aging process and, 55–57
  brain as decision engine, 47–49
  gender-based differences, 52–55, 56–57
  hormones, 53–54, 75–76, 100, 101
  memory and, 48–50, 56
  neurons, 49, 55
  See also brain
blaming and "bad" events, 300–302
blind spot, definition of, 6
brain
  addiction and, 280–281
  age-based differences, 51–52
  aging process and, 55–57
  changing your mind and effect on, 49
  as decision engine, 47–49
  dopamine deficit, 100–101
  hemispheres of, 53, 54–55
  during illness, 50–51
  image technology and neuro-economics, 75
  information processing, 47–50
  limbic system, 280–281
  memory and, 48–50
  pleasure and, 252–253
  teenagers and, 52, 99–100
  worrying patterns and, 198–199
  See also biology and behavior
Broderick, Joan E., 307

brokers
- assessing need for, 256–260
- coordination with psychologists, 8
- criteria for choosing, 262–264
- definition of, 259
- emotions of, 66
- interviewing of, 262–263
- licensing of, 259
- limitations of, 5–8, 254–255, 259–260
- types of, 261–262
- *See also* investing, approaches to

Buffett, Warren, quotations, 249, 326

childhood stage, 83–98
- allowance payments for chores, 85, 334
- blaming selves, 301
- clinical stories, 86, 90–94
- explanation of, 334
- industriousness and later success, 85–86
- influences during infancy, 84–85
- long term effects of trauma, 14
- parental limits and, 85–86

the Churner, 261

communication
- ability to discuss money scripts, 95, 168–169, 213, 223–224
- back to back method, 223–224
- empathic listening, 223–224
- gender-based differences, 54
- mutual understanding, 207–208
- negative comments, 74
- with prospective heirs, 322–324, 327–328
- respect, 207–208

computer dating, 190

confirmation bias, 72

consequences of actions, thinking about, 52

conservative risk profile, 265

the Conserver, 120–121

Consumer Federation of America, 163

couples relationships, 207–227
- adjusting to partner's money script, 223–224
- clinical stories, 208, 210–212, 216–217, 219–222
- empathic listening, 223–224
- lying/deception in, 208–213
- marriage commitment and, 210–213

courage, as signature strength, 20

the Cowboy, 261

credit card debt, 192–193, 281–283

Dalai Lama, 145

the Dealer, 121–122

Deaton, Angus, 307

debt
- clinical stories, 283–284, 285–286
- from credit card use, 192–193, 281–283

emotions and, 284–285
historical perspective on, 281–283
See also gambling and debt
dementia, 50, 57
denial/dissociation, 16
The Developing Mind (Siegel), 53
dihydrotestosterone (DHT), 75–76
discount brokerages, 256
dissmell-disgust, 15
divorce, and money scripts, 229–235
dopamine deficit, 100–101
Dylan, Bob, quotation, 317

emotional isolation, of single adults, 196–197
emotions
acknowledging of, 128, 344
addiction and, 275–276
as amplifiers of experiences, 15, 114–115, 275–276
beliefs and, 16
brain function and, 50
debt and, 284–285
definition of, 14–15
identification of, 1–2, 7–8
innate, 14–15
money scripts and, 15–17
perceived threats and, 13–14
positive emotions, 14, 15
See also money scripts; negative emotions
empathic listening, 223–224
Employee Benefit Research Institute, 294
empowerment
healthy narcissism and, 2
self-understanding and, 1–2
therapy and, 7–8
See also sense of self
endowment effect, 70–71, 253
enjoyment-joy, 15
entitlement, sense of, 16, 147–148
Erikson, Erik, 298, 306
euphoria, 272, 279
experience, information processing and, 50
extreme expressiveness, 2
See also money types

Fads and Fallacies in the Social Sciences (Goldberg), 53–54
fatigue, brain function and, 50
fear-terror, 14
Federal Reserve, on credit card debt, 283
fiduciary responsibility, 259–260
financial advisors
assessing need for, 256–260
criteria for choosing, 262–264
definition of, 259–260
interviewing of, 262–263
licensing of, 259–260
Financial Industry Regulatory Authority (FINRA), 259
financial planners
certification of, 260
coordination with psychologists, 7–8
definition of, 260
retirement planning and, 298

financial self
elements of, 334–335
of the Money Master, 343–344
See also money scripts; *specific stages of life*
Foreman, George, quotation, 293
401(k), 219, 256, 293, 300
Franklin, Benjamin, quotations, 161, 333
Frick, James W., quotation, 27

gambling and debt, 271–287
addictive behavior, 274–279
allure of, 271–272
chip on the shoulder mentality and, 278
clinical stories, 272–273, 274–275, 276–277, 278–279
healthy approach to, 276
leveraging investments as, 276–277
self-loathing and, 278–279
See also debt
Gandhi, Mahatma, quotation, 1
gay and lesbian relationships, 199–201, 219–220
gender
aggression and, 53–54
brain function and, 52–55
changing social attitudes about, 54
gene expression and, 56–57
hormones and, 53–54, 75–76
gene expression, 56–57
Generation X, 142–143
generativity vs. stagnation, 298, 306, 312–313
Goldberg, Steven, 53–54
Gottman, John, 74
gratification, ability to delay, 280–281
Great Recession (2008), 48, 300
grieving, 235, 237
growth risk profile, 265
Gurney, Kathleen, 342

happiness
of meaning/purpose, 21
in older age, 307
Seligman's levels of, 18–22
wealth creation and, 18–19
healthy narcissism, 2
heirs, discussions with, 322–324, 327–328
hemispheres of brain, 53, 54–55
herd instinct, 71–72, 253, 282
the Hoarder, 115, 210–213, 219–220
the Holistic Advisor, 261–262
hormones
gender and, 53–54, 75–76
of teenagers, 100, 101
trust-distrust dynamic and, 75–76
How We Decide (Lehrer), 76
humanity/love, as signature strength, 20

illness, brain function and, 50–51
industriousness in childhood, 85–86

infancy stage, 84
information processing
brain function and, 47–50
confirmation bias, 72
emotions and, 14–15
obstructions to, 50–51
inheritances. *See* legacies
interest rates, 135, 163–164, 282, 298
interest-excitement, 15
Internal Revenue Service (IRS), 293
interviews, of financial professionals, 262–263
investing, approaches to, 249–269
assessing need for professionals, 256–260
author's personal story, 249–252, 254–255, 264–265, 267
choosing financial professionals, 261–264
commitment requirement, 257–258
emotions and, 266
investment clubs, 255, 257–258, 267
leveraging as gambling, 276–277
one-time consultations, 258
risk tolerance profiles, 265–266
suitability rule, 259

Jefferson, Thomas, 19
jobs, signature strengths in, 21

Kahler, Rick, 16
Kahneman, Daniel, 62
Keller, Helen, quotation, 229
Kiplinger's Personal Finance, 257
Klontz, Brad, 16
Klontz, Ted, 16
Kohut, Heinz, 307

Lachmann, Frank, 84
Lao-Tzu, quotation, 343
left-hemisphere tasks, 53, 54
legacies, 317–330
clinical stories, 320–321, 323–327, 328
discussions with heirs about, 322–324, 327–328
financial bequests, 322–323
writing wills, 201
Lehrer, Jonas, 76
Lennon, John, quotation, 99
lesbian and gay relationships, 199–201, 219–220
leveraging of investments, 276–277
life expectancy, 293, 298
life review process, 298–299
limbic system, 280–281
the Listener, 261, 262
listening skills, 223–224
lizard brain, 280–281
long-term care insurance, 195
long-term memory, 48
loss, 65, 235, 237
loss aversion, 63–64, 66, 73–74, 76–77, 253

Madoff, Bernie, 17
magazines, 257
marriage, 189, 210–213
    See also couples relationships
McKinsey & Company, 294
Mellan, Olivia, 31, 113–114, 150
memory, 48–50, 56
men
    aggression and, 53–54
    gene expression in, 56–57
    hormones and, 53–54, 75–76
    risk of dementia in, 57
mental accounting, 66–70, 220–222, 253, 298
midlife stage, 177–185
    clinical stories, 178–179, 180–181
    as reflection stage, 178, 181–182
    See also retirement stage
Millennials generation, 142–143
moderate risk profile, 265
Money, 257
the Money Avoider, 117–118, 164–167, 180–181
money beliefs, and effects in life stages, 133–246
    during 19-21 age period, 133–140
    during 21-30 age period, 141–158
    during 30s age period, 161–176
    during 40s/50s age period, 177–185
    clinical stories, 134–136, 142, 143–153, 165–166, 167–168, 178–179, 180–181, 191–192, 193–194, 195–196, 197–198, 199–200, 208, 210–212, 216–217, 219–222, 231, 232–233, 236
    couples relationships, 207–227
    divorce and, 229–235
    financial balance, 167–168, 219–220
    Rule of 72 and, 163–164
    singlehood, 189–204
    widowhood, 235–238
    See also specific stages of life
the Money Master, 333–346
    author's personal story, 341
    clinical stories, 336–340
    description of, 342–343
    low emotionality of, 343–344
the Money Monk, 30–31, 117, 164–165, 216–218
money scripts
    overview, 27–46
    ability to discuss, 95, 168–169, 213, 223–224
    childhood and. *See* childhood stage
    clinical stories, 27–28, 30, 32–43
    as consolation, 33–34
    definition of, 16
    as entitlement, 38–39

healthy examples of, 17
infancy, influences during, 84–85
as necessary evil, 30–31
negative emotions and, 16–17, 124
as obstacle to altruism, 41–42
as other's responsibility, 42–44
reward deficiency syndrome, 100–101
rewriting of, 148–154
as security, 27–29
as self-confidence, 39–40
as self-esteem, 34–36
as self-importance, 36–37
as substitute for love, 32–33
teen years and. *See* teen years stage
unhealthy examples of, 16–17
See also money beliefs, and effects in life stages
money types, 113–130
acknowledging emotions and, 128
clinical stories, 114–126
the Amasser, 118–119, 178–180, 219–220
the Binger, 116
the Conserver, 120–121
the Dealer, 121–122
the Hoarder, 115, 210–213, 219–220
the Money Avoider, 117–118, 164–167, 180–181
the Money Monk, 30–31, 117, 164–165, 216–218
the Money Worrier, 125–126, 216–218
the Risk Avoider, 122–123
the Risk Taker, 119–120
the Spender, 114–115, 164, 210–213
the Money Worrier, 125–126, 216–218
Mundis, Jerrold, quotation, 113
mutual fund companies, 256

Nadeau, Robert, 54–55
NAIC (National Association of Investors Corporation), 255
negative emotions
constructive purpose of, 15, 254, 333–334
listing of, 14–15
money scripts and, 16–17, 124
steps to overcome, 124
See also emotions
neuroeconomics, 75–76
neurons, 49, 55
neurotransmitter chemicals, 280

oxytocin, 54, 75–76, 101

parental role, in setting limits, 52, 85–86, 144–145, 154–155
peers, 99–102, 142–143
pensions, 293
perceived threats and emotions, 13–14

personal accountability, 16, 17
the Phantom, 261
planners. *See* financial planners
Ponzi schemes, 17
positive emotions, 14, 15
See also emotions
Positive Psychology Center (University of Pennsylvania), 18
positive psychology, Seligman on, 18–22
prefrontal cortex, 52, 76, 100–101
preparation, worrying vs., 198–199
probability, gambling and, 272
protective selfishness, 194
pursuit of happiness, 19
pursuit of meaning, 20

real estate boom, 48
Registered Investment Advisers (RIAs), 259–260
regression to the mean, 62
regrets, 299, 307
religious beliefs, 17
religiousnous, 20–21
respect, 207–208
Retirement Advisors, 260
Retirement Specialists, 260
retirement stage, 293–315
annihilation anxiety, 307, 309–310
average savings levels, 294
blaming and "bad" events, 300–302
children's college costs and, 310–312
clinical stories, 294–296, 300, 303–305, 308, 310–311
downsizing financially during, 301–302, 312
financial planning and, 298
generativity vs. stagnation, 298, 306, 312–313
happiness in, 307
human capital as resource in, 302
life expectancy and, 293, 298
life review process, 298–299
planning for, 181–182
quality of relationships in, 303–306
self-esteem from work during, 296–297
reward deficiency syndrome, 100–101
RIAs (Registered Investment Advisers), 259–260
right-hemisphere tasks, 53, 55
the Risk Avoider, 122–123
the Risk Taker, 119–120
risk tolerance profiles, 265–266
risk-taking by teenagers, 100–103
Rule of 72, 163–164
ruthless competitiveness, 16

sadness-grief, 15
savings plans, 163–164, 170–171
scarcity, shock of, 29, 42
Schwarz, Joseph E., 307
self-absorption, excessive shopping and, 34–36

self-esteem
acknowledging emotions and, 128
development of, 286–287
gambling and, 273–274
money scripts and, 34–36
working during retirement stage and, 296–297
See also specific clinical stories; specific money types
self-loathing, 279
self-worth. *See* sense of self
Seligman, Martin, 18–22
Senior Advisors, 260
sense of self
annihilation anxiety and, 154, 307, 309–310
deficits in. *See* money scripts
definition of, 14
importance of, 309–310
limits/boundaries setting by parents and, 154
of the Money Master, 342–344
perceived threats and, 14
shame-humiliation, 15
S/he Brain: Science, Sexual Politics, and the Myths of Feminism (Nadeau), 54
shopping excessively, 33–36
short-term memory, 48
Siegel, Daniel J., 53
signature strengths (Seligman), 19–21
singlehood stage, 189–204
advantages of, 190–191
after death of marriage partner, 235–238
after divorce, 230–235
clinical stories, 191–192, 193–194, 195–196, 197–198, 199–200
emotional isolation of, 196–197
for gays and lesbians, 199–201, 219–220
protective selfishness and, 194
social networks, 190, 202
status quo bias and, 202
SmartMoney, 257
smoking addiction, 280
social networks, 143, 190, 201, 202
the Spender, 114–115, 164–167, 210–213
spending excessively, 34–36
stagnation. *See* generativity vs. stagnation
start-up adult stage, 141–158
clinical stories, 142, 143–153
parental limits and, 144–145, 154–155
peer influences on, 142–143
technology and, 142–143
status quo bias, 65, 202, 253
Steinberg, Lawrence, 99–100, 102
Stone, Arthur A., 307
substance use, brain function and, 50
success, childhood industriousness and, 85–86
sunk hole fallacy, 64, 253
surprise-startle, 15

the Teacher, 261, 262
the Technician, 261
teen years stage, 99–110
 brain function and, 52, 99–100
 clinical stories, 101, 102, 103–104
 explanation of, 334–335
 hormonal changes and, 100, 101
 parental limits and, 52
 peers and, 99–102
 risk-taking by, 100–103
temperance, as signature strength, 20
testosterone, 53–54
Thaler, Richard, 66–67, 70–71
therapy
 author's approach to, 2, 6
 money as core issue in, 6, 7–8
 See also specific clinical stories
thinking patterns, effects of, 2
thirtysomethings stage, 161–176
 clinical stories, 165–166, 167–168
 Rule of 72 and, 163–164
 savings plans, 163–164, 170–171
 settling down phase and, 161–164, 169
threats, physical vs. psychological, 13–14
touch, sensing of, 56
Tracy, Brian, quotation, 13
transcendence, as signature strength, 20
TransUnion, on credit card debt, 283
trust-distrust dynamic, 75–76
Tversky, Amos, 62
Twain, Mark, quotation, 271

U.S. Air Force study, 62

Vaillant, George, 85
Vanderveen, Peter, 272

wealth, 18–19, 324–326
Wealth Advisors, 260
Whittier, John Greenleaf, quotation, 171
widowhood, 235–238
wills, 201
wisdom, as signature strength, 20
women
 aggression and, 53–54
 divorce and, 230
 gene expression in, 56–57
 hormones and, 53–54, 75–76
 risk of dementia in, 57
work life, signature strengths in, 21
working memory, 48–49
worrying patterns, 198–199

Zagorsky, Jay, 207
Zak, Paul, 75–76
Ziglar, Zig, quotation, 141

CPSIA information can be obtained at www.ICGtesting.com
Printed in the USA
LVOW05s2351050114

R8145300001B/R81453PG368145LVX1B/1/P